Policies and Pleasaunces

Policies and Pleasaunces

A GUIDE TO THE GARDENS OF

SCOTLAND

KATIE CAMPBELL

BARN ELMS

for Michael

···

Barn Elms Publishing
Flint House, 11 Chartfield Avenue, London SW15 6DT
www.barnelms.co.uk

First published 2007

Policies and Pleasaunces: A Guide to the Gardens of Scotland
Copyright © Barn Elms Publishing 2007
Text copyright © Katie Campbell 2007

British Library Cataloguing in Publication Data.
A catalogue record of this book is available from
the British Library

Set in Berthold Walbaum
Printed in Malta by Compass Press

ISBN 978 1 899531 08 0

Maps by Linda Dawes
© Maps in Minutes ™ 2004
© Crown Copyright, Ordnance Survey

Designed by Jessica Smith

Cover photograph by Allan Pollock Morris

Contents

How to Use This Guide

This book separates Scotland into four regions, the South-West, the South-East, the North-West and the North-East, listing the gardens alphabetically within each region. To find any garden, simply refer to the regional maps or the index. Since 1975 Scotland's counties have been redrawn and renamed several times; the most recent version consists of 32 Council Areas – it is these that are used in the addresses, maps and index.

Telephone numbers, email and website addresses have been provided where possible. However, since many of the gardens are privately owned, opening times and admission charges may change, so you should check before setting out. Some gardens may extend their opening arrangements for displays of particular features, such as snowdrops, daffodils or autumn leaves. Because these openings are irregular they have not been included in the guide, but information is generally available on the individual gardens' websites. We recommend that you use the directions given in conjunction with a detailed road map. Access by public transport is often described on the relevant website or can be obtained by telephone or email.

The gardens in this guide are all open to the public, though in a few cases access must be obtained by contacting the owners or visiting when the garden is open under the auspices of the charity Scotland's Gardens Scheme. Details are available through the annual publication *Gardens of Scotland*, which is available from Scotland's Gardens Scheme (address below).

A number of gardens in the guide are owned or administered by the National Trust for Scotland (NTS). These often have their own websites but are all included in www.nts.org.uk. Access is free for NTS members and members of the National Trust of England, Wales and Northern Ireland; concessionary rates are offered to members of National Trust organizations of other countries. For further information contact the NTS at 0131 243 9300.

Finally, it should be remembered that gardens evolve. Properties change ownership, new layouts or plantings are introduced and features are replaced. Thus the structural and horticultural details of the gardens described in this guide are as subject to change as the opening times and admission prices.

Useful addresses

National Trust for Scotland (NTS)
Wemyss House, 28 Charlotte Square, Edinburgh, EH2 4ET

T: 0131 243 9300
E: information@nts.org.uk
W: www.nts.org.uk

Scotland's Gardens Scheme
42a Castle Street, Edinburgh, EH2 3BN

T: 0131 226 3714
E: sgsgardens@btconnect.com
W: www.gardensofscotland.org

Visit Scotland (Head Office) (Scottish Tourist Board)
Ocean Point One, 94 Ocean Drive, Leith, Edinburgh, EH6 6JH

T: 0131 332 2433 or 0845 22 55 121
E: info@visitscotland.com
W: www.visitscotland.com

or

Visit Scotland
Thistle House, Beechwood Park North, Inverness, IV2 3ED

T: 01463 716996

or

Visit Scotland Centre
19 Cockspur Street, London, SW1Y 5BL

T: 0131 332 2433

Historic Scotland (Head Office)
Longmore House, Salisbury Place, Edinburgh, EH9 1SH

T: 0131 668 8600
E: hs.inspectorate@scotland.gsi.gov.uk
W: www.historic-scotland.gov.uk

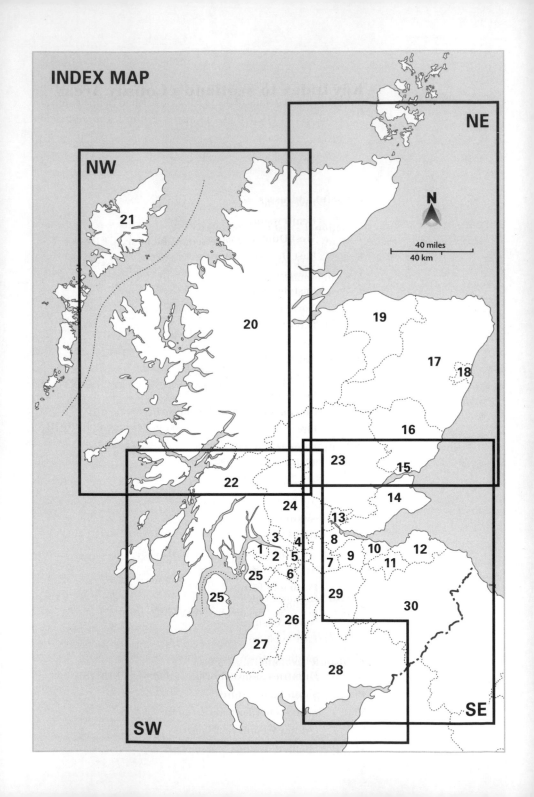

Key Index to Scotland's County Areas

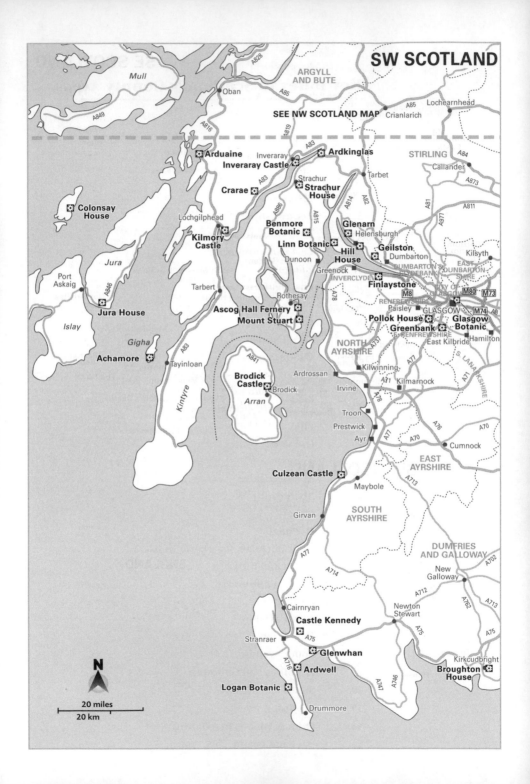

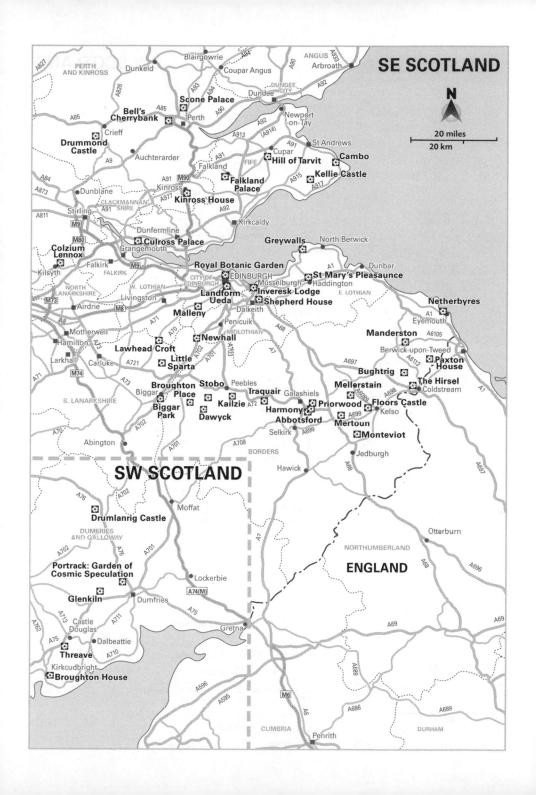

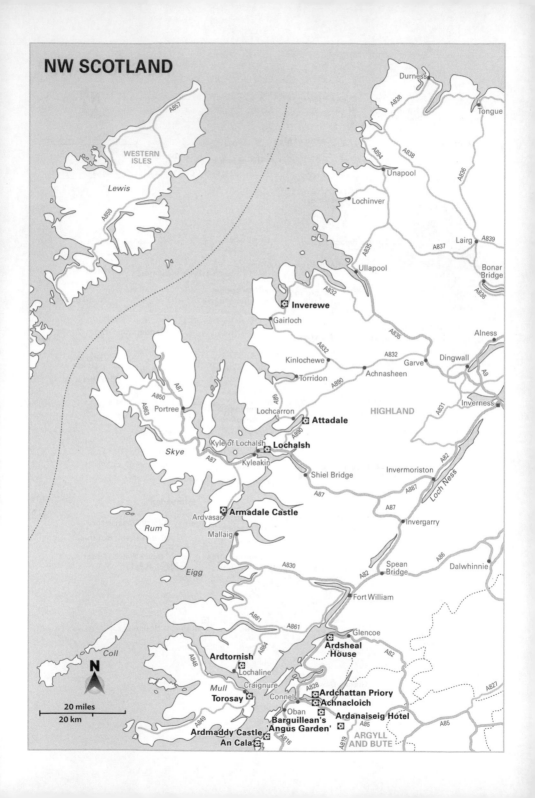

NW SCOTLAND

WESTERN
ISLES

Lewis

Durness

Tongue

A838

A838

A894

A836

Unapool

A835

Lochinver

Laird

A839

A837

Bonar
Bridge

A836

Ullapool

A835

Alness

A832

Inverewe

Gairloch

A832

Garve

Dingwall

A832

Kinlochewe

Achnasheen

A9

Torridon

A890

HIGHLAND

Inverness

A850

A87

Portree

Lochcarron

A890

Attadale

A831

A863

Skye

Kyle of Lochalsh

Lochalsh

A890

Kyleakin

Shiel Bridge

Invermoriston

Loch Ness

A887

A82

Ardvasar

Armadale Castle

A87

A87

Rum

Mallaig

Invergarry

Eigg

A830

A82

Spean
Bridge

A86

Dalwhinnie

Fort William

Coll

A861

A861

Glencoe

A82

**Ardsheal
House**

Mull

Ardtornish

A884

A848

Lochaline

A827

Craignure

A828

Ardchattan Priory
Achnacloich

Torosay

Connel

Ardanaiseig Hotel

Oban

**Barguillean's
'Angus Garden'**

A849

Ardmaddy Castle
An Cala

A816

A85

A85

A819

ARGYLL
AND BUTE

N

20 miles
20 km

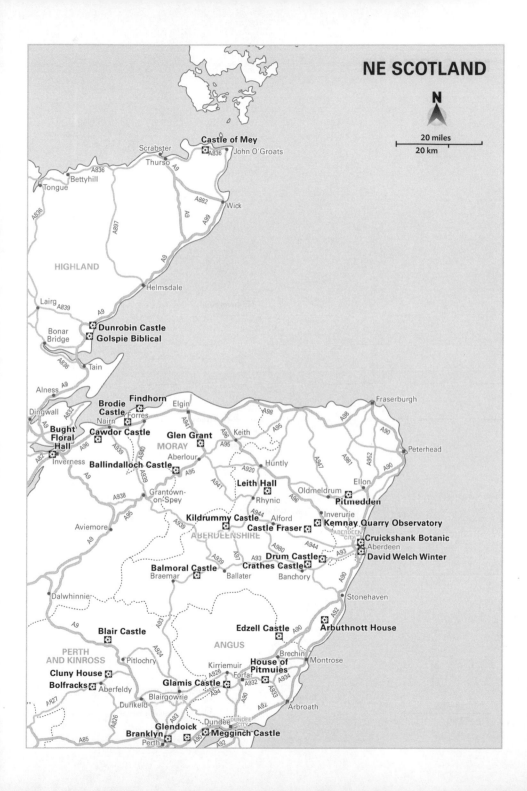

NE SCOTLAND

N

20 miles
20 km

Castle of Mey

Scrabster
Thurso   John O'Groats
A836
A9

Bettyhill
A836
Tongue
A882

A897
A9   Wick
A9
A99

HIGHLAND

A9

Helmsdale

Lairg   A839
A9

Bonar   **Dunrobin Castle**
Bridge   **Golspie Biblical**

Tain
A836

Alness   A9

Dingwall   **Findhorn**
Brodie   Elgin   A98
Castle   Forres   A95
Nairn
Bught   **Cawdor Castle**   **Glen Grant**   Keith   A95
Floral   A96   A939   A940   MORAY   A96   A90   Peterhead
Hall   Aberlour   A95
Inverness   **Ballindalloch Castle**   A95   Huntly   A947   A981   A952
A9   A938   A920   Ellon
Grantown-   **Leith Hall**   A90
on-Spey   Rhynie   Oldmeldrum
Aviemore   **Kildrummy Castle**   Alford   Inverurie   **Pitmedden**
A939   A944   **Castle Fraser**   **Kemnay Quarry Observatory**
ABERDEENSHIRE   A980   A944   ABERDEEN   **Cruickshank Botanic**
A929   A97   A93   **Drum Castle**   CITY   **David Welch Winter**
Dalwhinnie   **Balmoral Castle**   **Crathes Castle**   Aberdeen
Braemar   Ballater   Banchory
A9   A93   **Blair Castle**   Stonehaven
A93   **Edzell Castle**   A90   **Arbuthnott House**
PERTH   ANGUS
AND KINROSS   Pitlochry   Brechin   A92
A924   Kirriemuir   **House of**
Cluny House   Forfar   **Pitmuies**   Montrose
Bolfracks   Aberfeldy   **Glamis Castle**   A932   A934
A827   Blairgowrie   A94   A90   A93
Dunkeld   Arbroath
A826   Dundee
A85   **Glendoick**   CITY
Branklyn   **Megginch Castle**
Perth   A90   A92

Introduction

Despite its northern setting and unpromising terrain,
Scotland contains some of the world's most glorious gardens.
From intimate enclosures to large, open parks, from formal
parterres to wilderness walks, from botanical gardens to woodland arboreta, for nearly a thousand years this small, remote
nation has absorbed and reinterpreted the world's horticultural
trends. **Ardchattan** and **Priorwood** are built on the remnants
of medieval monastic gardens. **Edzell** is a rare example of
Scottish Renaissance horticulture. **Culross Palace** has been
restored to depict a seventeenth-century urban garden, while
the romantic parkland at **Castle Fraser** demonstrates the
eighteenth-century landscape style. The grandeur of nineteenth-
century formalism is displayed in **Torosay**, while such recent
creations as Charles Jencks's **Portrack: The Garden of
Cosmic Speculation** and **Kemnay Quarry Observation
Point** place Scotland at the cutting edge of contemporary
landscape design.

Philosophy, fashion and a turbulent history have shaped
Scotland's horticultural heritage, while varied weather and
terrain have contributed an enormous range of gardening styles.
The east coast is dry, cold and relatively flat, with bitter winds
blowing in from the continental landmass. These unpromising
conditions gave rise to inward-looking gardens sheltered within
high, enclosing walls, such as those of **Cambo**, **Greywalls** and
Netherbyres. Protected from the elements, these idyllic enclosures recall the earliest Persian paradise gardens, similarly
screened from the hostile world beyond.

The rich agricultural lands of Aberdeenshire and Angus in
the north allowed more open, expansive estates, such as
Ballindalloch, **Cawdor** and **Drum**, while the alluvial plains of
the rivers Tay and Tweed created lush farmland stretching into
the interior. James Justice, in *The Scots Gardener's Directory*
(1754), attested to the fertility of the land around the Firth of
Forth when he exhorted Scots nurserymen to break Holland's
floral monopoly, recommending Leith as an ideal spot to

establish rival bulb fields, given its plentiful supplies of cow dung, sand, tanners' bark and 'a dark, grey, sandy, Virgin Soil'.

Further inland, central Scotland is wooded, hilly and bitterly cold, with late frosts and frequent snow. Conifers play a major role in the gardens of this region – from **Blair Castle** in the north through to **Dawyck** in the south. **Little Sparta**, one of today's most celebrated gardens, incorporates the surrounding Pentland Hills to suggest sea waves in its maritime metaphors, while **Stobo** and **Kildrummy** both capitalized on their steep ravines to create the oriental gardens prized in the late nineteenth and early twentieth centuries.

The Borders region to the south is a fertile stretch of rolling hills. Traditionally the battleground between England and Scotland, for much of its history this was a lawless place of brigands, feuds and fortified dwellings. Early deforestation, followed by medieval sheep farming, stripped the hills of cover, while the ensuing soil erosion created vast swathes of boggy ground. The union of the crowns of England and Scotland in 1603 ensured stability, after which the land was drained, enclosed and fertilized, and today it hosts some of Scotland's most magnificent gardens. Grand estates like **Floors**, **Mellerstain** and **Manderston** reflect the influence of the English landscape movement, while smaller properties such as **Monteviot** and **Mertoun** accommodated the existing countryside rather than reshaping it to conform to a classical ideal.

Scotland's west coast is notoriously wet and mild. Warmed by the Gulf Stream, the rugged terrain encourages an informal approach, with woodland gardens creating a dramatic backdrop for the startling colours of rhododendrons, azaleas, camellias and magnolias, which flourish in the acid soil. Though salt-laden gales blow year round, dense shelter belts create microclimates in which such tender species as embothrium, enkianthus and olearia flourish. Ayrshire and Dumfries and Galloway in the far south offer gentle agricultural land. Further north, **Brodick** on the Isle of Arran, **Achamore** on Gigha and **Crarae** on the mainland represent three of the world's greatest rhododendron gardens; here, in the wooded glens of their littoral estates, passionate horticulturists hybridized new species, creating delightful woodland walks embellished with snowdrops, daffodils, primulas and meconopsis – the azure-coloured Himalayan poppy which perfectly echoes the west coast sea and sky.

The Clyde estuary houses many of Scotland's most notable

gardens. Created for affluent Glaswegians, these gardens exploited the new flora arriving from the Americas. Elegant eighteenth-century gardens like **Geilston** were built on trade with the New World, while enormous nineteenth-century estates like **Benmore** were financed by the riches of the industrial revolution. Smaller, domestic gardens like **Hill House** reflect the twentieth-century suburban style.

Further north, the Highlands host a surprising range of gardens. Such magnificent creations as Inverewe prove that, sheltered from wind and wild animals, an astonishing array of plants can survive if the land of this barren shore is enriched with local seaweed. The gardeners at **Castle of Mey**, at the northernmost point of mainland Britain, manage to coax spectacular vegetables from the cold, hard ground, and the last tendrils of warmth from the Gulf Stream expend themselves off Scotland's north-east coast, enabling the cultivation of massive gunnera at **Dunrobin** on the Moray Firth.

Though American conifers, South African heaths and Asian shrubs all play their part, perhaps the greatest glory of Scotland's gardens is their flowers. Whether in the vast walled enclosures of **Glamis**, **Crathes** and **Culzean** or the smaller domestic enclaves of **Broughton Place** and **Shepherd House**, Scotland's floral brilliance is the envy of the world. Constrained by the short summer, though nurtured by long hours of daylight, Scotland's flowers, often massed in spectacular, towering herbaceous borders, shimmer and glow through their brief season.

Most of the gardens in this survey are open daily through the summer, a few only by appointment, but all are reasonably accessible to the interested visitor. Whether informal woodlands carpeted with wild flowers or magnificent rhododendron glens, traditional pleasaunces or grand formal parterres, they each confirm the assertion of the Scottish architect Robert Lorimer that, in the Scottish garden, 'something of the golden age still lingers...'

Shaping the Scottish Landscape

In prehistoric times Scotland's climate and terrain were very different from today. Mild and dry, the country was swathed in native forest of Scots pine, birch, rowan, aspen and juniper. The Romans named the region *Caledon*, meaning 'wooded heights', though deforestation had began in Neolithic times with trees being cut for fuel and timber and to create agricultural land. Later, in an effort to thwart bandits, thieving birds and dangerous beasts such as bears and wolves, camouflage-providing hedges were grubbed up and woodlands were burned down. Overgrazing by sheep, cattle and deer prevented any chance of new growth, creating the treeless moorlands which predominate today.

Meanwhile, climate change around 1500 BC caused the weather to become wetter, windier and cooler. While the Romans are said to have introduced horticulture to Scotland when they invaded the country in AD 80–84, their brief tenure – they abandoned the territory north of Hadrian's Wall at the end of the second century – suggests they didn't have much time for gardening. In the fifth century the early Christians arrived from Ireland to settle the west coast, while the Anglo-Saxons settled the south-east; these two groups eked an existence from the land, but the first sophisticated horticultural knowledge came with the Anglo-Norman clerics of the thirteenth century.

Despite the constant skirmishes throughout the countryside, monastic communities were generally left in peace to cultivate their medicinal herbs, till their fields and harvest their orchards. Among the local people, however, horticulture was rare. Early accounts confirm that the Scots had little interest in fruit and vegetables; the Glasgow scholar John Major, in his *History of Greater Britain* (1521), wrote of them, 'Neither do they plant trees nor hedges for their orchards, nor do they dung the land.' In his *A Description of the Western Islands of Scotland* (1695) Martin Martin wrote despairingly of his native Western Isles, 'In many places the soil is proper for wheat; and their grass is good...If the natives were taught and encouraged to take pains to improve their corn and hay, to plant, enclose, and manure their ground, drain lakes, sow wheat and peas, and plant orchards and kitchen gardens etc they might have as great plenty of all things for the sustenance of mankind as any other people in Europe.' Nonetheless, until well into the eighteenth century, the national diet consisted largely of kale and porridge supplemented with peas, with fish for the poor and meat for the rich.

Among royals, however, gardens have long been a sign of power and prestige. Records suggest there was a royal garden as early as the twelfth century, in the reign of King David I. In 1507 the king's chaplain designed a garden for the Abbey of Holyrood House and in 1530, when James V returned from three years in France, he brought a French gardener to oversee the grounds of **Stirling Castle**. Though it is impossible to give an accurate date, it was probably during the reign of James V and his French wife, Mary of Guise, that the King's Knot was created: a formal garden with walks, terraces and an octagonal mount still visible today. Two centuries later, Daniel Defoe observed, in his *A Tour thro' the Whole Island of Great Britain* (1724), 'In the park adjoining the Castle were formerly large gardens, how fine they were I cannot say; the figure of the walks and grass-plats remains plain to be seen...they had, indeed, statues and busts, Vasa and fountains, flowers and fruit...'

With Henry VIII's dissolution of the monasteries in the 1540s, followed by the Reformation of the 1560s, Scotland reaped her share of rewards. A new aristocracy was created and loyal courtiers, invited to purchase monastic lands, set about creating country seats for themselves. The Museum of Scotland's Dean House panel, part of a late sixteenth-century painted ceiling rescued from an Edinburgh town house, provides an indication of contemporary horticultural taste. Depicting the senses as muses in various outdoor settings, it presents 'Taste' languishing before a formal garden with canal, arbour, pavilion and gravel walks, while a reedy, swan-embellished stream drifts off in the distance. James Gordon of Rothiemay's *Bird's Eye View of Edinburgh* (1647) depicts formal gardens behind the tenements and town houses of Canongate. While some have simple vegetable patches, others are filled with orchards, clipped trees and geometric parterres of varying degrees of complexity, indicating that by the middle of the seventeenth century the affluent middle classes were copying the horticultural pretensions of the nobility. But this was not the common trend. In his *A Short Account of*

Scotland (1689) Thomas Morer wrote of the Scots, 'Their avenues are very indifferent, and they want their gardens, which are the beauty and pride of our English seats.' The splenetic Thomas Kirke asserted in his *A Modern Account of Scotland* (1769), 'Woods they have none, that suits not with the frugality of the people, who are so far from propagating any, that they destroy those they had, upon the politick maxim that corn will not grow in the land pestered with its roots.' As late as 1772 Dr Johnson, travelling with Boswell between Aberdeen and Montrose, was repelled by the bleakness of the landscape: 'This wide extent of hopeless sterility...the oak and the thorn is equally a stranger, and the whole country is extended equally in nakedness' (*Journey to the Western Islands of Scotland*). Johnson's contempt for Scotland, however, is legendary, and the Reverend William Gilpin, more sympathetic to rugged, natural beauty, in his own account of 1776, retorted, 'Dr Johnson has given us a picture of Scotch landscape painted, I am sorry to say, by the hand of peevishness. It presents us with all its defects; but none of its beauties' (*Observations on several parts of Great Britain, particularly the High-Lands of Scotland*).

Nonetheless, exhortations to ameliorate the land through tree planting and field enclosure were widely ignored and even progressive landlords met great resistance from their tenants, who believed that trees and hedges took nutrients from the land, blocked the sun and provided refuge for thieving birds. A remarkably short-sighted system of leases – which tended to last for only one year at a time – provided a further disincentive for farmers to improve their plots. Even such beneficial introductions as the stalwart potato were strongly resisted by crofters, who feared the American import was a ruse by landlords to deprive them of their oatmeal.

Certainly gardening requires peace if not prosperity, and when James VI ascended to the English throne in1603 he put an end to three centuries of almost constant warfare. Slowly architecture and horticulture responded to the new-found peace as the defensive towers of the thirteenth- to sixteenth-century baronial period gave way to the country house and pleasure ground. Where the fortress had been sited in high or open ground, the country house could be placed in a designed landscape with elegant approaches and ornamental parklands.

Rural development continued through the seventeenth century. During the Commonwealth, many Royalists withdrew from public life to cultivate their estates. Though elaborate gardens with parterres, statuary and hydraulics would have been inappropriate in this anti-monarchist period, tree planting was begun around the policies (the immediate surroundings of the house) to provide shelter and interest. After the Restoration, the renewed promise of peace brought major land improvements. Newly enriched courtiers returned from exile with continental ideas on garden design. In 1670 the Royal Botanical Garden, Edinburgh, was established, and thirteen years later John Reid wrote *The Scots Gard'ner*, the first book to promote horticulture specifically for the Scottish climate and terrain.

This interest in the land flourished through the eighteenth century. With the 1707 Act of Union, Scotland sacrificed independence for stability. Many landowners, benefiting from confiscated Jacobite properties, settled down to develop their new estates; others with Jacobite sympathies discreetly retreated to their country seats.

The year 1723 saw the founding of the Society of Improvers of the Knowledge of Agriculture in Scotland by, among others, the Dukes of Atholl, Hamilton and Perth, and the Earls of Haddington, Stair and Wemyss. This was the first body of its type in Europe and it paved the way for all manner of farmers' clubs and agricultural associations. In 1729 William Mackintosh published his treatise on agricultural reform: *An Essay on Ways and Means for Enclosing, Planting etc. Scotland.* Enlightened landlords began increasing the length of tenancies to encourage the improvement of individual plots. Fields were enclosed in stone walls or hedging, and large-scale tree planting began in earnest, both for future profit and for present pleasure. By 1813 the Scots-born John Loudon was asserting, 'Agriculture in Scotland is conducted upon more scientific principles than in England...It has attained to a higher degree of perfection, and...consequently, buildings and other adjuncts necessary to its operations are better calculated for effecting the proposed end.' Gradually the produce of the newly modernized estates began supporting the country house and its entertainments – shooting, fishing, riding, golfing and garden making.

The agricultural improvements of the eighteenth century required more workers on the land, which promoted a move away from labour-intensive formal gardens. Undoubtedly the new fashion for romantic parkland accelerated this shift, though Scots landscapists always tended to enhance natural features rather than sweep them away to create the pastoral landscapes favoured in England. The native Scots style was essentially picturesque, with walled gardens, small ornamental parks and sheltering woodlands.

In the early eighteenth century Andrew Fletcher demonstrated a uniquely Scottish approach to design in his garden at Saltoun. A patriot who opposed the 1707 Act of Union, he followed neither the landscape style which was beginning to be promoted in England nor the formal style of the Continent. Instead he proposed a series of non-symmetrical enclosures, with harmony imposed through unifying sight lines to distant eye-catchers. After the Restoration, Sir William Bruce, Scotland's first major architect, promoted French formality and symmetry but gave further unity to his design by creating a distant focal point on the major axis. His garden at **Balcaskie** focused on the Bass Rock, his design for Hopetoun drew in the rounded hill of North Berwick Law, while his plan for **Kinross** hinges on the romantic ruin of Loch Leven Castle rising from the loch beyond.

In 1727 Sir John Clerk of Penicuik, in his prescient poem *The Country Seat*, praised the change in taste from formalism to naturalism a full four years before Pope's influential *Epistle to Lord Burlington* exhorted garden makers to consult the 'genius of the place' in all. By 1754 James Justice's *The Scots Gardener's Directory* ignored ornamental gardens, concentrating instead on practical advice for the development of the walled kitchen garden. In 1762, in his *Elements of Criticism*, Henry Home, Lord Kames, ridiculed the formal garden, deploring topiary and 'statues of wild beasts vomiting water'. Happily a native conservatism, and perhaps an antipathy to English fashion, ensured against the wholesale destruction of formal gardens that occurred in England and on the Continent.

From the mid-eighteenth to the mid-nineteenth century much of the Scottish countryside was transformed from a barren wilderness to a picturesque landscape of enclosed fields, sheltering forests and elegant country houses. Though this was part of a nationwide programme of agricultural improvement, in northern Scotland it was predicated on the Highland Clearances, the brutal expulsion of tens of thousands of subsistence farmers from their ancient lands so cattle and crops could be replaced by more lucrative sheep. Ironically, these Highland sheep farms proved unable to compete against the imports of wool and meat from the colonies in Australia, New Zealand and Argentina.

At this point much of the land was turned into deer forest and grouse moor to satisfy the sporting fantasies of affluent industrialists.

The twentieth century was a time of mixed blessings for Scottish horticulture. The First World War saw an exodus of Scots gardeners to the wealthy estates of America. The demise of Scotland's great agricultural estates through high taxation, cheap agricultural imports, increased wages, the loss of the labouring class and massive urbanization seemed to spell the end of the grand garden. Recently, these forces have been countered by an interest in ecology, heritage and conservation. While some old families struggle valiantly to maintain their properties, many of Scotland's largest estates have been turned into corporate headquarters, municipal offices, nursing homes or country hotels – institutions for which gardens are important. Meanwhile, Scotland's buoyant tourist industry, supported by such institutions as the National Trust for Scotland and the Historic Scottish Inventory, will probably ensure the continued maintenance and restoration of Scotland's horticultural heritage.

But the future holds further promise. The establishment of Scotland's first national garden, Calyx, at **Bell's Cherrybank** demonstrates a widespread interest in horticulture. Scotland is also home to two of the most innovative contemporary gardens, Charles Jencks's **Portrack: The Garden of Cosmic Speculation** and the late Ian Hamilton Finlay's **Little Sparta**. These suggest that Scotland will play a major role in promoting the garden design of the future as well as preserving the horticultural traditions of the past.

The Western Horticultural Tradition

The history of gardening is one of assimilation as succeeding groups absorbed the knowledge of the past and integrated their own philosophies, techniques and plant material with existing traditions. Gardening would have evolved initially from agriculture, which began about 10,000 years ago when the inhabitants of Mesopotamia – 'the land between two rivers', present-day Iraq – started to make use of the rich alluvial soil between the Tigris and Euphrates. Egyptian tomb paintings from the second millennium BC show ornamental gardens. By the first millennium BC the Assyrians were importing rare trees and flowers from distant territories to create exotic gardens for pleasure and display. The Persians fenced in vast areas of woodland to create hunting parks or *pairadaeza*, from which the English word paradise derives.

By the first century BC, the Romans had raised horticulture to a great art form, incorporating statuary to celebrate their gods, perfecting the art of topiary to transform trees into ornamental forms, linking dwelling with garden through porticoes, arcades, terraces and garden pavilions, and locating their villas on hilltops to encompass views of the surrounding country. The Romans also celebrated rural life and writers such as Virgil, Cicero and Pliny the Elder wrote influential treatises on farming.

With the decline of the Roman Empire from the late fourth century AD, horticulture in Europe once more became a utilitarian undertaking. The barbarians from the north had little time for pleasure gardens, while the early Christians despised the pagan sensuality of the Roman gardens and smashed much classical statuary to use in road-building.

In the Middle Ages, horticultural knowledge was safeguarded in the monasteries, where vast libraries preserved classical texts. Indeed, for centuries monks were the major horticulturists, experimenting with medicinal herbs in their physic gardens while cultivating simple orchards and vegetable patches to feed the community. Castles and fortified farms also maintained gardens to provide food. As a rule, these were walled to protect against enemies, thieves and wild beasts, with a central well for water. Often there would be a green court for grazing horses and even, climate permitting, a vineyard for grapes. As times grew more stable, gardens became more elaborate, with scented flowers lining the paths and decorative vines among the fruit trees which were grown against heat-retaining walls.

By the eleventh century Moorish influences began seeping into Europe with the Norman conquest of North Africa and Sicily. Arabic irrigation techniques were adopted, as were decorative fountains and pools, while plants such as roses, citrus fruits and many flower bulbs were introduced to Europe during the Crusades. The sacking of Arabic libraries released further classical texts, inspiring an interest in the sciences of the past.

The hold of the Church diminished with the movement known as the Renaissance (c. 1350–1550), whose very name refers to the rebirth of classical values. Humanist interests in man and his potential replaced slavish obedience to God, and gardens once again became places of pleasure, science and philosophical speculation. References to classical antiquity expressed the erudition of the owner; topiary and statuary were rediscovered, while symbolism and allusion were used to create allegorical programmes aligning gardens with the glories of myth and antiquity. Formal areas near the dwelling were laid out symmetrically around a central axis, with geometric patterns giving visual expression to the new interest in mathematics. Bowling greens and stretches of lawn were provided for sports and leisure. Exploration and colonization introduced horticultural imports from the New World and plants became valued for their colour, form and scent, not simply for their utilitarian possibilities.

In the succeeding Baroque period (1550–1700) gardens expanded even further, reflecting the advances in science, engineering and philosophy. The word is thought to derive from *barocco*, meaning 'an irregular pearl', and during this period the order and harmony of the Renaissance were replaced by a restless energy as religious wars racked Europe and the power of the Church was further undermined by scientists like Galileo and Newton, and philosophers like Bacon and Descartes. Elaborate patterns replaced simple geometry in parterres and flower beds, while sculpture became vigorous and muscular. Military engineering was used to create grand terraces, bastion walls and ramps or staircases; hydraulic engineering allowed for vast

water pools and fantastic fountains. Green theatres, wildernesses and labyrinths satisfied the urge for variety, drama and
movement. Long perspectives displayed the science of cartogra-
phy and appeared to extend the garden to the distant horizon,
while multiple cross-walks and parallel avenues pushed the
garden into the surrounding countryside.

By the eighteenth century people were seeking an alternative
to the grand formal style. Political conflicts, such as the English
Civil War, challenged the idea of absolute authority, and anxious
rulers began projecting a more conciliatory image that suggested
the integration of man and nature, and indeed of aristocrat and
peasant. Rather than imposing symmetrical, axial, geometric
designs on the landscape they worked with nature, enhancing
and celebrating natural forms. Pioneered in England, this new,
informal approach became known as the English landscape or
garden style (1700–1850). Though initiated by William Kent,
who famously 'lept the fence and saw all nature was a garden',
it was perfected by Lancelot 'Capability' Brown, whose sweeping
parklands came to epitomize the English countryside. Evolving
during a time of massive land enclosures, the landscape style
was easier to create and cheaper to maintain than the vast symmetrical parterres, elaborate topiary and multiple enclosures of
the previous era.

After the landscape style had swept away many important formal gardens a reaction set in. By the mid-nineteenth century,
garden owners began seeking more variety and individuality,
adopting a dizzying range of features including Moorish, Indian,
Chinese, Swiss and Japanese elements. At the same time revival-
ist movements arose in reaction to this eclecticism. English
designers such as Reginald Blomfield promoted the English
manor-house style, Scottish designers such as Robert Lorimer
looked to the Scots baronial past and French designers such as
Henri Duchêne imitated the grandeur of Versailles. However, all
these movements were variations on Renaissance formality,
with its use of statuary, topiary, geometric design and axial vistas.

Meanwhile, the popularity of alpine gardens and rockeries
revealed a lingering romantic fascination with mountain wilderness, while the profusion of arboreta demonstrated the widespread interest in the new trees, particularly conifers, being
imported from North Africa, Asia and the Americas. Throughout the century entrepreneurial plant-hunters plundered the
furthest reaches of the earth in search of novel plants, and in

Britain the abolition of the glass tax in 1845 led to a proliferation of greenhouses and elaborate conservatories to protect and display the exotica coming in from tropical regions. Towards the end of the century a new naturalism gained popularity in northern Europe, with William Robinson in England leading the movement against formal, architect-designed gardens in favour of wild and woodland gardens.

By the turn of the twentieth century the incomparable team of architect Edwin Lutyens and garden designer Gertrude Jekyll interpreted the prevailing Arts and Crafts movement to perfection. Combining vernacular architecture with exuberant planting, they established a harmonious relationship between house and garden. While rejuvenating the small country house, their style could be adapted to grand estates or small suburban dwellings.

By the mid-twentieth century two world wars had destroyed much of the European landscape, while social and economic changes made it impossible to maintain the grand estates and extensive villas of previous centuries. Urban expansion, rural depopulation, suburban development and extensive motorway systems altered the landscape. While modernism transformed post-war architecture, there was no equivalent innovation in garden design. Gradually, over the past fifty years, new styles have filtered into horticulture, but novelty is rare; landowners are essentially conservative and gardening is a conservative art form. Ecology, conservation and sustainability are today's major horticultural concerns, though the reclamation of industrial land, the search for sustainable styles and the interest in new materials all suggest that there may be more innovation in the century to come.

The Great Plant-Hunters

For a country of its size, Scotland has produced a remarkable number of great plant-hunters. In the eighteenth and nineteenth centuries scores of educated, ambitious young men achieved fame, if not fortune, in the jungles, valleys and mountains of Africa, the Americas and the Orient. Perhaps the national temperament predisposed the Scots to plant-hunting, an occupation that demanded intelligence, ambition, tenacity, a taste for solitude and hardship, and a passion for nature. In the early twentieth century George Forrest wrote from mountains of China, 'It is only Scots dourness which carries me on,' adding, 'For the cultivation of the patience...I recommend photographing of alpines in Yunnan.'

From the reign of James V in the early sixteenth century, Scotsmen travelling to the Continent as scholars, merchants and diplomats brought back seeds, plants and descriptions of foreign gardens. In 1670 Scotland's first physic garden was established in Edinburgh, stimulating a wide interest in foreign flora; indeed, a decade later John Reid in *The Scots Gard'ner* (1683) recommended such European imports as anemones, tulips, carnations, cowslips, crocuses and gillyflowers.

Professional plant collecting didn't begin in earnest, however, until the eighteenth century, with the exploration of the New World. The Society for Importation of Foreign Seeds, established in Edinburgh in 1765, was probably the first British syndicate to pay collectors for seed. Seeking new specimens, these intrepid botanists made dangerous journeys into hostile and uncharted territories. They were often under-resourced and alone, or in the company of local guides with whom they could barely communicate. Though David Douglas and Robert Fortune are Scotland's best-known plant-hunters, the names Drummond, Forrest, Masson, Menzies and Sherriff, incorporated in today's plant labels, immortalize less famous practitioners. The lives of Douglas, Fortune and Masson are described below on pp. 150, 170 and 205.

Thomas Drummond (1790–1837), a nurseryman from Forfar, arrived in Canada in 1825 as assistant naturalist on Sir John

Franklin's second Arctic expedition. Travelling by foot, canoe and horseback through the Canadian west, he had only an Indian guide for companion, and at one point he was forced to spend two months alone in the winter with limited supplies. On their return he and his guides got lost. Their dogs succumbed to exhaustion, so they had to carry their own supplies. They ran out of food and when they suffered snow blindness, which prevented them from shooting game, they survived by scraping meat from the deer hides they were using for warmth. Undaunted, the following year Drummond joined David Douglas on his west coast journey. Since Drummond's collections were mostly for scientific study rather than propagation, he has been largely ignored by posterity, though his name adorns several garden plants, chief among them the low, evergreen mountain avens, *Dryas drummondii*.

George Forrest (1873–1937) was born in Falkirk and trained at the Royal Botanic Garden, Edinburgh. In 1904 he was sent to China's Yunnan province to collect first for the commercial company Bees Seeds Ltd and later for a private syndicate. Despite surviving a massacre by Tibetans anxious to rid their borders of Chinese and Europeans alike, Forrest remained in the region for seventeen years. Employing native collectors, he also explored Sichuan, eastern Tibet and upper Burma, introducing more than 300 new rhododendrons, more than fifty primulas, several camellias and the prized gentian *Gentiana sino-ornata*. He also collected some fine meconopsis, many lilies and a plethora of dwarf plants.

Archibald Menzies (1754–1842) studied medicine and botany, and was appointed naturalist on Captain George Vancouver's world tour in the 1790s. Charged with recording the natural history of all countries visited, he was also expected to assess the chance of British plants and settlers surviving in each region. When the ship's surgeon became ill, Menzies replaced him and was applauded by Vancouver for not losing a single crew member. Among his introductions, the most famous are probably the monkey puzzle tree, *Araucaria araucana*, from South America and the Sitka spruce from north-west America.

Among lesser-known compatriots, John Fraser (1750–1811) explored the east coast of America, from where he gathered *Uvularia grandifloria*. In the same region, John Lyon (*c.* 1770) discovered *Iris fulva*, *Dicentra eximina* and *Pieris floribunda*. When James Main (1775–1846) arrived in Canton in China to discover foreigners were prohibited from leaving the treaty ports, he purchased plants from local nurseries. Though this approach was less glamorous than the methods of his plant-hunting peers, Main still introduced many camellias and tree peonies to Britain, as well as *Spiraea crenata* and *Chaenomeles speciosa*. Fred Balfour (*c.* 1920), an amateur who developed an impressive arboretum at **Dawyck**, joined an expedition to America's west coast, where he discovered Brewer's spruce, *Picea breweriana*. John Jeffries from Fife collected for the Oregon Committee of Scotland in 1851, sending home seed of *Tsuga mertensiana* and *Abies lowiana*. In 1854 William Murray from Perthshire sent his employers, the Edinburgh nursery firm of Messrs Lawson, the first seed of *Cupressus lawsoniana*.

In the twentieth century plant hunting was made easier by advances in transport and communications. While most of the showiest species had already been discovered, there are always new and rare plants to be found. In 1929 George Sherriff (1898–1967) and Frank Ludlow (1895–1972) met in India, where Sherriff was a vice-consul and Ludlow was a teacher. In 1933 they made their first expedition from Sikkim to the capital of Bhutan. Over the next two decades they made five more journeys into the Himalayas and Tibet, collecting many primulas, meconopsis and rhododendrons, as well as the fashionable *Euphorbia griffithii*. Sherriff's wife, Betty, made several expeditions with her husband. On a 1933 expedition in Bhutan, she dreamed of a new poppy; the next morning, following the directions in her dream, she discovered an unusual form of *Meconopsis grandis*, the seeds of which are still known as 'Betty's Dream Poppy'.

SOUTH-WEST SCOTLAND

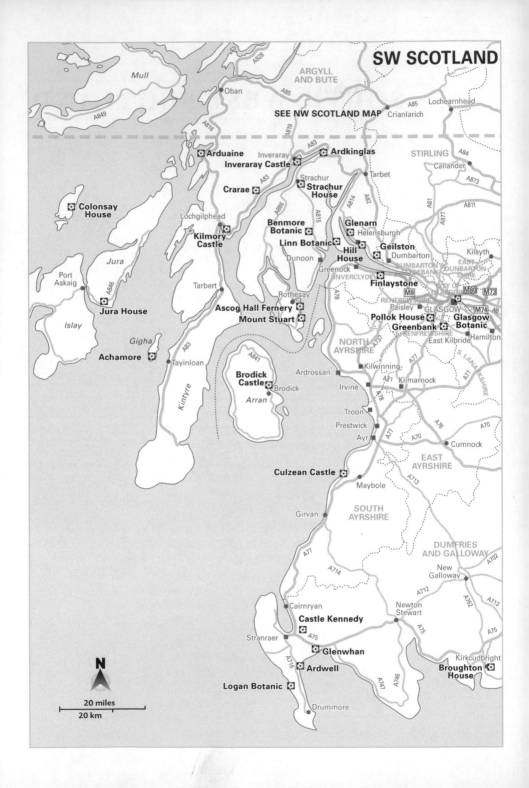

SW SCOTLAND

ARGYLL
AND BUTE

Mull

Oban

A828

A85

Lochearnhead

A85

SEE NW SCOTLAND MAP

Crianlarich

A849

A816

A819

STIRLING

A84

Callander

A873

Arduaine

Inveraray
Inveraray Castle

Ardkinglas

A83

Colonsay
House

Lochgilphead

A886

Crarae

Strachur
Strachur
House

A815

A814

A82

Tarbet

A81

A977

A811

Benmore
Botanic

Glenarn

Helensburgh

Kilmory
Castle

Linn Botanic

Dunoon

Hill
House

Geilston

Dumbarton

Kilsyth

EAST
DUNBARTON-
SHIRE

Jura

Greenock

INVERCLYDE

Finlaystone

M8

M80

M73

Port
Askaig

A846

Tarbert

Rothesay

A78

RENFREWSHIRE

GLASGOW

M74

A8

Jura House

Ascog Hall Fernery

Pollok House

Paisley

GLASGOW
Botanic

Islay

Mount Stuart

Greenbank

RENFREWSHIRE

East Kilbride

Hamilton

Gigha

A83

NORTH
AYRSHIRE

A737

S. LANARKSHIRE

Achamore

Tayinloan

Kilwinning

A71

Kilmarnock

A77

Ardrossan

Brodick
Castle

A841

Brodick

Irvine

A78

A76

A70

Arran

Troon

Prestwick

A77

A70

Cumnock

Kintyre

Ayr

EAST
AYRSHIRE

A713

Culzean Castle

Maybole

A713

Girvan

SOUTH
AYRSHIRE

DUMFRIES
AND GALLOWAY

A702

A77

New
Galloway

A714

A712

A713

Cairnryan

Newton
Stewart

A762

A75

Castle Kennedy

A75

Stranraer

A75

A716

Glenwhan

Kirkcudbright

Ardwell

A746

Broughton
House

Logan Botanic

A747

Drummore

N

20 miles
20 km

Achamore Gardens

Achamore, Isle of Gigha,
Argyll and Bute, PA41 7AD

Isle of Gigha, Argyll and Bute

T: (01583) 505354   E: admin@gigha.org.uk   W: www.gigha.org.uk

Open all year,
dawn–sunset

Fee £3.50, children £1

Ferry from Tayinloan,
Kintyre, 1½m S from
ferry terminal

Only 6 miles long by 1¼ miles wide, the aptly named Gigha (from the Norse *gudey*, meaning 'Good Isle' or 'Isle of God') houses one of Scotland's most impressive early twentieth-century gardens. Warmed by the Gulf Stream, Gigha has moderate rainfall and almost no frost, though the brutal winds blowing in from the Atlantic would deter many horticulturists. Towards the end of the nineteenth century the island was bought by Captain William Scarlett, the 3rd Lord Abinger, who built Achamore House in 1884, planting spruce and sycamore woodlands to provide shelter and cover for game. Sixty years later the intrepid Sir James Horlick bought the island as a space to cultivate rare and exotic plants. Restoring the now decrepit house, he moved in after the war, and over the next thirty years, with the advice of plantsman James Russell, he evolved a magnificent garden – a

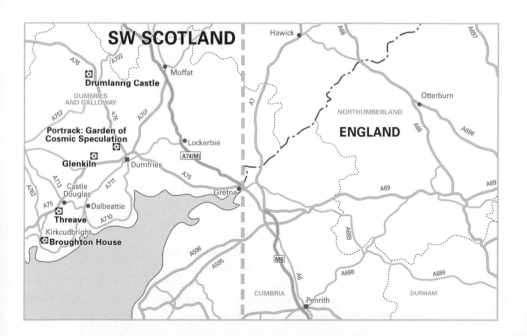

feat which is even more impressive when one realizes that all paths were created, glades cleared and beds dug with only wheelbarrows and horse and cart, as there were no tractors on the island.

Here, as in Horlick's earlier garden in Berkshire, rhododendrons form the backbone of the design. The 50-acre woodland is intercut with narrow paths leading to sheltered glades filled with species and hybrid rhododendrons, including Horlick's own crosses, such as the small, violet-flowered 'Songbird'. Rather like a labyrinth, the woodland presents an intriguing promise of anticipation and surprise which Edward Hyams, in the inaccurately named *The English Garden* (1964), suggests is best appreciated by 'wandering slowly, alone, and preferably lost, for several days, from glade to glade'.

On his death in 1970, Horlick left part of his rhododendron collection to the National Trust for Scotland – some of it is now at **Brodick Castle** on the island of Arran. The estate passed through various owners and in 2002, in a historic buy-out, the inhabitants of the tiny community purchased the island for themselves to prevent its acquisition by an unsympathetic owner.

The estate is entered by a pebbled footpath from the village hall. The entrance glade, planted with Brazilian *Gunnera manicata*, South African kniphofia and a large Japanese katsura, *Cercidiphyllum japonicum*, offers a hint of the exotic treats to come. An area of camellias, azaleas and hydrangeas, known as Colin's Garden, lies just inside the estate walls; from here the paths meander on two marked routes through the woodlands, encompassing such delights as the Spring Bank, with its early-flowering rhododendrons, and the George Taylor Garden, with two beautiful enkianthus trees, whose lovely spring flower clusters give over to vibrant autumn colours.

For rhodophobes, the walled garden, which is divided into two enclosures, is the horticultural highlight. The south garden houses lawns and peacocks, a rustic pergola and herbaceous borders, with a magnificent Mexican *Pinus montezumae* basking against the one wall. The north garden has some notable conifers, including the striking *Abies delavayi* with its implausibly blue cones; a gift to Sir James from the garden at **Crarae**, it was grown from seed collected by Kingdon-Ward on his last expedition to the Himalayas in 1952. Just beyond the north garden is a wonderful cone-shaped *Atherosperma moschatum*, a gift from the **Royal Botanic Garden, Edinburgh**; in its native Tasmania, Aboriginals make a tea from the aromatic leaves.

Now under the auspices of the Isle of Gigha Heritage Trust, Achamore Gardens is managed by head gardener Malcolm McNeill, with the help of one assistant. When McNeill arrived at Gigha as a garden boy forty-seven years ago, there were eight full-time gardeners, two devoted to the kitchen garden alone. Despite the reduced labour force, the walled garden is immaculate and the grounds of this plantsman's paradise are admirably maintained.

Ardkinglas Woodland Garden

Ardkinglas, Cairndow, Argyll and Bute PA26 8BH

Open all year, dawn–sunset

Fee £3

On A83, Loch Lomond to Inveraray road, signposted

Argyll and Bute

T: (01499) 600261   E: ardkinglas@btinternet.com   W: www.ardkinglas.com

Founded in the eighteenth century, Ardkinglas reflects the widespread fascination with the conifers that began pouring in from the New World to supplement Britain's native Scots pine, yew and juniper. Ardkinglas probably derives its name from the Gaelic words aird, kin and glas, meaning respectively 'a height', 'a head' and 'greyish green'. The 25-acre garden is dramatically sited on an outcrop at the head of the grey-green River Kinglas, overlooking Loch Fyne. A single beech, *Fagus sylvatica*, and several common oaks by the garden entrance are among the earliest surviving trees on the estate. The sorbus glade nearby, planted in 1996, demonstrates that the planting programme continues to this day.

By the mid-nineteenth century the estate was renowned for its woodlands; a gazetteer from 1819 noted, 'A beautiful stretch of Loch Fyne, with the woods and policy of Ardkinglas coming into view, refreshes the eye and spirit...' Native trees such as rowan, ash, oak and Scots pine have always been allowed to regenerate naturally, and the mixed plantings provide shelter for a collection of exotic plants cultivated in the nineteenth-century woodland garden. It is from this period that most of Ardkinglas's Champion Trees arise. Under a recent scheme initiated by the Tree Council to make the British population more aware of its arboreal treasures, the council has designated fifty Champion Trees around the country. Ardkinglas's best known British Champion, the largest tree on the estate, and perhaps in the whole of Britain, is the giant fir, *Abies grandis*. Planted in 1875, it was measured in 1989 and found to have a height of 205 feet and a girth of nearly 20 feet. Nearby is a golden-plumed Sawara cypress, *Chamaecyparis pisifera* 'Plumosa Aurea', from China, and various other Champion Trees are dotted about the grounds. The estate is also known for its rhododendron collection: the Bodnant Bank is cloaked in red hybrids raised by Lord Glenkinglas, while older species fill the new North American garden.

As the Victorian passion for conifers is supplanted by a modern desire for variety, the woodland lochan is being planted with deciduous trees to increase diversity and seasonal interest. A carpet of naturalized bluebells, *Endymion non-scriptus*, ensures further spring enchantment, while woodland walks provide spectacular vistas of the loch and the Kinglas. More paths lead to the ruins of an old moss-covered mill.

In 1999 a rustic gazebo was constructed of local timber on a hill overlooking the loch. Filled with arboreal inscriptions, this features prose and poetry ranging from the medieval St Bernard ('More things are learned in the woods than from books; animals, trees and rocks teach you things not to be heard elsewhere') to the recent humorist Spike Milligan ('There's a Nong Nang Ning/Where the trees go ping!') via Blake, Burns, Evelyn, Johnson, Keats, Stevenson and Thoreau.

Arduaine Garden (NTS)

Argyll and Bute

T: (01852) 200366   E: mwilkins@nts.org.uk
W: www.arduaine-garden.org.uk

Arduaine, Kilmelford,
Argyll and Bute
PA34 4XQ

Open all year, 9.30–sunset

Fee £5, conc. £4

Off A816, 20m S of Oban,
17m N of Lochgilphead

With its name meaning 'green point', this 20-acre garden is squeezed between the waters of the Jura Sound and the craggy slopes behind. The story goes that in 1897 James Arthur Campbell, returning to Scotland from his tea plantations in Ceylon, sailed along the west coast in search of the ideal location for a house and settled at Arduaine. Another version claims that one evening, while shooting on the island of Jura, he noticed the intense green of the mainland point with the sun setting behind it and determined that that should be his home. Whatever finally induced him to purchase this particular promontory, Campbell began creating a garden here in 1903, inspired by Osgood

Mackenzie, who was then developing his own garden at **Inverewe**, further up the coast.

Douglas firs, planted to create shelter, were quickly decimated by hungry rabbits. Other trees and bamboo followed, and in the shelter of the wooded glen the garden began to take shape. The first area to be cultivated, known as the Inside Garden, was a kitchen garden sited on a plateau open to the sea. A boundary of trees was planted to screen out the salty sea spray and, despite strong winds, such tender plants as the New Zealand cabbage tree, *Cordyline australis*, thrive in this frost-free pocket. Neat, ordered beds and internal borders characterized the garden in its early years.

A long border followed, with a second, lower, long border attesting to the inter-war fashion for herbaceous planting. Campbell caught the rhododendron bug and by the late 1920s the estate boasted 220 different rhododendrons, mostly species. The glen itself is packed with rhododendrons, with tender *R. maddenia* concentrated along the Gully Path where the steep slope encourages frost to drain away, while a canopy of Japanese larch provide overhead protection. The Grassy Ride is flanked by further treasures, including the spring-flowering *R. sinogrande*, with its enormous frothy white flower domes. The broad track which runs from the glen to the sea contains the unusual Chinese *R. genesterianum*, with dense, plum-coloured flowers. Several watercourses thread through the estate; the Top Pond harbours a rare and venerable *R. arboreum* subsp. *zeylanicum*, while the Heron Pond below is separated from the sea by a band of Scots pines and *R. ponticum*.

The High Garden, with its south-facing views along the coast, is approached via the Arboretum Walk, which still displays some of its original plantings of *R. arboreum*. A steep cliff path winding beside bracken-covered hills provides a striking contrast to the lush garden below. Bracken, known as the 'curse of Argyll', thrives on the grazing lands, where it is poisonous to livestock.

Through the middle years of the twentieth century Arduaine Garden succumbed to neglect; wartime lack of staff, post-war financial constraints and severe storms contributed to its decline. In 1971 it was taken over by Edmund and Harry Wright, nurserymen from Essex. They dug new ponds, expanded the herbaceous beds and increased the rhododendron collection. In 1992, unable to maintain it properly, they gave the estate to the National Trust for Scotland, who accepted it, despite the lack of an endowment, because of the importance of its plant collection.

Ardwell

Dumfries and Galloway

T: (01776) 860227   E: info@mull-of-galloway.co.uk
W: www.mull-of-galloway.co.uk

Ardwell, Stranraer,
Dumfries and Galloway
DG 9LY

Open 1 Mar to 30 Sep, 1–5

Fee £1.50, children 75p

10m S of Stranraer, off A76

This austere eighteenth-century house is surrounded by work-ing farmland and deciduous woods. Frost is rare and rainfall averages 40 inches per year; the mildness of the climate is demonstrated by a tender *Datura sanguinea* flourishing against the wall. Alpines flourish among paving stones, while a catholic mix of decorative shrubs, clipped Irish yew and cabbage palm, *Cordyline australis*, embellish the side terrace. A sunken lawn to the front suggests an earlier formal parterre. The path to the walled garden is lined with magnolias, camellias and eucryphias, ensuring colour from spring to autumn. The donkey green, no longer nourishing donkeys, is filled with spring and autumn bulbs. The huge walled garden is largely laid to lawn, though seasonal fruit, vegetables and plants are for sale. An unusual inner wall surrounds a small water feature, probably originally a dipping pond. Two marked walks meander round the policies, each of which takes about twenty-five minutes.

Ascog Hall Fernery

Isle of Bute, Argyll and Bute

T: (01700) 504555   E: enquiries@ascoghallfernery.co.uk
W: www.ascoghallfernery.co.uk

Ascog Hall, Rothesay,
Isle of Bute
PA20 9EU

Open Easter to end Oct
except Mon and Tues,
10–5

Fee £3, children free

From Rothesay, 3m S
on A844

The term 'fernery' applies equally to enclosed glasshouse and outdoor planting; Ascog Fernery has both. Though the nineteenth-century passion for ferns stretched from America to Europe, it was most pronounced in Britain, where ferns, used as house plants, could tolerate the low light levels of the dark Victorian interior. The fashion for ferns inspired an interest in other foliage plants, as the gardens of Ascog Hall demonstrate.

This rich Victorian garden was originally laid out in 1870 by Edward La Trobe Bateman, who had just returned from Aus-tralia, where he made his name as an artist and garden designer. With island beds, sinewy paths, green lawns and evergreen shrubberies, Bateman managed to create picturesque perspectives in what was essentially a flat setting. Today the garden has been restored, with gravel paths, undulating rockeries and bog gardens dripping with frondy Victoriana – ceanothus, ivies, old shrub roses, ferns and palms thrive in the damp, mild climate. In contrast, a tennis court has recently been transformed into a gravel garden filled with contemporary grasses and other sun-loving plants.

The real treat at Ascog, however, is the sunken fernery, built of red sandstone from the Bute shore and glazed with a greenhouse roof. Created in 1870, this grotto-like enclosure is delightful in both its architectural features and its exotic collection. A waterfall at one end cascades into a central pool surrounded by waterside plants, while planting pockets carved into the walls create the shady, humid conditions required by many of the ferns. Divided into geographical regions, the fernery houses an impressive collection of subtropical and temperate ferns, including an ancient *Todea barbara* thought to be 1,000 years old. An article about the fernery from *The Gardener's Chronicle* in 1879 enabled the owners to replicate the original plant list, contributing to the authentic Victorian feel.

Benmore Botanic Garden

Benmore Botanic Garden, Dunoon, Argyll and Bute PA23 8QU

Open Apr to Sep, 10–6; Mar and Oct 10–5

Fee £3.50, children £1

Off A815, 7m N of Dunoon on Cowal peninsula

Argyll and Bute

T: (01369) 706261   E: benmore@rbge.org.uk   W: www.rbge.org.uk

Benmore, one of three specialist outposts of the **Royal Botanic Garden, Edinburgh**, is sometimes known as the Younger Botanic Garden, after Harry George Younger, who gifted it to the nation in 1928. Spectacularly sited over the River Eachaig, this woodland garden is renowned for its flowering trees and shrubs.

The 140-acre grounds are entered through a magnificent avenue of giant redwoods, *Sequoiadendron giganteum*, planted in 1863 by Pearce Patrick, a wealthy American who had purchased the estate the previous year. As a precautionary measure, Patrick's gardeners initially planted silver firs between the trees to provide shelter, since the sequoia had been introduced to

The Sequoia

The stately sequoia, *Sequoiadendron giganteum*, or giant red-wood, which features so prominently in Scotland's west coast gardens, derives its name from the native American Indian Sequoyah (c. 1760–1843). Though often romantically described as an Indian chief, Sequoyah was in fact the son of a European man and a Cherokee woman. Raised in the tribe, he was a champion hunter until an accident crippled him. Despite the ridicule of his tribesmen, Sequoyah set about devising an alphabet for his people, thus enabling them to record their history, communicate long distance and participate in the written culture of North America. When he became involved in national politics, advocating ecological approaches and native rights, Sequoyah was often known as George Gist, taking the surname of his father, who is believed to have been a German trader. Happily it was his native name which was given to the redwood tree.

Britain less than a decade before and nobody knew how well it would fare. Of the original fifty sequoias all but one survive – that having been felled by a devastating gale in 1968.

Inspired perhaps by Pearce Patrick's magnificent avenue, a subsequent owner, Greenock sugar magnate James Duncan, cloaked the hills with six million trees after draining the land and shifting the course of the Eachaig. In 1889 Duncan sold Benmore to the Edinburgh brewer Henry Younger, who used his new wealth to develop the estate over the next three decades, until his son donated it to the nation.

The Victorian love of rhododendrons is evident in Benmore's collection: one of the world's finest, it contains over 250 species, with many more cultivars and subspecies. Following the prevailing fashion for all things oriental, the Youngers transformed James Duncan's duck pond into a water garden with waterside plants, a bronze fountain and a central island, planted with Japanese maples and a towering katsura tree.

The large, formal walled garden once hosted elaborate greenhouses; sadly over the years these succumbed to violent storms. Today the garden is laid to lawn, with coniferous shrubs and an impressive herbaceous border. There is also a charming gazebo, known as Puck's Hut from the carved faun on its roof. Designed by Sir Robert Lorimer in the 1920s, it is a memorial to Isaac Bayley Balfour, Regius Keeper of the Royal Botanical Garden, Edinburgh, who conceived the idea of a west coast outpost and then went on to develop Benmore's arboretum and rhododendron collections. Originally sited in nearby Puck's Glen, the building was moved to the shelter of the walled garden after the 1968 gale laid waste the glen.

Today Younger's oriental theme is continued in the Bhutanese Glade and a new Japanese Glade which is under development. The Chilean Glade and the Tasmanian Ridge add yet more variety and well-signed paths lead round the estate.

Brodick Castle,
Isle of Arran,
North Ayrshire KA27 8HY

Open walled garden:
Good Fri–31 Oct, 10–4.30;
1 Nov–21 Dec, Fri–Sun
10–3.30;
castle: Good Fri–31 Oct,
11–4.30

Fee £10, conc. £7
(incl. castle)

2m N of Brodick

Brodick Castle Gardens (NTS)

Isle of Arran, North Ayrshire

T: (01770) 302202   E: brodickcastle@nts.org.uk   W: www.nts.org.uk

Brodick is a Norse word meaning 'broad bay' and sure enough Brodick Castle – parts of which date from the thirteenth century – stands high over the Firth of Clyde, guarding the Isle of Arran on a site which has been a defensive stronghold since the fifth century. Ancestral home of the Duke of Hamilton, Brodick has seen its share of turmoil. In 1306 Robert the Bruce is said to have attended his followers at the castle after their disastrous ambush by the English in the Battle of Methven. In the sixteenth century the 2nd Earl was the guardian and regent of Queen Mary. In the seventeenth century the 1st Duke was executed in the Civil War; when his successor died in battle three years later, Cromwell's troops seized the castle and occupied it for a time, adding a battery to the east and an extension to the west of the medieval tower. In 1844 the architect James Gillespie Graham was commissioned to double the size of the castle, adding the high tower, crenellations and other baronial touches. Today the castle sits in an austere, emerald lawn backed by a range of shrubs, including eucryphia and olearia.

The walled garden was built as a kitchen garden in 1711, though its current planting of roses and herbaceous borders dates from the 1930s, when the daughter of the house married John Boscawen, who sent many temperate plants from Tresco

Abbey, his estate in the Scillies. The circular garden in the lower section replaces a rose garden and pavilion. Further woodland plantings derive from the great twentieth-century plant-hunters, such as Reginald Farrer, George Forrest and Frank Kingdon-Ward, whose introductions from the Himalayas and the Orient thrive in the warmth of the Gulf Stream.

The walled garden opens on to a pond planted with primulas, meconopsis, *Gunnera manicata* and other damp-loving plants. In the woods beyond, a nineteenth-century ice house virtually disappears into the hillside – in Arran's mild climate, ponds seldom froze and it usually had to be stocked with ice from the mainland. Elsewhere the Bavarian summer house, dramatically sited on a rocky promontory, provides spectacular views of the sea. Built by the 11th Duke of Hamilton for his wife, Princess Marie of Baden, the pavilion is the only remaining one of four which once dotted the grounds. Its interior is decorated with patterns of pine cones, while the outside is embellished with the twisted stems of *Rhododendron ponticum* – a novel use for this plant, which runs rampant through the west coast.

The loamy soil and high humidity of the region appeal to the rhododendrons which form the backbone of the woodland garden; of particular note are the magnificent tree rhododendrons, such as *R. macabeanum*, with its huge trusses of creamy yellow flowers in spring, and the small, tender, scented *R. nuttallii*. *R. falconeri* is another treasure, with its glorious mahogany-coloured bark. Heathers flourish in the acid soil, as do hydrangeas, which grow in striking shades of blue.

Marked trails point out such treasures as Britain's largest *Leptospermum scoparium* or New Zealand tea tree, so called by early settlers who used its aromatic leaves as an infusion. Some of the estate's enormous silver firs, *Abies alba*, were felled during the Second World War and floated in the Clyde for target practice. There are also several *Magnolia campbellii*. These giant Himalayan tulip trees can reach heights of 150 feet; though Brodick's are a mere 60 feet tall, when their huge water-lily-like flowers open in spring they can be seen several miles away across the bay. Brodick also houses the Horlick collection of rhododendrons given by Sir James Horlick from his garden at **Achamore**.

Woodland walks encompass the Mill Pond, originally the castle's water source. Above it the Mill Burn powered the saw mill and later the hydroelectric station supplying power to the estate. The spruce plantation sits on the site of an early village which was abandoned during the Highland clearances, when crofters were evicted to make way for grazing. The fire pond fills an earlier lime quarry and the remains of a charcoal furnace can be found in the woods.

The meadows near the castle are grazed by picturesque Highland cattle, while the Heronry Pond recalls the ancient sport of falconry. Though originally used to procure game for the table, by the Middle Ages falconry had become the sport of kings, involving enormous expense and elaborate ritual. Herons, considered noble birds, were among the most prized prey, so large estates would establish heronries to ensure an ample supply. Though falcony remained a favourite sport of the Stuart kings, its decline began in the seventeenth century with agricultural improvements and the enclosure of waste lands. The introduction of shotguns to the sporting field spelled the end of falconry and by the twentieth-century falcons themselves were hunted down as vermin.

Broughton House Garden (NTS)

Broughton House,
12 High Street,
Kirkcudbright, Dumfries
and Galloway DG6 4JX

Dumfries and Galloway

Open garden: 1 Feb to
31 Mar daily, 11–4;
house and garden:
Good Fri to 31 Oct, 12–5
daily, except closed on
Tues and Wed in Apr, May,
Jun, Sept and Oct

Fee garden: free in Feb
and Mar; otherwise
house and garden: £8,
conc. £5

Signposted in
Kirkcudbright

T: (01557) 330437 E: broughtonhouse@nts.org.uk W: www.nts.org.uk

Created by E. A. Hornel in the early twentieth century, Broughton House Garden is a charming amalgam of Scots and oriental influences. Hornel was one of a group of artists known as the Glasgow Boys who developed a form of Scottish Impressionism at the end of the nineteenth century. Eschewing conventional classical subjects, they turned instead to social realism, seeking inspiration in rural life.

Although he was born in Australia, from the age of two Hornel lived in Kirkcudbright. Named for the eighth-century kirk of Cuthbert, the picturesque harbour village had been a fashionable artists' colony since the 1880s, patronized by people who couldn't afford to winter in London or Edinburgh. By 1900 Hornel had achieved enough success to purchase Broughton House, which, though terraced, was one of the most prestigious dwellings in the region. After turning the outbuildings into a studio and gallery, he discovered a love of gardening, and as his reputation grew he bought up adjoining properties to expand his horticultural canvas to about an acre.

Like many at the time, Hornel was fascinated by Japanese prints. He pursued his interest on two trips to Japan, bringing back irises and peonies among other plants. In a 1907 letter from Ceylon he bemoans the fact that he is missing the annual display of his Moutan peonies. Though notoriously difficult to propagate, these tree peonies, *P. suffruticosa*, are ideally suited to the temperate climate of south-west Scotland and give a spectacular show for a fortnight in spring.

While public access is through a narrow lane between the High Street and the harbour, Hornel would have approached the garden directly from his studio, which overlooks a sunken courtyard. Formerly the laundry, this area was cloaked by Hornel in jasmine and clematis. The pond beyond is planted with lilies, fringed with irises, flanked by a stone lantern and traversed by a red balustrade, giving it a distinctly Japanese air. Elsewhere a wisteria tunnel, cherry and sorbus trees and a dripping fountain fed by a rainwater tank enhance the oriental feel.

Bits of architectural salvage including curling stones, stone troughs, millstones, a multi-faceted sundial and a twelfth-century granite cross add a Scottish touch, while a rosery, box-edged flower beds, open lawns and harbour views locate the garden firmly in the Edwardian era. There is also a delightful summer pavilion which can be revolved to follow the sun.

The greenhouse at the bottom of the garden is where Hornel and his sister cultivated orchids. The original was destroyed in the gales of 1998 and the current reconstruction houses plants from the Antipodes in honour of Hornel's birthplace. The tree fern *Cyathea australis*, the cycad *Macrozamia communis* and the bottlebrush *Callistemon* add an exotic air, while *Pandorea jasminoides* and *Kennedia rubicunda* shade a collection of pre-1930s pelargoniums. Ancient apple trees recall this area's earlier role as the kitchen garden.

Devotees of Hornel's paintings will recognize the dense planting and extraordinary variety of this enchanting urban garden – snowdrops and cherry blossoms figure prominently in his work, as do aproned maidens frolicking amid birch groves.

Castle Kennedy Gardens

Castle Kennedy, Stranraer,
Wigtownshire, Dumfries
and Galloway DG9 8BX

Dumfries and Galloway

Open 1 Apr to 30 Sep, 10–5

T: (01776) 702024 E: info@castlekennedygardens.co.uk
W: www.castlekennedygardens.co.uk

Fee £4, children £1

5m E of Stranraer on A75

Castle Kennedy Gardens are a curious amalgam of French formality and British romance. Designed in 1730 by the 2nd Earl of Stair, they were clearly influenced by his experience as former British Ambassador to France. The 75-acre estate is set on an isthmus between the White Loch, filled with clear spring waters, and the Black Loch, fed by dark, peaty hillside burns. The gardens themselves revolve around the picturesque ruin of Castle Kennedy, a medieval tower house which burned down in 1716. The Earl, also a field marshal, might well have sympathized with the Covenanters, as he deployed his troops shaping the land, thus distracting them from the rebels. No doubt this provided valuable practice in creating earthworks and he lent his enterprise legitimacy by giving military names to his landscape features, a series of formal avenues, terraces, plateaus, mounds and ridges.

At the narrowest part of the isthmus, the Earl created an impressive 2-acre circular pond from an inlet in the White Loch. Thomas M'Alla, the contractor who oversaw the works, described it as 'a bason, like a great glas'; when it isn't covered in lilies, the pond is, indeed, a mirror to the surrounding rhododendrons and azaleas. The walled kitchen garden was part of the original eighteenth-century design, as was the canal at the entrance; probably dug for drainage, it links the two lochs and is spanned by an elegant arched stone bridge.

After the Earl's death the pleasure grounds reverted to wilderness and his reviled descendant, the 7th Earl, even cut down the avenues, though he spared the beech drive at the entrance, which remains to this day. In 1814 the 8th Earl discovered the original landscape plans in a gardener's cottage and set about restoring the grounds. Reflecting the Victorian fashion for conifers, he established the pinetum, which is now world-renowned. He also planted up the old avenues, each with a different species. A double line of noble firs, *Abies nobilis*, was dubbed by Joseph Hooker 'the blue avenue'. There is also a rare double avenue of monkey puzzles, *Araucaria araucana*, planted in 1844 with seed from South America. In 1860 the head gardener enthused in the *Scottish Gardener*: 'the distinct and unusual appearance of the tree, combined with the regularity and order, which is observable in the beautiful arrangement of its branches and foliage, causes it to harmonize well with architectural erections...' In the nineteenth century the avenues were under-planted with flowering shrubs; azaleas enliven the monkey puzzles, while the bright-red flowers of the Chilean fire bush, embothrium, and the white flowers of eucryphia provide other avenues with spring and summer colour.

As with so many west coast gardens, rhododendrons are a key feature. When the local forest was cleared for agriculture in the sixteenth century, it left a layer of rich acid soil. Combined with the benign influence of the Gulf Stream and annual rainfall of 45 inches, this makes ideal growing conditions for temperate, acid-loving plants. Many of the tree rhododendrons, *R. arboreum*, were grown from seed collected in the Himalayas by Joseph Hooker.

In 1867 a new castle, Lochinch, was built in the baronial style a mile away from the old castle ruins at the other end of the isthmus. This is linked to the old ruin by formal avenues, with the Round Pond in the centre and the woodlands unfolding in between. After the monumental scale of the Castle Kennedy gardens, the landscaping round Lochinch is more intimate and domestic. The sunken lawn beside the castle was originally a formal parterre boasting no fewer than fifty-eight beds, but changing tastes and reductions in staff have transformed it to a less formal area of eight large beds. Though no longer planted with heather, the Heather Garden recalls the Victorian passion for all things Scottish.

Today the walled kitchen garden by the ruin of Castle Kennedy is planted with fruit trees, herbaceous borders and flowering shrubs. The flat area in front of the castle – probably originally a formal parterre – is now a simple lawn. The canal banks are lined with an unusual planting of *Cordyline australis*, giving this area a contemporary feel. Early settlers in Australia found that the young leaves tasted of cabbage – hence the common name, 'cabbage palm', though these trees are not in fact palms at all and could be better described as 'tree lilies', with their pendulous trusses of creamy, scented flowers. The islets in Black Loch beyond are Bronze Age crannogs, or lake dwellings. Today they act as wildlife reserves, protecting animals from man as they once protected men from animals.

The Rhododendron

Given Britain's love of roses, it is hardly surprising that the nation should succumb to a plant known, literally, as the 'rose tree' – from the Greek *rhodon*, 'rose', and *dendron*, 'tree'. Though rhododendrons derive mainly from Asia – Burma, China, Tibet, India and the Himalayas – the first species to come to Britain was *Rhododendron hirsutum*, which arrived in 1656 from central Europe. A few species were introduced from North America and western Asia in the early eighteenth century, but it wasn't until 1763, with the introduction of *R. ponticum* from the eastern Mediterranean, that the plant became widespread. While initially valued for its ornamental properties, it was widely planted, especially in Scotland, as a windbreak and game cover.

In the mid-nineteenth century the genus was popularized when Joseph Hooker returned from his seminal journey through Sikkim and the Himalayas with thirty new species of rhododendron. His specimens, seeds and his book *Rhododendrons of the Sikkim-Himalaya* (1849–51) created a vogue that was particularly strong in western Scotland, where the damp climate and lime-free soil gave rise to world-renowned collections at **Crarae**, **Brodick** and **Achamore**.

In Scotland rhododendrons flourished to such an extent that they quickly naturalized, rampaging through the countryside, overwhelming native plants and transforming many natural and designed landscapes. While the commercial forestry industry now treats rhododendrons as weeds, they are still much loved by local gardeners. The genus, which includes over 600 species, encompasses evergreen and deciduous varieties, low, creeping shrubs and massive trees; it is easy to cultivate and hybridize and today it exists in almost every imaginable colour.

Colonsay House Garden

Isle of Colonsay, Argyll and Bute

Colonsay House,
Isle of Colonsay, Argyll
and Bute PA61 7YU

Open woodland garden:
all year; walled garden:
Easter to Sep, Wed and Fri

Ferries from Oban to
Colonsay six times a
week in summer, three
in winter

T: (01951) 200211 E: colonsay@dial.pipex.com

Developed since the 1930s by the Strathcona family, this informal 30-acre woodland garden is full of unusual and tender plants. Winter frosts are rare, while hours of summer sunshine are among the highest in the country, creating a mild climate in which rhododendrons, camellias, eucalyptus, crinodendrons, embothrium and mimosa flourish amid native trees. Despite lashing storms, the annual rainfall of 45 inches is half that of mainland Argyll and the acid soil is shallow and free-draining. Existing woods provided shelter, paths were cut through the undergrowth and a stream winding through the valley was planted up with gunnera to create a water garden. In spring the clearings are lined with Himalayan primulas, while bluebells and meconopsis coat the forest floor.

The formal walled garden beside the elegant eighteenth-century Colonsay House boasts a venerable tree fern, *Dicksonia antarctica*. Originally from Australasia, tree ferns grow very slowly, the trunk increasing only 1 foot per decade. Unique among flora, they do not produce roots, taking their moisture and nutrition from the fronds and upper trunk. Despite a native habitat of temperate rainforest, the tree fern has adapted to most conditions and is found in sheltered, humid sites throughout the country, though it still looks exotic against the bleak terrain of the western islands. With reductions in garden staff over the past fifty years, the walled garden has been divided into two enclosures and largely laid to lawn. An earlier rose garden that was thwarted by salt winds today hosts abutilons, olearias, hebes, leptospermums and other shrubs, enlivened by the enormous blue stems of *Echium pininana*, which must enjoy the island climate as they also thrive at **Achamore Gardens** on Gigha. Beyond this space is the Lighthouse Garden, focusing on the eponymous lens from the Rhuvaal lighthouse on Islay. A dome-like structure surrounded by a decorative stone terrace, its glass facets create myriad rainbows in sunshine, while in mistier weather it seems to glow like a craft from outer space. Produce from the organic vegetable garden at the far end is sold in the café, which serves lunch and tea in summer. Colonsay House also offers accommodation. A small stone statue of a stooped abbot crouching in the shrubbery opposite the car park is said to be a genuine medieval piece, possibly a tombstone from the fourteenth-century priory at Oronsay, a nearby island accessible by foot across the strand at low tide and well worth a visit. For botanists Colonsay hosts 500 species of local flora, including such rarities as the sea samphire, *Crithmum maritimum*, the marsh helleborine, *Epipactis palustris*, and the orchid *Spiranthes romanzoffiana*.

Crarae (NTS)

Crarae, Inveraray,
Argyll and Bute PA32 8YA

Open all year, 9.30–sunset

Fee £5, children £4

11m SW of Inveraray
on A83

Argyll and Bute

T: (01546) 886614 or 886388   E: fsinclair@nts.org.uk   W: www.nts.org.uk

This lush woodland garden encompasses about 50 acres sweeping across a steep glen bisected by the Crarae Burn as it rushes to Loch Fyne. Described as 'the nearest thing in Britain to a Himalayan gorge', the landscape at Crarae has been populated since prehistoric times, as demonstrated by the Neolithic chambered cairn nestling by the burn. The western edge of the estate was planted in the early nineteenth century with Scots pine and European larch, remnants of the old Caledonian Forest. The first garden on the property was designed in 1893 by Margaret, Lady Campbell, who demolished the local inn, then created a rock garden in the rubble (north-east of the present house). Though the house has been separated from the wider grounds and is closed to the public, the remaining estate was designed in the early twentieth century by Grace, Lady Campbell, inspired by her nephew, the great plant-hunter Reginald Farrer (1880–1920). At her death the garden was further embellished by her son Sir George Campbell (1894–1967).Though he didn't directly subscribe to any of the great plant-hunting expeditions, Sir George had a particular interest in rare trees and exchanged many specimens with friends. From R. S. Balfour at **Dawyck** he got a Chinese fir tree, *Cunninghamia lanceolata,* which is close to 65 feet high today, and from **Inveraray Castle** he brought a giant fir, *Abies grandis,* now about 100 feet high. Sir George possessed that classic British passion for rhododendrons and while his mother before him had introduced spectacular *R. falconeri,* he continued to embellish the woodlands with species rhododendrons.

Although Crarae's 400 rhododendrons are a major feature, there is much else on offer, including magnolias, a wide variety of deciduous trees, such as sorbus and acers, and a large grove of eucalyptus evolved from the twenty species, mostly Tasmanian, which Sir George planted nearly a century ago. Wild flowers gird the woodland in spring, while cotoneasters and berberis lend autumn glory. Crarae also holds the national collection of *Nothofagus,* the southern beech trees whose smaller leaves distinguish it from the common beech.

Culzean Castle Gardens (NTS)

South Ayrshire

T: (01655) 884455 E: culzean@nts.org.uk W: www.nts.org.uk

Culzean is the ancestral home of the Kennedy clan, one of Scotland's oldest families, which can trace its roots to Robert the Bruce. The site has been a defensive stronghold since time immemorial and the castle's fortifications date back to the thirteenth century. Sir Herbert Maxwell noted that 'the last place in the realm that any student of horticulture would choose for his tranquil vocation would be that lofty bluff on the firth of Clyde', but the North Atlantic Drift ensures a mild, humid climate and since the nineteenth century Culzean has been famous for its elegant grounds, its many garden buildings and its impressive walled garden. Named for the sea caves beneath the castle, the estate was known in the fifteenth century as the House of Cove; this was altered to Cullean in the seventeenth century, with the current spelling adopted in the eighteenth.

It was also in the eighteenth century that Culzean's horticultural fortunes began to rise. In 1777 the 10th Earl of Cassilis commissioned Robert Adam to turn his rustic defensive tower into an elegant country house. Adam was nearing the end of his career at the time. His ornate neo-classicism was losing favour in the south and, as he retreated to his native Scotland, he evolved a new style, drawing on ancient Scots, medieval and Roman traditions. In this new romantic mood, Adam created the ruined arch, the viaduct and the cliff-top home farm, as well as the four-square castellation which encircles Culzean's medieval tower. His oval 'saloon' at the back of the castle is surrounded with French windows; these open onto a balcony over the sea, turning the drawing room itself into a virtual belvedere.

The entry was carefully contrived so approaching visitors would see the castle framed in the ruined arch – a conceit inspired by contemporary drawings of Hadrian's villa. Crossing the viaduct, they would then be confronted with the equally spectacular sight of the Firth of Clyde beyond. The Firth was notorious for smugglers, and Culzean's fortified sea caves were routinely used to hide tea, spirits and other contraband goods from the revenue officers. Indeed, the Kennedys had long conspired in the 'running trade', in part to express their contempt for the Hanoverian kings, being ardent Jacobites and loyal to the exiled Stuart dynasty.

Culzean Castle, Maybole,
South Ayrshire KA19 8LE

Open castle and walled garden: Good Fri to 31 Oct, 9.30–5.30

Fee castle and walled garden: £12, children £8

12m S of Ayr on A719 or 9m S of Ayr on A77 and 3m to W

As early as the seventeenth century, the defensive ditch in front of the castle was used as a pleasure garden; in 1693 the local minister noted that the house was 'flanked on the south by very pretty gardens and orchards, adorned with excellent terases and the walls loaden with peaches, apricotes and cherries and other fruit'. With Adam's eighteenth-century renovations, this garden was expanded and formalized to accommodate the central fountain and lawn. The Earl also hired Thomas White, a fashionable designer of the Capability Brown school, to landscape his grounds. White and his son are credited with around 100 landscapes in Scotland and northern England, among them **Castle Fraser** near Aberdeen.

When the 12th Earl inherited, he added two orangeries. One, to the south of the lawn, dates from 1818 and today contains potted citrus trees, as well as abutilons, fuchsias, plumbagos and passionflowers. The second was transformed into a camellia house, probably in the middle of the century before gardeners realized that camellias are in fact hardy. Today it holds both camellias and citruses, acknowledging its twofold past.

In the Edwardian era the formal garden held two tennis courts, though these were subsequently grassed over to create the long lawn. Today, roses, clematis and other climbers cloak the buttressing wall while a striking border of kniphofia, red-hot pokers, flanks the lawn, protected from the ferocious gales which batter the coast.

The huge walled garden, sited half a mile from the house, was a model of late eighteenth-century horticulture. Sheltered by elegant beech woodland, its stone walls were lined with heat-retaining brick, while the central dividing wall was filled with flues to warm the fruit trees espaliered against it. Today one side contains the traditional mix of fruit, flowers and decorative herbaceous borders; the other, turned into a rose garden at some point when the house required less produce, has recently been transformed into a low-maintenance wilderness of exotic plants and sinewy paths. The walled garden is reached by an avenue lined with silver firs, *Abies alba*, a feature applauded by Sir Herbert Maxwell, who notes that so often these trees are isolated in mixed plantations where their towering crowns are battered ragged by the wind; assembled together in close rank as they are at Culzean, their noble height and straight, silvery trunks can best be appreciated.

The Swan Pond near the walled garden was created in 1823

in a low-lying meadow. An enormous, ornamental lily pond, it provided summer boating and winter ice for the estate's two ice houses. The rustic fowl house nearby held a pheasantry, several poultry runs, an aviary and accommodation for a labourer to oversee the birds. The pagoda was added in 1860, a precocious example of the oriental taste that would sweep British horticulture after the opening of Japan to the West in 1868. Designed as a swan house, it was later converted to an aviary, with a tea room above.

The policies beyond reflect the evolution from the landscape to the rococo style as smooth fields and elegant groves became increasingly ornamented with incidents, entertainments and exotic specimens. For garden historians, there are more than forty architectural features, ranging from the austere Dolphin House – a seaside laundry, which housed three maids along with boilers and tubs – to the domed beach hut that recalls the early nineteenth-century vogue for sea bathing. The deer park, established in the nineteenth century, was briefly home to a variety of unusual animals from emu to buffalo. Culzean also boasts no fewer than three curling ponds, one of which was in use until the 1940s.

By the mid-nineteenth century Culzean was famous throughout the country; in 1862 the *Encyclopaedia of Gardens* ranked it the best estate in Ayrshire. By the Second World War, however, cheap agricultural imports, escalating taxes and labour shortages made Culzean, like many Scottish estates, unmanageable. It was donated to the nation in lieu of taxes, with the request that the top floor be made available to General Dwight Eisenhower in gratitude for his war services. It is now owned by the National Trust for Scotland, which has restored the castle, gardens and 600-acre grounds as a fascinating example of a grand Scottish country estate.

Drumlanrig Castle Gardens

Dumfries and Galloway

T: (01848) 331555 E: bre@drumlanrigcastle.org.uk W: www.drumlanrig.co.uk

Drumlanrig Castle, home of the Douglas family, is one of Scotland's most important domestic Renaissance buildings. In 1684 William, 3rd Earl of Queensberry, having been created 1st Duke

Drumlanrig Castle, Thornhill, Dumfries and Galloway DG3 4AQ

Open gardens: 31 Mar to 30 Sep, 11–5; castle: 4 May to 30 Jun, 12–4; 1 Jul to 22 Aug, 11–4

Fee gardens: £4, children £3; house and gardens: £7, children £4

3m N of Thornhill, 17m from Dumfries on A76

of Queensberry as a reward for his loyalty to Charles II, decided
to erect a dwelling worthy of his new status. Drumlanrig was the
result. Nearly a decade in the making, it was built of local pink
sandstone and set on a hill at the end of a long ridge – *druim* and
rig are both Gaelic for 'ridge'. Surrounded by sheltering woodlands, with commanding views over the River Nith, the 40-acre
garden was designed at the end of the century in the French formal style popular at the time, especially among those Royalists
who had joined the king in exile.

The impressive entry, known as the Great North Avenue, was
extended in the eighteenth century, and in 1977 an inner row of
lime trees was planted to replace the older trees when they die.
The 600-foot-long terrace was built in the early eighteenth century. Its massive supporting wall originally hosted fruit trees,
though today it supports, among other climbers, an ancient
fan-trained *Ginkgo biloba.*

In 1720 Daniel Defoe, sent by the government to gauge trade
possibilities with the North, gave a vague description of Drumlanrig's gardens: 'At the extent of the gardens there are pavilions
and banqueting-houses, exactly answering to one another, and
the greens trimm'd, spaliers and hedges are in perfection.' The
Rev. Peter Rae, writing about the same time, was more effusive
if no clearer. Calling Drumlanrig's gardens 'very beautiful', he
described a nine-square grid with the castle in the middle, surrounded by a kitchen garden, a parterre, a forecourt, an outer
court, a flower garden, a regular garden, a designed garden and
'my Duchess's garden'. This accords with John Reid's prescription
in *The Scots Gard'ner* (1683): 'Make all the buildings and plantings ly so about the house, as that the house may be in the centre.'
The grid pattern is still discernible in today's simplified layout.

There are references to a 'caskade' in late seventeenth-
century plans and an early eighteenth-century illustration shows
water pouring down a stepped cascade into a canalized section
of the Marr Burn. In 1776 the Rev. William Gilpin, pioneer of the
picturesque movement, was appalled by Drumlanrig's opulent
formality: 'It is amazing what contrivance had been used to
deform all this beauty.' Of the cascade he exclaimed, 'So vile a
waste of expense as this whole scene exhibits we rarely meet
with. Deformity is spread wide through every part of it.' By the
end of the century the cascade was abandoned and the canal
transformed into a lake; soon after it was returned to its natural
course within the Marr Burn.

Drumlanrig also contains a rare wilderness, a formal grove of deciduous trees traversed by hedge-lined paths and enhanced with fountains. While most wildernesses were transformed into naturalistic forests in the eighteenth century, then filled with conifers during the nineteenth-century vogue for pinetums, Drumlanrig's wilderness has remained largely untouched by changes in fashion.

By the mid-eighteenth century a renovation programme had grassed over most of the formal gardens, including both the east and west parterres. In the nineteenth century these were replanted, the east parterre becoming an American Garden with formal beds sporting acid-loving exotics, while the west parterre was restored to a formal design filled with colourful bedding plants. Both gardens were grassed over again during the Second World War, though in 1978 the east parterre was restored to a 1735 plan with simplified scroll patterns and large stone urns. Twelve years later the west parterre was redesigned as a rose garden with topiary yews defining the space and nepeta filling out the roses.

The Shawl Garden was originally formal with a floral border round a central fountain; grassed over in the eighteenth century, it was revived in the nineteenth century as a decorative garden with tightly clipped heathers of different colours planted in intricate patterns. In the twentieth century this was simplified; though the layout remains the same, the heathers have been replaced by heuchera, alchemilla, stachys and sedums, with coloured gravels fleshing out the design.

As with other grand formal gardens such as **Drummond**, it is impossible to tell how much of Drumlanrig's design is original, since the seventeenth-century conventions – terraces, parterres, allées, topiary – returned to fashion two centuries later. Around 1840 Drumlanrig's gardens were restored by two prominent landscape architects, Charles Mackintosh and David Thompson. While reinstating formal parterres, the designers introduced flowering shrubs, foreign conifers and various exotic plants. Five rustic summer houses, of which only four remain, were designed by Mackintosh.

Among the treasures of Drumlanrig's extensive woodlands are Britain's largest weeping beech, *Fagus sylvatica* 'Pendula', and her first Douglas fir, *Pseudotsuga menziesii*, grown from seed sent by the plant-hunter David Douglas to his brother, who was Director of Works at Drumlanrig. The country park has walks, nature trails and cycle routes, the stable yard has a visitor centre with information on local wildlife, and there is a children's play centre tucked in beside the Victorian greenhouses.

Finlaystone, Langbank,
Renfrewshire PA14 6TJ

Finlaystone

Renfrewshire

Open all year, 10–5

Fee £3.50, children £2.50

T: (01475) 540505   W: www.finlaystone.co.uk

Off A8, 2m W of Langbank

Finlaystone is one of several large private Scottish gardens that opened to the paying public in the twentieth century in an effort to survive. Parts of Finlaystone House date to the fourteenth century; for 400 years the estate belonged to the Earls of Glencairn and in the late eighteenth century Robert Burns stayed here as guest of the 14th and final earl, writing, 'I'll remember thee, Glencairn and a' that thou hast done for me.' Though today's garden was largely designed in 1900, it is filled with Celtic symbolism, reflecting its romantic past.

Sitting on a gentle slope, facing north across the Clyde, the house is surrounded by tall deciduous trees which thrive in the mild, damp climate. Originally the gardens sloped right down to the shore, where the vegetable garden was set in the rich alluvial plain. In the mid-nineteenth century, when the railway line cut off the river, the pleasure gardens had to be reoriented to the south, with a new kitchen garden created closer to the house.

At the turn of the twentieth century a formal rose garden and shrubberies were added to the grounds, creating a designed landscape of about 10 acres. An elegant lawn stretches to the west of the house, flanked on the river side with a gravel path and a stone balustrade. Pride of place is given to an ancient yew said to have sheltered John Knox in 1556 as he celebrated the first Communion of the Reformed Church in the west of Scotland. Sadly, a dendrologist has recently cast doubt on this story, suggesting that the tree is less than four and a half centuries old; in any case, in the renovations of 1900 the historic yew was moved 40 feet to the west to let more light into the drawing room, where a family member did her sewing. At the end of the lawn a yew hedge, castellated in the 1920s by an enthusiastic French aunt, encloses a sunken garden centred on a stone font.

To the east of the house the New Garden, dating from 1959, offers ornamental woodland encompassing a picturesque burn which races past the old laundry. Waterfalls, weeping cherries and azaleas lend an oriental air, while in autumn the roseate colours of the bog-loving umbrella plant, *Peltiphyllum peltatum*, illuminate both banks of the stream.

To the south, a modern copy of a Pictish boar leads to the walled garden. Though long extinct on the British mainland, the boar was an ancient symbol of courage, ferocity, strength and health, adopted by the bellicose Scots on battle shields and family crests.

The large walled garden beyond has been recently re-designed. Vegetables and espaliered fruit along the southern edge recall its earlier utilitarian purpose, while a rose-planted pergola round a central fountain designed in the form of a Celtic cross provides pleasure amid utility. Herbaceous borders, a café and nursery fill in the rest of the space, and ornate wrought-iron gates frame the formal lawn and the Clyde beyond. A cross-axis leads from the fern avenue, past the 'smelly garden', to a knot garden created on the site of an earlier rosery. A bog garden beyond was made from a leaky formal pond and the axis ends in a Celtic foot maze. Laid out in 1980, inspired by a pattern from the eighth-century *Book of Kells*, the maze was designed in one continuous line with six circles interlocking six semicircles. Beyond the formal gardens, azaleas, rhododendrons and other acid-loving shrubs give way to 70 acres of woodland walks.

Geilston Garden (NTS)

Argyll and Bute

T: (01389) 841867   E: information@nts.org.uk   W: www.nts.org.uk

Geilston is a prime example of the country estates that evolved along the banks of the Clyde financed by the fortunes made by Glasgow merchants. This 10-acre estate contains a walled pleasure garden, a beech-enclosed vegetable garden, a woodland garden, a water garden, a heather garden, ornamental shrubs and

Geilston, Cardross, Argyll and Bute G82 5EZ

Open Good Fri to 31 Oct, 9.30–5

Fee £5, conc. £4

Off A814, 18m N of Glasgow at west end of Cardross

double herbaceous borders. An elegant avenue of red-twigged limes, planted in the 1980s, has replaced the eighteenth-century lime avenue which led from the main road to the house. Though parts of it date from the fifteenth century, the house was rebuilt in 1766 for James Donald, who made his fortune importing tobacco from the New World colony of Virginia and exporting manufactured goods in return. The walled garden, greenhouse, *doocot* and stables are all part of his embellishments.

During the nineteenth century the estate was purchased by the Geil family, who rose from merchant class to landed gentry, imparting their name to the estate en route. In 1922 Geilston was bought by Glasgow iron merchant James Hendry, whose daughter Elizabeth bequeathed it to the National Trust for Scotland in 1989. The ship weathervane on the *doocot* recalls the mercantile past on which the estate's fortunes were based.

To the west of the steadings is a huge vegetable garden. Enclosed within a tall beech hedge, it surrounds an old stone dipping tank which would have been used for watering plants. An 1860 Ordnance Survey indicates that the space was originally divided into six sections by paths: today the space is quartered with internal beech hedging, the central arm flanked by herbaceous beds; one quarter is given over to an orchard, another to vegetables, an old ornamental bed has been retained, and a tennis court to the east has recently been turned to lawn.

The walled garden extends directly from the house in traditional fashion and an inscribed keystone indicates that the space was built in 1797. The land within has not been levelled and steep slopes create areas of intimacy, with woodland walks along the inner edge of the wall. A central lawn surrounds a magnificent Wellingtonia, *Sequoiadendron giganteum*, while espaliered apple trees and climbers cover the wall beyond. A heather garden beside the house features *Calluna vulgaris*, Scotland's most common heather. Here the pink 'J. H. Hamilton', the purple 'Tib', the crimson 'Firefly' and the white 'County Wicklow' create a subtle palette, enlivened by the lime-green foliage of the rarer *Erica carnea* 'Aurea'. Given the ease with which heathers can be cultivated and maintained, it's remarkable that such gardens are not more common in Scotland. A double herbaceous border leads from the heather garden down to the Victorian glasshouse against the lower wall. The potting shed nearby has an unusual window cut into the back, overlooking the water and woodland garden beyond.

The Geilston Burn rushes beside the walled garden, while woodland walks meander past a Victorian well-head. Mixed plantings of ornamental trees and shrubs give way to woodland under-planted with spring bulbs and that perennial favourite, the bluebell. In one of those classic examples of nations divided by a common language, the Scottish bluebell, *Campanula rotundifolia*, is known in England as a harebell, while England's bluebell, *Hyacinthoides non-scripta*, is in fact a type of hyacinth. This linguistic confusion lends weight to the arguments of elitists who advocate the use of Latin in the naming of plants.

Glasgow Botanic Gardens

Glasgow

T: (0141) 334 2422   W: www.clyde-valley.com/glasgow/botanic.htm

Glasgow Botanic Gardens, 730 Great Western Road, Glasgow G12 0UE

Open all year (times vary, so phone first)

Fee free

Corner of Great Western Road and Queen Margaret Drive, 1½m NW from city centre

Glasgow Botanic Gardens pack a lot into a relatively small space: a visitor centre, herbaceous borders, a 'Year Round Border', a fern garden, a rose garden, an 'Unusual Vegetables' garden, a chronological border, woodland walks along the River Kelvin and eleven linked greenhouses containing a wide range of cacti, an impressive collection of orchids and the national collection of species begonias.

The most impressive feature, however, is the Kibble Palace, a picturesque Victorian construct built by John Kibble on his estate in Coulport, then later dismantled and floated down the Clyde to Glasgow. Originally used as a concert hall, it was purchased by the Botanic Gardens authorities in 1873 and re-erected just within the garden gates as a conservatory. Covering an area of 23,000 square feet, it is one of the largest glasshouses in Britain and features an impressive collection of tree ferns from Australia and New Zealand.

One of the garden's most interesting horticultural features is the New Herb Garden. A scented-plants section contains such rarities as holy grass, *Heirochloe odorata*, whose vanilla-scented leaves were strewn before religious processions, and *Pelargonium odoratissmum*, whose apple-scented leaves are still used in perfumery, aromatherapy and potpourris. A bed of dye plants contains the buttercup, *Ranunculus acris*, the tip of whose shoots are boiled for purple dye, and *Genista tinctoria*, dyer's green-weed, whose stems, leaves and flowers give a yellow dye that produces the elusive colour green when used over indigo. The Scottish Bed features Scotland's emblem, the spear thistle, *Cirsium vulgare*. It also holds the field pea, *Pisum sativum*, which, dried and used for split pea soup or ground into flour, sustained generations of hearty Scots peasants. This bed also demonstrates the inventive use made of the most humble plants: the flowers of the cowslip, *Primula veris*, were boiled to create a sedative, while its roots were used to treat rheumatism; sorrel, *Rumex acetosa*, was eaten in salad and used as a poultice on bruises, while its roots gave a red dye; the daisy, *Bellis perennis*, was made into an ointment for wounds, scurvy, fever and liver inflammation. A Wheat Bed displays wild emmer, one of the ancestors of modern wheat, and einkorn, a primitive wheat grown in the Neolithic times and still used today in Turkey.

The Chronological Border groups plants according to the century in which they were introduced to Britain. The sixteenth-century section contains peonies from central Europe and honesty from the Balkans; from the seventeenth century came evening primrose from eastern North America and nasturtiums from Peru. The eighteenth-century brought bergenia from Siberia, hypericum from Turkey, candytuft from western Asia, red-hot pokers from South Africa and wintergreen from eastern North America. The nineteenth century had euphorbia from Turkey, *Heuchera maxima* from California and *Mahonia aquifolium* from western North America, while twentieth-century introductions include *Geranium renardii* from the Caucasus, *Primula florindae* from Tibet and honeysuckle, *Lonicera pileta*, from China, demonstrating that the world still harbours undiscovered horticultural treasures.

The World Rose Garden offers choice bits of information on the world's favourite flower and there is also a memorial by Scotland's fire brigades to their comrades who died in the 2001 bombing of New York's Twin Towers.

The Kaleyard

For centuries kale – also known as colewort or cabbage – was the staple of the Scots diet; indeed,so ubiquitous was the vegetable that Scotland's cottage gardens were widely known as 'kaleyards'. Jamieson's *Dictionary of the Scottish Language* reports that the word kale was often used to signify the whole meal, so an invitation to dinner might be expressed as 'Come and tak' your kale wi' me', while in Edinburgh the two o'clock bell signifying the dinner hour was commonly called the 'kale-bell'. Until eighteenth-century agricultural improvements led to the development of market gardens, most town houses and urban tenements had their own kaleyards, though beyond the occasional digging in of old turfs or roof thatch, these were poorly maintained, with little drainage or fertilizer.

With the nineteenth-century romanticization of Scottish peasant life the kaleyard became a favourite subject in literature and art. The literary triumvirate of J. M. Barrie, S. R. Crockett and the Rev. John Watson, with their novels of humble but spiritual peasant folk, were referred to as the 'kaleyard school'. Wisely, perhaps, both Barry and Watson used pseudonyms – Barry writing as 'Gavin Ogilvy' and Watson as 'Ian McLaren'. Barry soon moved on to more mature works – for example, *Peter Pan* – and the term itself became one of censure, suggesting a sentimental, melodramatic and essentially plotless style. Similarly a group of East Lothian painters favoured the subject; the simple folk and earthy crops depicted in such works as Arthur Melville's *A Cabbage Garden* (1877), James Guthrie's *A Hind's Daughter* (1883) and W. Y. McGregor's *The Vegetable Stall* (1884) celebrated the Scots peasant and his noble relationship with the soil.

This passion for kale was largely restricted to the Lowlands; Highlanders considered the cultivation of kale to be effeminate, preferring instead common nettle. The Grants, who lived near the Lowlands, were mocked as 'soft, kail-eating Grants', while a Gaelic poem about the Battle of Killiecrankie describes the defeated soldiers as 'men of kail and brose'.

Glenarn

....

Argyll and Bute

T: (01436) 820493   E: masthome@dial.pipex.com

Glenarn, a typical nineteenth-century woodland garden, over-looks Gareloch in the Clyde estuary. Renowned for its magnolias and rare and tender rhododendrons, the garden is planted with the exotic imports that were introduced by intrepid plant-hunters of the time; among its many treats is a *R. falconeri* grown from seed supplied by Joseph Hooker in 1849. Redesigned in the 1920s, the garden now boasts a rock garden and scree beds rising vertiginously above the Victorian villa. Elegant tables

Glenarn, Rhu,
Helensburgh,
Argyll and Bute
G84 8LL

Open 21 Mar to 21 Sep,
dawn–sunset

Fee £3, children £1.50

2m N of Helensburgh on
A814, in Rhu go up Pier
Road, turn right on
Glenarn Road, signposted

are fashioned from millwheels and bits of architectural salvage mounted as sculpture. A flock of beehives and an impressive row of compost boxes attest to their owners' horticultural canniness. Steep, narrow paths meander through the woodlands past olearias, hydrangeas and other nineteenth-century favourites under-planted with snowdrops, crocuses, daffodils, primulas and the usual array of spring flowers.

Glenkiln Estate, Shawhead, Dumfries and Galloway

Fee free

5m W of Dumfries on A75 to Henderland, 1m N to Shawhead, then 2m NW to Old Water Reservoir, no signs, no enclosures

Glenkiln Estate

Dumfries and Galloway

Although not strictly speaking a garden, Glenkiln's landscape can compete with any number of rhododendron-filled glens or herbaceous borders. From 1951 to 1976 the late Sir William Keswick embellished his estate with modern sculptures, fulfilling his long-held ambition of creating the world's first collection of sculpture in a natural setting. The six pieces are sited in the amphitheatre created by ancient hills, around an enormous reservoir.

The collection is essentially a homage to Keswick's friend the sculptor Henry Moore, but it also features work by Sir Jacob Epstein and Auguste Rodin. The sculptures are sited with a sensitivity no institution could replicate; indeed, Keswick himself declared that the sculpture 'possessed its surroundings', while Moore claimed that Keswick was the first patron to appreciate the power of his works in a natural setting. Moore was one of the first contemporary sculptors to create work specifically for the outdoors. Returning to the ancient Greek traditions, he saw sculpture as an art of the open air, best seen in daylight; he once famously declared, 'I would rather have a piece of my sculpture sit in a landscape, almost any landscape, than in, or on, the most beautiful building I know.'

It is a spine-tingling sensation to drive along a winding road through magnificent rural scenery and suddenly come upon an etiolated, upright creation standing by the roadside. Recalling an Iron Age totem, this striking object is Moore's bronze *Standing Figure.* Half a mile further down the reservoir, silhouetted against the sky on the ridge of Brennan Hill, is what appears to be a Celtic cross. Originally known as *Upright Motive No. 1*, this piece was created by Moore as a vertical assemblage of shapes, the end product being a sort of worn body with a vague cruciform silhouette. So intimately has the piece melded with its environment that it has become known to locals and art historians alike as *The Glenkiln Cross.*

Further along, Moore's hieratic *King and Queen* presides serenely over the slope; perfectly scaled to the surrounding hills, it represents an ideal integration of art and nature. A base of local stone links the sculpture with the geology of the site and it is a surprise to discover that the piece was not actually made for the setting. These monumental watchers do not refer to specific historic or literary characters; they sit, like archetypal gods or guardians, their presence ennobling the landscape. This partic-ular work inspired the landscape designer Sir Geoffrey Jellicoe, whose 'seats of contemplation' at the Kennedy Memorial in Runnymede were a direct response to the pose and setting of Moore's *King and Queen.*

Discreetly placed at the head of the reservoir is Rodin's bronze *St John the Baptist,* striding forcefully forward as though preaching to a multitude. His upraised arm evokes the classical pose of a warrior poised to strike, his plinth suggests a primitive altar and his burn-side setting recalls his role as the baptizer of Christ. More difficult to find is Jacob Epstein's *Visitation.* Set in a grove of pine trees nearby, this modest maid cowers before the implicit angel. These last two, more literal, pieces provide a Christian counterweight to the pantheistic spirituality evoked by Moore's rather abstract, primitive creations.

The final piece in the collection, Moore's *Two Piece Reclining Figure,* demonstrates that though the sculptor emerged from the European tradition of figurative art epitomized by Michelangelo, his major inspiration was always Mother Nature herself.

Glenwhan Gardens

Dumfries and Galloway

T: (01581) 400222   W: www.glenwhangardens.co.uk.

This is a relatively recent garden, created in the past quarter century. Though Glenwhan, in Gaelic, means 'glen of the rushes', the estate sits on a rocky outcrop, 300 feet above sea level and buffeted by the wind on all sides. Despite this unpromising

Glenwhan, Dunragit, Stranraer, Wigtownshire, Dumfries and Galloway DG9 8PH

Open 1 Apr to 31 Oct, 10–5

Fee £4, children £1

7m E of Stranraer, off A75 at Dunragit

setting, the owners, inspired by the horticultural splendour at **Logan** nearby, decided to attempt a garden. After fencing in 12 acres with a protective shelter-belt of deciduous and coniferous trees, they created two small lochs to drain the land. The warmth of the Gulf Stream helped to create a microclimate which, with its annual rainfall of 45 inches and a pH factor of 4.5, is favourable to acid-loving plants.

Existing bracken and gorse were used to shelter tender species, 100 hardy rhododendrons and deciduous azaleas were planted in the woods, and temperate plants such as the Chilean embothrium and New Zealand eucryphias and olearias now flourish throughout the property. A primula walk and a bluebell ride provide early colour and scent; camellias, hollies and hydrangeas bulk out the woodland plantings, while trilliums flourish underneath.

Glenwhan is a personal garden, filled with quirky statues and convenient benches. Lakeside planting is dominated by a magnificent gunnera bog and a rustic rose trellis. There are also some lovely birches, such as *Betula* 'Hergest', with its golden peeling bark. Exotic ducks, hens and peacocks, a summer house and a gazebo, a dog cemetery, rock, water, herb and heather gardens, a small nursery and a seasonal tea room supplement the varied pleasures.

Greenbank Garden, Flenders Road, Clarkston, Glasgow G76 8RB

Open all year, 9.30–sunset, but closed 25 and 26 Dec, 1 and 2 Jan

Fee £5, conc. £4

6m S of city centre, from Clarkston Toll take Mearns Road, signed

Greenbank Garden (NTS)

Glasgow

T: (0141) 616 5126   E: information@nts.org.uk   W: www.nts.org.uk

Greenbank Garden is the National Trust for Scotland's western headquarters. The small but elegant Georgian estate was first developed in 1764 by Glasgow merchant Robert Allason, who made, then lost, his money supplying ships for the American War of Independence. A shelter belt of woodland encloses the grounds; within it the house gives on to a large, open lawn from which an avenue of clipped yew trees leads to a 2½-acre walled garden. Used as a demonstration garden, this space is subdivided into more than thirty different sections, displaying a range of ornamental plants, annuals, perennials, shrubs and trees of particular interest to small-garden owners. Despite lingering frosts and impervious clay soil, over 3,000 species are carefully maintained to provide year-round interest. The topiary garden features an owl and a pussy cat, snails and slugs, and, bizarrely, a honey jar. Tightly knotted parterres suggest possibilities for tiny back yards. There is also a modern grass garden, a traditional herb garden, a pond garden, a cactus garden, a dried-flower section, summer and winter borders and a gravel garden. At the centre of the enclosure is an unusual 1620 lectern sundial which was set to eighteenth-century Glasgow time as Greenwich Mean Time was not invented until 1884.

Greenbank conducts trials for *Gardening Which?*, growing plants for two years to test their suitability for the Scots climate. The trial beds are flanked with peony borders; a Scots favourite, the peony derives its name from the Greek physician Paeon and possibly owes its popularity to the fact that its roots and seeds were prescribed for various women's complaints, including childbirth. Bergenias figure prominently, as Greenbank holds the national collection; somehow, thanks to the expert skills of Greenbank's gardeners, this dull but dutiful evergreen manages to look contemporary when paired with grasses or fronted with nepeta.

Among several water features, the best-loved is the 'Fame Fountain', a 1930s bronze nude created by Charles d'Orville Pilkington Jackson for Glasgow's 1938 Empire Exhibition. An apple store and bee boles in the walls attest to the earlier incarnation as a kitchen garden; raised beds and wheelchair access make it suitable for disabled horticulturists, while woodland walks pass fields of picturesque Highland cattle. The northeast shelter belt is planted as a woodland garden, specializing in snowdrops and daffodils. Major Hamilton, one of the early twentieth-century owners, was a great lover of narcissi and introduced many rare and costly bulbs, some of them from **Brodie Castle**, which now maintains the national collection of Brodie daffodils.

Hill House,
Upper Colquhoun Street,
Helensburgh,
Argyll and Bute G84 9A5

Open Good Fri to 31 Oct,
1.30–5.30

Fee £8, conc. £5
(incl. house)

Off B832, E of
Helensburgh, 23m NW of
Glasgow

Hill House (NTS)

....

Argyll and Bute

T: (01436) 673900   E: information@nts.org.uk   W: www.nts.org.uk

Hill House, home of the publisher Walter Blackie, is a rare example of modernist landscape garden design. It has all the features one would expect from a cosmopolitan member of Glasgow's affluent Edwardian bourgeoisie: rose garden, orchard, kitchen garden, woodland with wild flowers, lawns, tennis court, topiary and herbaceous borders. But despite these traditional features, the layout is unmistakably modern.

Like many affluent intellectuals at the beginning of the twentieth century, Blackie joined the exodus from the city, choosing to raise his family in the idyllic seaside retreat of Helensburgh, 20 miles from the centre of Glasgow. There he purchased a potato field facing south over the Clyde estuary and commissioned one of the most innovative designers of the day, Charles Rennie Mackintosh (1868–1928), to plan his country estate.

Though adored in Secessionist Vienna, Mackintosh was famously undervalued in his homeland during his lifetime. Nonetheless he has since been rediscovered and shamelessly promoted by Glasgow's publicity machine in a phenomenon wryly known as 'Mockintosh'. This should not blind visitors to his genius, nor to its expression at Hill House. Mackintosh's botanical drawings demonstrate that his interest in plants extended way beyond what was required by the Art Nouveau flourishes of the time. In 1899 he had designed the landscape as well as the architecture for Windyhill in Kilmacolm; here a simple, formal, asymmetrical plan demonstrates his precocious appreciation of the modern aesthetic which would define avant-garde landscape design in the century to come.

Though it is not entirely clear what input Mackintosh had in the garden at Hill House, he is generally assumed to have overseen the design while Blackie attended to the details. Here again, a modernist formality prevails. The narrow house stretches across the top of the site, leaving unobstructed views over the estuary to the south. The western entrance has a semicircular drive, elegantly articulated with a half-circle of standard hollies curving round the lawn and discreet blue mop-head hydrangeas lining the wall. The circle motif is reiterated in the unusual

circular lilac garden to the east and the half-moon topiary along
the retaining wall. It is also echoed in such architectural details
as the eastern turret of the house, which recalls the pepperpot
tower of the sixteenth-century **Castle Fraser**, and in the gardener's hut to the south-east, which recalls barrel-shaped early
Scots *doocots*.

The utilitarian features – greenhouses and kitchen garden –
are hidden away in the inhospitable northern section of the site.
The sloping lawn to the south is divided by a thick lime hedge,
while an off-centre path joining the two spaces demonstrates the
modernist interest in occult formality. Replacing symmetry with
balance, modernist designers attempted to achieve harmony
through abstraction. Mackintosh's avant-garde impulse is honoured today in the recent addition of a kinetic sculpture by
George Rickey. A gift of the artist, this has been placed on the
north front of the house in a space which Mackintosh designed
to display a feature, though the well-head he suggested had been
rejected as too expensive and nothing was ever found to replace
it in Blackie's time.

A small, formal rose garden offsets the lilac circle, while
beyond, a wild-flower meadow meanders along the eastern edge
of the garden, past an unusual mound planted with bluebells
and crowned by three birch, *Betula pendula*. To the west an
informal planting of flowering trees leads to a lily pond, and a
rock garden, providing an oriental flavour. The flat, lower lawn
used to hold the croquet lawn and tennis court.

The house itself is white, abstract and monumental, like a
bold piece of sculpture presiding over the garden. As Antoni
Gaudí was doing in Spain and Frank Lloyd Wright in America,
Mackintosh attempted to evolve a contemporary national style,
combining vernacular motifs and materials with modern
simplicity. Elegant and sculptural despite its modernist austerity,
Hill House draws on the Scottish baronial tradition with its
white, harled surface, dramatic roofline and judicious use of
leaded glass.

But it is in the interior that Mackintosh really excelled, and
here the horticultural metaphors flourish. Indeed, with its integration of floral surfaces and forest-like structures, Hill House
can be interpreted as an indoor garden. Visitors enter through a
glazed trellis-work screen. From here the hall progresses like a
formal allée lined with dark, oak beams. Ahead the foyer is an
open glade, beneath a copper chandelier suggestive of the sun.

The two main public rooms lead off the hall. In the first of these, Blackie's study, an arboreal atmosphere prevails with oak bookshelves, desk-drawer pulls embellished with metal butterflies and reed-like decorative panels with pieces of purple glass embedded in them producing mysterious glimmers of light.

The second public room, the sitting room, also entered from the dark hall, is a dramatic, light-filled space with the panorama of the Clyde unfolding beyond. Painted in white with touches of pink and green, this room juts into the garden, like an ornate pavilion. The central bay window is draped in translucent curtains decorated with roses, while stylized stems carved into side panels, a trellis pattern on the carpet and roses stencilled on the walls reinforce the arbour-like atmosphere.

The horticultural imagery extends to the first floor, where the hall lamp resembles a delicate ironwork birdcage within the grove of wooden supports. In the main bedroom the symbolism reaches its apogee in an erotic motif where masculine, trellis-like, ladder-back chairs appear to provide the support for delicate, feminine roses stencilled on the wall behind. Gender equality presides as floral forms vie with trellis-work grids on carpet, walls, furniture and shutters. Even the door jamb is bent to a horticultural purpose, being flanked on either side by niches to hold flower posies. In the garden beyond, conventional trellises and arbours further link exterior with interior in this unique integration of horticulture and architecture.

Despite international acclaim, Mackintosh failed to create a viable architectural practice. Turning instead to the decorative arts, he ended his days designing fabrics, book covers and furniture while indulging, for pleasure, in landscape painting and botanical illustration. Though virtual obscurity followed his death, in 1971 the Royal Incorporation of Architects in Scotland (RIAS) purchased Hill House and its Mackintosh-designed furnishings. Eleven years later the estate was taken over by the National Trust for Scotland. The top floor is rented, but the rest of the house and garden are open for visitors. In 1988 Mackintosh's horticultural prowess was acknowledged when David Austin bred a tough, bushy, lilac-pink rose with a powerful scent and named it Charles Rennie Mackintosh.

Inveraray Castle Gardens

Argyll and Bute

T: (01499) 302203   W: www.inveraray-castle.com

Inveraray is home to the powerful Clan Campbell, Dukes of Argyll and staunch Royalists who, after the 1707 Act of Union, supported the English monarchs against repeated rebellions by the Scots. Inveraray draws its name from the River Aray: *inver* being Gaelic for 'a river mouth', while *aray* is thought to come from the Norse for 'a gravelly bank'. The policies were first land-scaped in the seventeenth century with advice from John Evelyn, the virtuoso writer, designer and arboriculturist, whose influence is evident in the formal lime avenue which marked the entrance to the original castle. The avenue may have been planted by the 8th Earl of Argyll to commemorate his bringing of Charles I to Scotland in 1641 – a fruitless journey, since the King failed to gain allies in his fight against Parliament and was forced to make concessions to the powerful Covenanters in their resist-ance to the anglicizing of the Scottish Kirk. The avenue, which was largely replanted in the nineteenth century, still contains a few of the original trees.

The current turreted castle, with its triumphal central tower, was inspired by John Vanbrugh's designs for Blenheim and Cas-tle Howard. Built of local blue-green schist in the mid-eighteenth century, it replaced an earlier fifteenth-century fortified dwelling. While the old castle was immortalized in Walter Scott's *The Legend of Montrose* as the 'noble old Gothic castle of Inver-aray', the kindest response to the new castle was Dr Johnson's comment, on his 1773 journey through Scotland, 'what I admire here is the total defiance of expense...' It has been said that the castle's fantastical roofline complements the rugged hills behind, though by that criterion the earlier towers, courtyards and embattled walls so admired by Scott would have been an even better complement.

In 1756 Walter Paterson, head gardener for the new castle, levelled the ground in front to create a flat, featureless, plinth-like lawn with neither the romance of a landscape park nor the elegance of a formal garden. Such austerity could never have survived the Victorian era and in 1848 the 8th Duke had the grounds redesigned by W. A. Nesfield, the most fashionable landscapist of the day.

Inveraray Castle,
Inveraray, Argyll and Bute
PA32 8XE

Open castle: 1 Apr to 31 Oct, 12–7.45;
woodland walks: all year

Fee castle: £6.30,
children £4.10;
woodland walks: free

On A83 just before Inveraray from N

Nesfield created a new approach, removed much of the dark, sheltering laurel shrubbery and divided the lawn to create a formal garden with three horizontal bands bisected by a central allée. The near band is laid out in the pattern of the St Andrew's Cross; known, therefore, as 'the flag border', it is filled with shrubs and herbaceous plants to give year-round interest.

Beyond the flag border is the rose garden, replanted in 1980s with such delights as the China rose 'Perle d'Or' and *R. rugosa* 'Blanc Double de Coubert'. Beneath a magnificent cucumber tree, *Magnolia acuminata*, to the right of the lawn, sits a millstone, known as the Blar-en-Buie; local legend reports that some misguided soul once removed a rowan tree growing from its centre and was cursed thereafter, the rowan being sacred in Celtic folklore. Further down the lawn an early eighteenth-century neo-classical statue of Verity struggling with Felicity provides the edifying spectacle of writhing, naked, female flesh. Matching this is a more sober sculpture of the Campbell sisters, daughters of the 5th Duke, carved by Lorenzo Bartolini (1770–1850).

Beyond the formal area, the garden opens out to woodland. Rhododendrons and azaleas thrive in the mild climate, despite rainfall which averages 90 inches per year. Among the many ancient trees are a yew whose boughs extend across the whole of the glade and a dramatic circle of western red cedar, *Thuja plicata*. The inevitable monkey puzzle flourishes beside one path, and a junction is marked by a pair of cannons from a Spanish galleon of the Armada fleet, sunk in 1588 off the coast at Tobermory.

Today the 2 acres of formal garden and 14 acres of policies are admirably tended by a single gardener. Though the formal garden is open only by appointment, it is visible from both castle and grounds. From the castle, four marked walks lead through the wooded hillside, providing fascinating glimpses of 3,000 years of landscape history. The 8-foot-high 'standing stone' beside the formal avenue is probably a route marker from the second millennium BC. From the first millennium BC is a crannog or small island near the shore of the loch, constructed of wood and stone to provide its occupants with a dwelling safe from enemies and wild beasts. A medieval ironworks and charcoal pits nearby were probably in use until the seventeenth century. From the sixteenth century is Bushang Cottage, whose name is said to derive from *beau champ*, meaning 'beautiful field' – the exclamation of the French-speaking Mary Queen of Scots when she visited in 1563.

The eighteenth century provided many embellishments, including the sham tower, designed 'in the imitation of a ruin' by Roger Morris and William Adam. Adam, father of the more famous Robert, also designed a 'rusticated grotto' and a pictur-esque circular *doocot*, which forms the end point of a vista and provides a ground-floor sitting room complete with fireplace. Scotland's first truly classical architect, William Adam, began his career as assistant to Sir William Bruce, who designed, among other things, the formal garden at **Kinross**. Adam's firstborn, John, was also a successful architect who created the unusual elliptical, arched stone Garden Bridge, dating from 1758. From the nineteenth century a rustic thatched pavilion allowed romantic riverside musings, while the fish pond acted as a back-up reservoir for the hydroelectric scheme, one of the first in the country, which provided light for the castle.

Among various arboreal treasures is a Spanish or sweet chestnut over 300 years old and thought to be the first of the species planted in Scotland. There is also a Lebanese cedar planted by Queen Victoria on her 1875 visit, and a gigantic west-ern red cedar, planted in 1853, which claims the widest girth of any red cedar in Scotland.

Jura House Garden

Isle of Jura, Argyll and Bute

T: gardener (01496) 820315   E: mirjam@aol.com
W: www.jurahouseandgardens.co.uk

Jura House, Ardfin,
Isle of Jura,
Argyll and Bute
PA60 7XX

Open all year,
dawn–sunset (tea tent
June to Aug, Mon–Fri
11–5)

Fee £2.50, children £1

5m east of Port Askaig
ferry terminal, off A846

The island of Jura is one of Britain's last remaining wildernesses. An ornithologist's paradise, it attracts shore, field, wood and farm birds, as well as birds of prey such as kestrels, merlins, harriers, falcons, buzzards and golden eagles. Foliate lichens also prolif-erate, attesting to the lack of pollution. Jura House (not open to the public) is set in a sheltered spot on the south side of the island with spectacular views to the island of Islay – and beyond to Ireland on a good day.

Today the walled garden is the preserve of Dutch gardener

Peter Cool, who runs it on organic principles. Accessed from the car park by a path meandering through native woodland, the garden is built on a sloping site and bisected by a stone-lined burn. Traditional kitchen garden features – vegetables, fruit trees, pergolas, lawns and herbaceous borders – are interspersed with a large collection of exotics, mostly from Australasia.

Entering through a conventional rose garden with box edging and yew hedges, the visitor is suddenly assailed with the palm-like leaves of a Tasmanian tree fern, *Dicksonia antarctica.* A bizarre, primitive-looking plant, its trunk is constructed of fibrous roots protecting a central vascular core whose tubes conduct water and minerals from the soil to nourish the fronds. Acid-loving eucryphia, magnolias, eucalyptus and rhododendrons fill out the planting. Sculptural benches created from slabs of weathered wood invite contemplation of the garden and the sea beyond. An orchard abuts the lower wall, sheltered from the salt spray by a tall fuchsia hedge. A spectacular wild-flower meadow surrounds the nearby tea tent and a path leads down to a delightful sandy beach, with wind-sculpted trees hugging the headlands and imperturbable swans drifting amid the jagged rocks.

Signed walks along the shoreline pass through the 'machair', dune grassland, home to wild goats and rabbits. Barely visible are the ruins of an old crofting village demolished in the nineteenth century because it obstructed the view from the laird's house. Thyme grows in the steep scree slopes, as does stonecrop, *Sedum acre,* which was eaten, as a salad, by crofters as well as being used to treat worms and scrofula.

A second, hillside walk reveals unusual dykes built of flat stones and round boulders, thought to be the work of a Lowland builder. Serrations in the hills indicate the ancient farming system of 'lazybeds'. An exhausting process whose name derives from *ley,* meaning 'fallow ground', this entailed digging narrow trenches and piling the resulting earth on to adjacent strips to create deep beds. Often used for growing potatoes, lazybeds were employed on shallow ground to provide drainage and increase soil depth.

When first introduced into the Highlands in 1700, potatoes were fiercely resisted by the crofters, who thought the lairds were trying to deprive them of their beloved barley. Much more efficient than cereal crops, potatoes supported four times as many people, acre for acre, as oats or barley. Eventually, cereals were abandoned as potatoes became the main food source, so when the potato crop failed the effect was devastating. A series of poor harvests in the mid-nineteenth century culminated in the potato famine, which forced waves of emigration, depopulating both the Highlands and Ireland.

Two portal-like standing stones on the path mark the site of a Neolithic chambered cairn from around 2000 BC, used for housing cremated remains. Further along, a Bronze Age burial cairn lies on a plateau by the stream.

Kilmory Castle Garden

Argyll and Bute

T: (01546) 602127   E: alison.mcilroy@argyll-bute.gov.uk
W: www.argyll-bute.gov.uk

Kilmory Castle,
Lochgilphead,
Argyll and Bute PA31 8RT

Open all year,
dawn–sunset

Fee free

Off A83, just before
Lochgilphead

'Whatever Kilmory may be now, it was a curious place full of surprises and oddities': the words of the novelist L. B. Walford in the late 1800s are as valid today as they were then. Kilmory, from the Gaelic Cille Mhoire or St Mary's Chapel (*kil* from *cille*, meaning 'cell' or 'chapel'), is an ancient religious site. A cemetery was sited here 5,000 years ago and the ruins of St Mary's Chapel are still in the grounds. The baronial-style castle dates from the early nineteenth century and in 1830, when Sir William Hooker, then Professor of Botany at Glasgow University, was engaged to improve the grounds, he restored the garden along the lines of an existing 1770s plan. Though now overgrown and unkempt, an impressive yew avenue suggests earlier precision.

Many of the plants with which Hooker filled the estate were brought back from his expeditions abroad; at one time the garden boasted over 100 rhododendron specimens and one plant from every country in the world. In keeping with the taste of the time and the limitations of the climate, rhododendrons, conifers and ferns prevailed, all of which still thrive in the high rainfall and acidic soil. In 1855 the *Scottish Gardener* magazine enthused: 'In open glades and in spaces cut out of the jungle of low growing trees...to a stranger's astonishment, are found growing in great profusion and variety, ferns indigenous and exotic...' When Sir William was appointed director of Kew Gardens, he took many rhododendron cuttings with him.

During the first half of the twentieth century Kilmory succumbed to the neglect and decay that befell many properties at the time. In 1974 the Argyll District Council purchased the estate, using the castle for council offices and restoring the walled garden and grounds. The children's playground and picnic benches attest to municipal ownership, but a sensory trail encourages disenfranchised urbanites to reconnect with nature, while a wonderful burn-side walk meanders through a ferny forest to the lake beyond. Beside the Victorian potting sheds a didactic herb garden claims that aniseed was used as an antiseptic and expectorant, horseradish was a laxative and cured rheumatic pain, lemon balm was taken for digestive disorders and camomile was used to reduce inflammation and brighten hair.

Linn Botanic Gardens

Linn Botanic Gardens, Cove, Helensburgh, Argyll and Bute G84 0NR

Open all year, dawn–sunset; parking limited

Fee £3.50, conc. £2.50, children £1, under 5s free

6m S of Garelochhead on B833, 1m N of Cove on shore of Loch Long

Argyll and Bute

T: (01436) 842242/842084   E: linnbotanicgardens@btinternet.com

Originally the grounds of a Victorian villa overlooking Loch Long, the present garden was hived off and has been developed since the 1970s. The Linn of the title refers to the boggy ground below the cliff, which was routinely flooded by two burns before it was cleared in the late nineteenth century. Certainly water is the prevailing element: the rushing waterfall of the glen competes with the still waters of the loch, while the central water garden incorporates ponds and fountains. Trees are helpfully labelled and many rare plants are to be found in the woodland, though the 'Botanic' in the title might mislead; this is not a place of order and didacticism, but rather a densely cultivated wilderness. A walk of just over half a mile is carefully signed to keep visitors going in the same direction along the narrow path. A bamboo garden, begun in 1990, now houses thirty species, alpines clothe the cliff face, lilies line the Long Pond created from a tennis court in the early 1970s and recently a New Zealand heath was planted in a former lawn. A rustic gazebo and various benches provide shelter and rest, while a nursery offers plants for sale.

Logan Botanic Garden

Dumfries and Galloway

T: (01776) 860231 E: logan@rbge.org.uk W: www.rbge.org.uk

Logan, the southernmost satellite of the **Royal Botanic Garden**, Edinburgh, derives its name from the Gaelic *laggan*, meaning 'a small hollow'. Logan sits on a low-lying, gale-tossed peninsula warmed by the Gulf Stream, with an annual 40 inches of rainfall spread evenly throughout the year. Carved from a large agricultural estate, more than half of the garden's 24 acres are given over to protective windbreaks, as the sea, with its salt spray, is never more than a mile away on either side.

Approached through a field of cattle, Logan hides a multitude of surprises behind its sedate Victorian façade. Since the RBGE acquired the garden in 1969, they have been preserving and expanding the collection of southern hemisphere exotics amassed by the McDouall family at the beginning of the twentieth century. The ruined tower incorporated into the garden wall is a remnant of the medieval castle which burned down at the end of the fifteenth century. The walled garden was built as a kitchen garden around the late eighteenth century and 100 years later it was transformed into a pleasure garden when James McDouall married Agnes Buchan-Hepburn, a passionate gardener who brought collections of lilies, roses and decorative shrubs to the marriage.

Agnes introduced the first exotic to Logan in the form of a eucalyptus tree, but it was her two sons who gave the garden its current structure, using plants they collected from temperate regions as well as those acquired from professional plant-hunters such as Reginald Farrer and George Forrest. Today the walled garden is a delightful mixture of exotic plants and Edwardian features with Italianate urns, lily pools, gravel paths and formal avenues supplementing palms, tree ferns, eucalyptus and myriad brightly coloured, strange-shaped flowers and shrubs. Birds use the palm fibre for building nests, while bees sip from the *Echium nervosum*. Picturesque millstones are set into the garden paths and the poolside boasts sections of basalt columns from the Giant's Causeway on Ireland's Antrim coast – acquired when such acts of cultural pillage went unnoticed.

In 1909 the McDouall brothers planted the avenue of cabbage palms, *Cordyline australis*, in the upper walled garden. They

Logan Botanic Garden, Port Logan, Stranraer, Dumfries and Galloway DG9 9ND

Open Apr to Sep, 10–6; Mar and Oct, 10–5

Fee £3.50, children £1

14m S of Stranraer, off B7065

also planted the grove of tree ferns, *Dicksonia antarctica*, in the centre of the walled garden and lined the burn outside with *Trachycarpus fortunei*, Chusan palms. The burn itself hosts what is widely held to be Scotland's largest *Gunnera manicata*.

In 1927 the brothers pioneered the practice, widely followed in the first half of the twentieth century, of growing acid-loving plants in terraces of fresh-cut peat against peat walls. With the loss of peat bogs through the century, the use of such endangered material is now frowned upon; nonetheless Logan continues to replace its peat beds every ten to fifteen years to retain the authenticity of this historic feature.

Summer colour is created with the annual bedding out of more than 5,000 perennials – felicias, verbenas, penstemons and argyranthemums among others, mostly from southern Africa, South America and the Mediterranean. The garden walls support a rich collection of unusual climbing plants, including Chile's national flower, the delicate, bell-shaped *Lapageria rosea*. Resilient shrubs as pittosporum, olearia and the New Zealand flax, *Phormium tenax*, combine with more common beech hedging to provide further protection for tender plants. A fascinating section entitled Local Heroes celebrates plants at the edge of their geographical distribution area. The canny crofters living along the local Galloway coast used sea kale, *Crambe maritima*, as a stewed vegetable, while *Euphorbia paralias* was made into a purgative – hence its vulgar name 'sea spurge'; curiously sea holly, *Eryngium maritimum*, was used as both a cure for flatulence and an aphrodisiac.

Woodland gardens to the south and west hold Logan's enviable collection of *Rhododendron maddenia*; in most Scottish gardens these tender rhododendrons can survive only under glass, but here they flourish in the shelter of the garden wall and castle ruins. Eucalyptus, magnolias and camellias also appreciate the acid soil. There are dedicated Tasmanian and Chilean collections and Logan participates in the RBGE's International Conifer Conservation Programme, cultivating endangered temperate conifers. In 1980 the cabbage palms were replaced after seventy years of battering by salt gales. Because Logan's ideal conditions cause accelerated growth rates, shrubs mature quickly and soon need replacing.

Throughout the year the woodlands offer informal delights, with spring snowdrops giving over to early summer meconopsis, trilliums and primulas. These are followed by autumn leaves, berries and grasses, while in winter the garden's bones reveal their subtleties as the colour, form and texture of the trees take centre stage.

Mount Stuart

Isle of Bute, Argyll and Bute

T: (01700) 503877   E: contactus@mountstuart.com
W: www.mountstuart.com

In 1718 the 2nd Earl of Bute set out to create a magnificent garden; today that garden remains one of the most impressive in the whole of Scotland. Carefully choosing a site on the sheltered east side of his island, he laid out his 300-acre estate with formal gardens, elegant woodlands and magnificent views over the Firth of Clyde. The splendid lime avenue leading to the shore was created by the 3rd Earl in the mid-eighteenth century, one of many wooded avenues framing distant landmarks. The immense 'Forty Five Avenue' leading past the house derives its name, not from the Jacobite uprising, but from the distance, in feet, between the trees across the avenue. The large flat lawn in front of the house was once a formal parterre with a bowling green to the south, a kitchen garden to the north and a series of vistas reflecting the Georgian taste for order.

The original walled garden which housed the 3rd Earl's prized collection of Mexican dahlias was replaced, in the nineteenth century, with a Victorian kitchen garden. In the 1990s this was redesigned by Rosemary Verey in her characteristic ornamental potager style. Since then the garden has been revamped, yet again. The current design, by television star James Alexander-Sinclair, reflects the contemporary fashion for loose, airy schemes, bold plantings and tall grasses. The walled garden centres round a glass pavilion, purchased from the 1988 Glasgow Garden Festival. As part of a larger conservation programme, this houses rare and endangered plants from the Far East and the Antipodes, including orchids, passionflowers, pitcher plants, gingers and bananas. Cut-flower beds surround the pavilion, while an orchard radiates to the south. Vegetable beds are decorative as well as utilitarian, planted for colour and form and

Mount Stuart, Rothesay, Isle of Bute, Argyll and Bute PA20 9LR

Open Easter weekend (Fri–Mon) and May to Sep, 10–6

Fee £3.50, children £2

5½m S of Rothesay ferry terminal on A844

The Ice House

Used for storing food, the ice house was an enclosed room, partly filled with ice that was either piled between layers of insulating heather, straw or sawdust or crushed and packed into a central void. Invented by the Chinese and known to the Romans, the ice house did not become part of the Scottish landscape until the eighteenth century, when agricultural improvements expanded the diet. The ice house required a good drainage outlet and an insulated entrance. Most were free-standing and were sited in a shaded position near the kitchen, with easy access for deliveries, and close to a loch or stream to absorb the melt-water. Caves and grottoes were also favoured locations though some were dug into river banks, as at the **Colzium Lennox Estate**; others were excavated from hillsides, hidden in ha-has or inserted into bridges, as at **Culzean Castle**. Curiously, the ice house at **Bughtrig** was accessed through the greenhouse.

Though ice houses were primarily used for storing meat and fish, as the Scots diet became more sophisticated vegetables, fruit and dairy produce were also kept on shelves or stored on trays suspended in the cool air above the ice. In the temperate climate of Scotland's west coast, ice had to be imported from colder inland regions. Since the ice collected from estate ponds in winter was liable to be muddy and full of leaves, it wasn't until the nineteenth century, when purer ice was imported from Scandinavia and America, that ice came to be used in cooking, ice creams and frozen puddings. In the finest houses, ice was also carved or moulded into elaborate images. While embellishing the table, these decorative sculptures also acted as an early form of air-conditioning.

enclosed within dwarf hedges. Culinary and municipal herb beds, fruit cages and a pleached hornbeam walk fill out the walled garden.

The nineteenth-century pinetum stretches to the west, featuring specimen conifers most of which originate in the forests of the American North-West – giant sequoia, Douglas fir, noble fir, western hemlock and western red cedar. Set out in a formal, geometric pattern, the saplings were protected by sheltering laurel hedges, which slowly died as the conifers grew and cut off their light and nutrients. Today Mount Stuart runs a conifer conservation programme in conjunction with the **Royal**

Botanic Garden, Edinburgh. Having planted 100 acres with endangered conifers from around the world, Mount Stuart is nurturing this 'living gene bank' for future restoration to the wild.

The Victorian preference for wilder, romantic landscapes is evident in the Wee Garden. Designed in 1823, this 8-acre enclosure, sited in the most sheltered part of the estate, houses temperate plants, including euchryphia, kalmia and *Cryptomeria japonica*. In the late nineteenth century there were also pet wallabies here.

From the same era comes the rockery, designed by the popular Edwardian designer Thomas Mawson (1861–1933). Mawson had to pipe water from 1½ miles away to create this boggy fantasy. He also designed the Calvary Pond to represent Jerusalem's Via Dolorosa with the Twelve Stations of the Cross, culminating in a 30-foot crucifix and a chapel beside the pond. Forgotten in the turmoil of the twentieth century, the pond was recently cleared and the path reopened, though the religious allegory survives only in the name. In 1995 the 200-year-old beech avenue was replanted, continuing a long tradition of restoration and innovation. Today four marked walks of differing lengths range across the formal and designed landscapes, providing a fascinating picture of three centuries of horticultural fashion.

Pollok House (NTS)

Glasgow

T: (0141) 616 6410　E: pollokhouse@nts.org.uk　W: www.nts.org.uk

The Pollok Estate provides an extraordinary rural experience 3 miles from the centre of one Scotland's largest cities. Though portions of the land, sold off in the nineteenth century, were developed into the southern suburb of Pollokshields, the estate still offers formal parterres, a walled garden, woodland and wildlife gardens, riverside walks, a deer park, cricket grounds and various playing fields. The current house, the fourth on the property, is a handsome Georgian mansion. Designed by William Adam, it was built by his sons Robert and John in 1747,

Pollok House, Pollokshaws Road, Glasgow G43 1AT

Open all year, 10–5, but closed 25 and 26 Dec, 1 and 2 Jan

Fee house; £8, conc. £5, gardens free

Signed from A736 in Pollokshaws

their father having died just after construction began. The wings and entrance hall are early twentieth century; the garden terraces and flanking pavilions also date from this period, while the elegant stone lions were carved by Hew Lorimer in the 1940s.

Sir John Stirling Maxwell was largely responsible for the design of the gardens. In 1888 he planted the lime avenue to the north of the house with twenty-one pairs of lime trees to mark his twenty-first birthday; he also designed the elegant parterres to the south and east of the house. Sir John shared the late Victorian passion for rhododendrons, having collected and bred many of the cultivars in the woodland garden; one Pollok cultivar, 'Jock', was named for his son-in-law, while 'Olive' was named for his head gardener's wife. The woodland garden also boasts the usual nineteenth-century favourites: magnolias, a handkerchief tree, *Davidia involucrata*, and an arbutus or strawberry tree. Sir John planted the wider woodland with a mix of deciduous species, including ash, beech, birch, oak, sycamore and chestnut, as well as rarer red and Turkey oaks.

In 1965 the house and garden were turned over to the Glasgow Local Authority, which maintains the grounds in an austere but imaginative fashion. The 2-acre walled garden to the east of the house is subdivided with clipped yew hedges to create a rockery, vegetable garden, rose garden and various enclosures, featuring herbaceous, perennial and bedding displays. Several impressive greenhouses grow tender fruit and vegetables.

The country park hosts a herd of Highland cattle, recalling the prize-winners bred by the Maxwell family in the early nineteenth century. It also provides 360 acres of wildlife and wild flowers, its spring bluebells being particularly popular. Known in Gaelic as *currac-cuthaige* or 'cuckoo's-cap', Scotland's bluebell has taken on a sort of mythic status as the 'people's flower'. Its modesty, its 'true blue' colour and its tendency to spring up in barren outcrops have endowed it with a grass-roots virtue celebrated in verse and song. In the centre of the parkland, ten minutes' walk from Pollok House, sits the Burrell Collection – a wonderful array of fine and decorative arts housed in a fabulous timber-and-glass gallery specifically designed to blend with the surrounding woodland.

Portrack:
The Garden of Cosmic Speculation

Dumfries and Galloway

One of the most significant landscapes of recent times, this private estate is open by appointment and anybody interested in contemporary design will be astounded by its originality. The 5-acre garden was first conceived in the mid-1980s by the architectural historian Charles Jencks and his wife, Maggie Keswick, an expert in Chinese geomancy. Bravely acquiescing to Jencks's belief that contemporary science is 'potentially the greatest impetus for creativity of our time', his in-laws allowed the family seat to be transformed from a traditional Victorian estate to an avant-garde centre for cosmic speculation.

After his wife's death in the early 1990s, Jencks continued imposing his arcane interests on the local landscape. Following a long-standing horticultural tradition, he uses his garden to create a microcosm of the universe. As Cardinal Gambara used the Villa Lante to illustrate the evolution of the world, as it was then understood, from original wilderness to Renaissance order, Jencks is using Portrack to explore today's most advanced scientific ideas. Fractals, entropy, quarks, black holes, DNA, chaos, catastrophe and quantum theories all find some form of horticultural expression in the grounds.

Underpinning the design is Jencks's belief that the universe is ordered through harmonic patterns of self-similar repetitions. This idea is expressed in the metaphor of waves – from the subtle rhythm of the Soliton Wave gates to the convex black and white tiling of the Fractal Terrace, from the grass and gravel curves of the Symmetry Break ha-ha to the sweeping calligraphy of the word play etched in paving stones.

Despite its perplexing theoretical underpinnings, the garden developed along pragmatic lines. A waterlogged meadow, drained to create a swimming hole for the children, became the paisley-shaped Slug Lakes; the resultant landfill was banked up into sculptural Snail Mounds. A discarded model by architect James Stirling was redeployed as a folly and placed in Crow Wood, thus transforming the mundane forest into a mysterious *sacra bosco* or sacred grove.

The walled Victorian kitchen garden was first designed as a 'physik' garden for herbs; this evolved into a 'physics' garden,

Portrack, Holywood,
Dumfries and Galloway
DG2 0RW

Open by written appointment and on certain days for Scotland's Gardens Scheme

Fee £6

5m N of Dumfries, 1½m off A76

examining the senses, before being redesigned as an 'ambi-grammi' garden, exploring the ambiguous nature of language through inscriptions which can be read both right-side up and upside down. Such wordplay recalls the poetic whims of Ian Hamilton Finlay's **Little Sparta** nearby.

Early on Keswick and Jencks planned a 'Skottish' garden as a sly response to the 'tartanization' of Scotland initiated by Sir Walter Scott at **Abbotsford** and promoted by canny Scots publicists ever since. The identification of particular tartans with particular clans is a relatively recent invention, promoted by manufacturers keen to sell as much fabric as possible. Portrack's Skottish Garden, based on the Keswick family tartan, was to feature lines of rocks, concrete, brick and stone interwoven with plants to create a rich plaid effect. Though this wry essay on national identity was never actually created, the humour behind it permeates the garden: a pebble foot maze is called the Maze Brain, a tennis court is called the Garden of Fair Play and decorative gate-pier finials represent different models of the cosmos.

While traditional gardeners might question the attempt to explain cosmogenesis through horticulture, no one can deny the sheer inventiveness of the enterprise. Whatever its intellectual pretensions, the garden remains an extraordinary horticultural achievement. The sound of trickling water, the scent of herbs, the textures of gravel, grass and stone underfoot, and the multiplicity of colours and forms make this garden a stimulant for the senses as well as the mind.

Strachur House Garden

Strachur House, Strachur, Cairndow, Argyll and Bute PA27 8BX

Open all year, 1–5

Fee £2.50, children 50p

14m N of Ardbeg on A815, at Strachur House Farm, signposted

Argyll and Bute

The large walled garden at Strachur House is a fine example of an eighteenth-century garden adapted for twenty-first-century circumstances. Set within a landscaped park, laid out by General Campbell in 1782, the garden leads off the back of Strachur House. In the absence of a huge labour force, much of the garden has been laid to lawn, the stonework is decaying and the flower borders have a casual, unkempt charm. Azalea beds, autumn beds, a golden bed and various other-coloured beds surround a central, sunken garden known as the Bear Pit. There is also an unusual anemone and agapanthus bed which provides a crisp balance of whites and blues. Trellises support hops, honeysuckle, roses and clematis; borders are filled with tulips, roses, lilies, campanulas and other Edwardian favourites. The central axis ends in a round enclosure backed by a semicircular yew hedge. Ancient beeches, yews and Japanese maples shelter the garden, while a burn-side rhododendron walk meanders through woodland. A neat vegetable patch beyond the walled garden has a grass path flanked by sweet peas under-planted with antirrhinums, creating a delicate pastel composition. The bleating of sheep in an adjacent field emphasizes the pastoral informality of this delightful garden.

Threave Garden (NTS)

Dumfries and Galloway

T: (01556) 502575   E: threave@nts.org.uk   W: www.ngs.org.uk

The name Threave is thought to derive from the Old Welsh for 'homestead', though Iron Age remains indicate that the area has been settled for millennia. The medieval castle was annexed by the crown after the unsuccessful Jacobite uprising of 1745 and in the mid-nineteenth century the estate was bought by a prosperous Liverpool businessman who turned it into a Scottish sporting estate in the fashion of the time. Leaving the castle ruins as a picturesque folly, he built a Scots baronial-style mansion on the highest piece of land. In 1948, when the estate was given to the National Trust for Scotland, there was talk of blowing up the house, as dwellings of that size were unfashionable and expensive to maintain. Happily, the Trust decided to retain the house, turning it into a School for Practical Gardening. The surrounding 65 acres of gardens, though primarily designed for trainee gardeners, are filled with ideas for the interested amateur. The varied terrain encouraged an informal layout which allows for a variety of different habitats and styles, including a pond and waterfall, scree beds, orchards, an arboretum and rose, woodland, peat and rock gardens.

The Victorian walled garden is of particular interest. Each wall has an information board stating the hours of sun per day and the average seasonal temperature, demonstrating that

Threave, Castle Douglas, Dumfries and Galloway DG7 1RX

Open garden: all year, 9.30–5; house: 1 Apr to 31 Oct, Wed–Sun 11–3

Fee garden: £6, conc. £5; house and garden: £10, conc. £7

1m W of Castle Douglas, off A75

within a single enclosure temperatures can range from the north-facing wall with a mere two hours of sun per day and an average summer temperature of 13°C (55°F) to the south-facing wall with nine hours of sun and an average summer temperature of 22° (71°F). Wisteria, *Solanum capsicum* and abelias thrive on the south-facing wall, while more forgiving morello cherries and redcurrants shelter against the colder north wall. Such hardiness explains why currants, along with gooseberries, were a popular part of the nineteenth-century Scots diet. Since sugar was expensive, berries were often fermented as wines rather than preserved as jam.

While the original glasshouse had coal fires within hollow walls to warm the fruit trees espaliered against it, this system was replaced in 1997 with state of the art technology, providing a cool house for tender rhododendrons, a temperate house for fuchsias and other temperate plants, and a tropical house for orchids, banana trees and dramatic *Strelitzia reginae* or birds-of-paradise. Cold frames flank the glasshouse, as do alpine troughs.

The patio garden, to the east of the walled garden, was designed as a student project in 1972; three decades later, this quiet mossy area is filled with statuary, while a *Eucryphia nymansay* provides summer flowers and an *Acer rubrum* gives autumn colour. The woodlands are full of herbaceous perennials and flowering shrubs, including many rhododendrons and azaleas, and a *Davidia involucrata* or handkerchief tree. The tall, conical *Metasequoia glyptostroboides* is one of the few deciduous conifers. Commonly called the dawn redwood, the tree originated in China; it was first described by fossil records in 1941 and was thought to be extinct until later that same year, when living plants were discovered.

SOUTH-EAST SCOTLAND

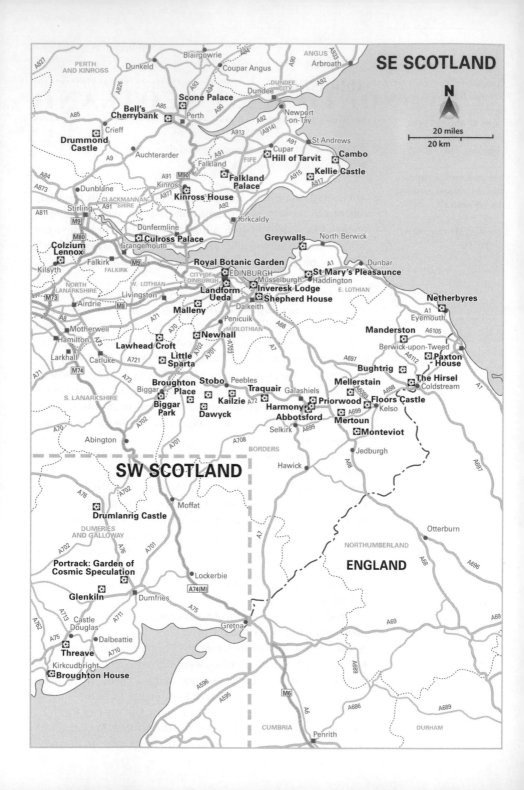

Abbotsford

Abbotsford, Melrose,
Scottish Borders TD6 9BQ

Open 19 Mar to 31 Oct,
9.30–5, except Sun in Mar,
Apr, May and Oct, 2–5

Fee gardens: £2, children
free; house and gardens:
£6, children £3

2m W of Melrose, off A7
on B6360

Scottish Borders

T: (01896) 752043   E: enquiries@scottsabbotsford.co.uk
W: www.scottsabbotsford.co.uk

Abbotsford, the estate created by Sir Walter Scott in the early nineteenth century, is a magnificent pastiche. With its reliance on both literary and historic allusions, the garden prefigures the work of Ian Hamilton Finlay at **Little Sparta**, but where Finlay's interests range from Greek mythology to Nazi regalia, Scott confined himself to Scottish folklore.

In 1811 Scott purchased Cartley Hole, a 100-acre farm dramatically perched on a hill overlooking the River Tweed and said to have been a haunt of the medieval poet Thomas the Rhymer. Legend, promoted by Scott in his collection of local ballads *Minstrelsy of the Scottish Border* (1802), describes how the comely Thomas was abducted by the Queen of Faeries, who released him, seven years later, imbued with the gifts of poetry and prophecy. By aligning himself with this thirteenth-century seer, Scott subtly reinforced his identity as interpreter of the Scottish soul.

In his perennial quest for romance and antiquity, Scott quickly rechristened his estate Abbotsford, alluding to a narrowing in the river where the monks of Melrose drove their cattle in days gone by. Over the years he acquired more land and developed castle and garden, littering both with Celtic motifs. A lasting tribute to his powers of design and promotion, Abbotsford soon became the favourite Scottish site for artists on both sides of the border, remaining so for several decades until it was usurped by **Balmoral** – an equally romantic fabrication – in the mid-nineteenth century.

Scott was one of a group of Scots intellectuals who feared that their nation had been steadily losing her identity since the 1707 Act of Union with England. Industrialization and rural depopulation had left Scotland's cities teeming, her countryside empty and large portions of her population living abroad. The Jacobite uprisings of 1715 and 1745 had both ended in failure, while Bonnie Prince Charlie, the last Scots hero, had died an heirless, alcoholic exile. Scott's *Minstrelsy of the Scottish Border*, along with Francis Grose's engravings in *Antiquities of Scotland*

(1789–92) and Robert Burns's transcriptions of old Scottish songs, was part of a movement to halt this cultural erosion.

In Abbotsford Scott did more than simply preserve endangered tales; he manufactured a Scottish heritage – virtually inventing a Celtic architecture, landscape and lifestyle. In 1822 he stage-managed George IV's visit to Edinburgh – the first royal appearance since Charles II's disastrous 1651 bid to regain the English crown. By squeezing the corpulent king into a kilt less than a century after such elements of national identity had been banned in the Disarming Act, Scott started a Europe-wide fashion for this unlikely garment.

While Scottish architects had long been classicizing unwieldy castles, Scott harked back to the baronial age, adding turrets, towers, bastions, gables, crenellations and chimneys to create a roofline as craggy as the surrounding hills. His interiors dripped with armour and antlers, suggesting the rugged lifestyle celebrated in his fiction, while his garden exhibited a rather schizophrenic combination of French formality and Italian exuberance amid romantic English parkland.

Condemning the English landscape style as 'not simplicity, but affectation, labouring to be simple', Scott surrounded his house with enclosures, walls, gates, pavilions and avenues. The entrance drive meanders through Victorian woodland of yews and conifers. Rowans also figure, as they were traditionally held to guard against evil.

The south courtyard around the main entrance is a rather dour space focusing on a fountain, the bowl of which came from the old Edinburgh market cross, pulled down in 1756 as an obstruction to traffic. Today's planting of pink petunias recalls that in 1660 the bowl was filled with wine to celebrate Charles II's restoration. The yew hedge on the south wall replaced an earlier rose pergola. Ovals cut into the hedge reveal five medallions from the old market cross, alternating with rectangular stones from a Roman settlement nearby.

A recently planted woodland walk winds off to the west, while the north front of the castle is austerely terraced into three grassy slopes overlooking the river. Rabbits are a perennial problem, as indicated by the copious game larder built into the top terrace, embellished with a ring of gargoyles and crowned with a romantic bastion lookout.

The east court, a large walled garden, is entered through a heavy, rustic, wooden door. With admirable loquacity, Scott lamented the English practice of banishing the walled garden far from the house: 'The garden, artificial in its structure, its shelter, its climate and its soil, which every consideration of taste, beauty, and convenience recommended to be kept near to the mansion, and maintained, as its appendage, in the highest state of ornamental decoration...has, by a strange and sweeping sentence of exile, been condemned to wear the coarsest and most humbling form. Reduced to a clumsy oblong, enclosed within four rough-built walls, and sequestered in some distant corner where it may be best concealed from the eye...'

Scott's walled garden exhibits the highest state of ornamental decoration. A herbaceous border thrives in the ruins of the old vinery, while a luxurious peony border attests to the Scottish love of this oriental flower. Roses, cotoneaster and variegated ivies line the walls and the corners are punctuated with clipped yews. The central lawn, surrounded with raised gravel walks, is divided into two sections; one features a plaintive sculpture of Morris, the excise man in Scott's novel *Rob Roy*, while the other focuses on an ancient sundial. Separating this garden from the south court is a screen copied from the cloisters at Melrose Abbey. Clipped yews on the western wall mark the entrance to the raised kitchen garden.

Here the traditional Scottish mixture of flowers, fruit and vegetables flourishes, with sweet peas scaling the floral borders to screen the mundane produce behind. An elegant orangery, designed by Sir Walter himself, marks the western end of the garden, while ancient espaliers and box edging create interior divisions. Behind the garden an old potting shed houses the boilers which used to heat the walls; today espaliered fruit trees thrive without the benefit of hot pipes – a dubious benefit of climate change.

Scottish thrift ensured that Abbotsford was designed for low maintenance long before the modern ecologists made this a guiding principle of sustainability. Today two full-time gardeners and two foresters maintain the whole estate. Within the castle, the library is said to have been built of cedar, supplied by James Waugh from **Harmony Garden** in Melrose nearby. Legend has it that the dying Scott insisted on being wheeled into the dining room so that his last hours could be spent contemplating the Border countryside which he popularized so lovingly in his fiction.

Bell's Cherrybank Gardens

Perth and Kinross

T: (01738) 472800   E: info@thecalyx.co.uk   W: www.thecalyx.co.uk

Founded by Bell's Whisky, this 6½-acre garden holds the National Heather Collection, with more than 900 varieties all clearly displayed. The huge range of plants is bound to inspire heather-lovers; for others there is an aviary, a water garden and a children's playground.

Cherrybank Gardens were recently donated to Scotland's

Bell's Cherrybank Gardens, Necessity Brae, Perth PH2 0PF

Open Jan and Feb, Thurs–Sat 10–4, Sun 12–4; Mar to Oct, Mon–Sat 10–5, Sun 12–5; Nov and Dec, Mon–Sat 10–4, Sun 12–4

Fee £3.75, children £2.50

Off A93 Glasgow road, on S edge of Perth, 1m E of Broxden roundabout

Scottish Gardeners

Despite her small size, northern setting and lack of horticultural traditions, Scotland has produced a disproportionate number of great gardeners. By the mid-eighteenth century many of Britain's grand estates, among them Blenheim Castle in Woodstock and Syon House in London, had Scotsmen as head gardeners. This unexpected situation is often attributed to the excellence of the Scots parochial school system, which ensured an educated workforce. The lack of deep-rooted national horticultural traditions probably encouraged innovation, while the hostile climate undoubtedly sent ambitious apprentices south to England, where the growing season was longer, the climate more clement, the apprenticeships shorter, the opportunities greater and the wages better. Accustomed as they were to the more brutal conditions of the north, Scots gardeners excelled in England, and when they graduated to positions of power they looked to their homeland for assistants.

In 1722 a Scot, Philip Miller (1691–1771), was appointed Curator of the Chelsea Physic Garden. He sought apprentices among his countrymen, one of whom, William Aiton (1766–1849), went on to create the Royal Botanic Garden at Kew, where he, in turn, appointed a fellow Scot, the twenty-three-year-old William McNab (1780–1848), as his foreman. Meanwhile, Miller was succeeded at Chelsea by another Scot, William Forsyth (1737–1804), who then went on to oversee the gardens at St James's and Kensington palaces. This clannishness engendered widespread resentment, and in the 1760s English gardeners attempted, unsuccessfully, to ban all apprentices from the north. Nonetheless, Scottish gardeners continued to be prized throughout Europe. Thomas Blaikie (1758–1838) established a thriving practice in France, supplying English plants to his French clients while helping to lay out the Bagatelle Gardens for the future King Charles X and the Parc Monceau for the Duc D'Orléans. James Fraser (1793–1863), whom J. C. Loudon described as 'an excellent botanist and gardener', settled in Ireland, where he designed many landscapes in the picturesque style. Even Catherine the Great of Russia insisted on having her own Scots gardener.

Garden Trust, which has acquired a further 50 acres and is planning to create Scotland's first national garden and horticultural centre. After an exhaustive consultation process the name Calyx was chosen for the project, a calyx being the whorl of leaves which protects the growing bud within.

A horticultural extravaganza, this £23-million project will combine scholarship with entertainment, developing both trial beds and lifestyle gardens to provide horticultural advice as well as design inspiration. While the trial beds will cater specifically for the Scots climate – testing fruit, vegetables and decorative plants – the lifestyle gardens will promote the work of national and international designers.

Although Calyx is not scheduled to open until late 2007, demonstrations and workshops are already under way. The project is expected to attract thousands of visitors, from at home and abroad – an example of the contemporary phenomenon of horticulture prompting tourism, which in turn promotes economic regeneration.

Biggar Park

South Lanarkshire

Biggar Park, Biggar, South Lanarkshire ML12 6JS

Open May to Jul by appointment and on certain days for Scotland's Gardens Scheme

Fee £3

¼m S of Biggar on A702

T: (01899) 220185

This popular garden is as rich and varied as would be expected from the owner of Dobbies, one of Scotland's largest commercial nurseries. When Captain and Mrs David Barnes arrived at Biggar Park thirty years ago, they found magnificent trees and lots of spring bulbs; the rest of this glorious 10-acre garden has evolved in the intervening decades. The line of conifers along the front boundary was recently put in to screen a newly built housing estate across the road. Planting round the eighteenth-century house was kept to a pink palette to tone with the warm, stone walls. A marshy area in front was transformed into a pond, while a striking red bridge gives an oriental atmosphere to the scene. This harmonizes with the Japanese garden which evolved around a fire pond dug during the Second World War in case of bombs. Acers, bamboo and pagoda-shaped topiary surround a central stone which looks ancient and oriental though it was dug out of a nearby field.

The estate is well served with statuary, much of it sent back in a job lot from Italy, where Captain Barnes was on a buying trip for Dobbies. A copy of Michelangelo's *David* turns a tranquil copper beech enclosure into an Italian garden. The woodland walk round the back of the house reveals other, less orthodox sculpture, including a grotesque owl whose beady eyes peek eerily from an ivy cloak. The serpentine path to the orchard is under-planted with snake's head fritillaries. Deriving their common name from the reptilian shape of the unopened bud and their genus name from the shaker, *fritillus*, in which the Romans shook their dice, these sinister lilies reinforce the sense of this area as a *sacra bosco* or sacred grove.

The walled garden, situated a discreet distance from the house, sports buttressing hedges which shelter colour-themed herbaceous borders. The garden itself, though less than an acre in size, is one of the highlights of the estate, with walls over 7 feet tall and views through an elegant red, wrought-iron gate to a volcanic plug in the distance. Though fruit and vegetables are combined in the traditional manner, this is a place of pleasure more than utility. Obscuring the original cruciform shape, the owners tripled the depth of the flower beds and created a magnificent 150-foot double herbaceous border down the centre. This is backed by roses, swagged on fat moss-covered ropes reputedly from the *Queen Mary*.

A fibreglass sculpture of a sword and hand, *Excalibur*, emerges from the central dipping pond. Herbaceous plants are staked on steel poles designed to support reinforced concrete, while the bright-green plant tags are rendered truly indelible with a sheep-tag pen, available from rural vets. The ubiquitous azaleas and rhododendrons are banished to the spring garden, where they can be appreciated in season, then quietly forgotten. The estate is planned for year-round interest, as swathes of meconopsis follow the daffodils, providing early colour before the herbaceous borders take over, to be succeeded in autumn by blazing acers.

Broughton Place,
Broughton, Biggar,
South Lanarkshire
ML12 6HJ

Open 9 April to Dec,
10.30–6

Fee honesty box

Slightly N of Broughton on
the A701, signed
'Broughton Gallery'

Broughton Place

South Lanarkshire

T: (01899) 830234

Broughton Place is an elegant example of twentieth-century historicism. Despite its air of antiquity, this baronial-style keep was designed in the 1930s by Basil Spence, and its stark monumentality is intriguingly evocative of the Modern movement. Approached by an impressive eighteenth-century beech avenue, the white walls provide a striking contrast to the startling green of the surrounding moors.

Over the years the house has been divided into apartments and today an art gallery provides the access to the delightful walled garden, built into a steep slope to the rear of the dwelling. Spence designed the charming corner *doocot,* the ground floor of which once doubled as a summer house for a tennis court on the other side of the wall. The remainder of the 2-acre space was laid out by the original owner, one of those indomitable Scots women who wrested a magnificent garden from thin soil 1,000 feet above sea level, whipped by winds and subject to protracted winter frosts.

The garden was laid out in the formal style with a wide central gravel path and stone steps linking lower lawn, central knot garden and upper orchard. Today an iris walk and stone troughs of billowing white saxifrage replace an earlier watercourse which had begun to disintegrate. Deep flower borders flank the central path and magnificent *Clematis montana* drape languidly across the wrought-iron gate at the end. The interior space is divided with hedges and stone walls to shelter such tender species as *Eucryphia glutinosa.* With the growing season limited by late springs and early autumns, the garden vibrates in July and August as peonies, iris, alliums, roses, delphiniums and the usual herbaceous glories rush to maturity. Poppies thrive on the light, free-draining soil and the garden boasts many mysterious cultivars from the middle of the twentieth century.

The influence of the art gallery is felt throughout, with unusual statuary, benches and garden accoutrements. The box knot garden is planted with feverfew – an ancient cure for headaches; indeed, the gardener insists that anyone who chews a few of the leaves will find all pain has vanished within half an hour. A southerner, he describes all Scots gardens as '*dreich*' – tedious, dreary, 'like the weather'. This useful bit of old Scots slang derives from *dree* – to endure or suffer; hence 'to dree one's weird' or suffer one's destiny. Surprisingly, despite the barren moors above it, the garden at Broughton Place is anything but *dreich*.

Bughtrig

Scottish Borders

T: (01890) 840678

Bughtrig, Leitholm, Coldstream, Scottish Borders TD12 4JP

Open 1 Jun to 1 Sep

Fee £2, children £1

¼m E of Leitholm on B6461

Bughtrig means 'a farm on a ridge'; *rig* figures frequently in names in this region. Remarkably, the property has belonged to only three families since the fourteenth century. The earliest traceable records show it was owned by the Dicksons, a Border family who, facing financial problems in 1695, sold it to prosperous merchants from the Netherlands; one hundred and forty years later, after a protracted family dispute, they sold it back to the Dicksons. In 1938 the property was bought by Admiral Sir Bertram Ramsay and his wife. When her husband was killed in service, Lady Ramsay sought solace in horticulture, developing the gardens until 1974, when the property passed to her son, who has continued to develop it with such whimsical touches as a Rupert Till wire hen and a cheerful trumpeting elephant by John Cox.

The house, built in the late eighteenth century, opens on to a large, semicircular lawn with a wonderful view of the Cheviot Hills. In the nineteenth century a shelter belt of specimen conifers was planted to create a microclimate, ensuring that Bughtrig is always several degrees warmer than the surrounding region. The 2½-acre walled garden is enclosed on three sides by hedges, with a fourth wall being formed by the façade of a former farm building. Beyond this lies a large fruit garden, probably created in the early twentieth century. Unusually, the ice house is accessed from a door in one of the greenhouses.

Though the garden was originally planted with the traditional Scots mixture of fruit, vegetables and flowers, the Ramsays gradually removed the vegetables and many of the fruit trees, creating a formal flower garden with box-edged beds, roses and peonies and a striking autumn border of bright-red *Lobelia cardinalis* 'Huntsman'. Interior divisions are formed by espaliers and beech hedges, while a charming grass walk, bordered by flowers and backed by a copper beech hedge, leads to a honeysuckle-draped pergola. One of the many roses on display is the large, lilac-coloured 'The Scotsman', donated by the newspaper of the same name.

Part of the old kitchen garden has recently been turned into a memorial garden, with a simple knot surrounding a statue of Admiral Ramsay, commemorating those who died in the Second World War during the Dunkirk and Normandy operations.

Cambo

Cambo, Kingsbarns,
St Andrews, Fife KY16 8QD

Open all year, 10–5

Fee £3.50, children free

Off A917, 16m from St
Andrews, between
Kingsbarns and Crail

Fife

T: (01333) 450054 W: www.camboestate.com

With its enchanting walled garden, woodland walks and isolated beach, Cambo is one of the most delightful private properties in Scotland. The eighteenth-century estate is approached through open parkland filled with grazing cattle, goats and horses – a charming introduction to the informal delights to come. Cambo takes its name from the Cambo Burn, which, unusually, runs through the walled garden. During the early twentieth century the stream was enhanced to create a picturesque oriental atmosphere, reinforced with weeping willows, a rustic stream-side pavilion and several ornamental bridges.

The garden itself is threaded with wide borders, grass paths, gravel walks and informal beds containing some intriguing colour combinations, such as deep-purple aquilegia and lime-green hostas. The cut-flower garden was recently replanted in an abstract, geometric layout, while prairie-style perennial planting ensures late-season colour. Among 250 rose varieties on display, the upper wall is clad with such coloured climbers as the creamy 'Gloire de Dijon' beside the pure-white 'Mrs Herbert Stevens' beside the deep-red 'Guinée'. The olfactory senses are further indulged with a lilac-walk featuring twenty-six varieties, including the double-white 'Mme Lemoine' and the double-purple 'William Robinson' – the latter's rich scent and verdant habit seem an appropriate tribute to the father of the informal garden style. There is also a spectacular old apple allée underplanted with nepeta, alliums and old-fashioned roses. A thick ribbon of chives flanks the strawberry bed, while a stream-side lawn provides a serene space amid the profusion of colours and scents.

Though large, the garden is intimate, with shrubs and trees kept to human scale. The space has not been levelled and the natural curves of the land contribute to the air of Edenic harmony. Beyond, a woodland walk provides a potent contrast to the cultivated garden. Renowned for its late winter snowdrops and early spring bulbs, the walk leads through ancient woodlands where Holly and Ivy, the resident Large White sows, keep the undergrowth in check. Suddenly the whistle of wind in the treetops gives way to the crashing of waves on rocks as visitors find themselves on a lonely beach beside the North Sea.

Colzium Lennox Estate

Stirling

T: (01236) 828150

Colzium Lennox, Kilsyth, Stirling G65 0PY

Open grounds: all year; walled garden: Apr to Sep, 12–7; Oct to Mar, weekends only, 12–4

Fee free

½m E of Kilsyth on A803

In 1937 Colzium House and 68 acres were left to the burgh of Kilsyth by William Mackay Lennox as a memorial to his mother. Like many large estates, Colzium was let out as a market garden during the Second World War, and it degenerated in the post-war period. In 1967, however, in a spirit of idealistic redevelopment, the burgh, with the help of the Countryside Commission for Scotland, began to restore and develop the estate for the enjoyment of the general public. Today the walled garden is an arboreal showcase with raked, serpentine paths winding through a dizzying array of shrubs and trees, all discreetly labelled and immaculately maintained. Sheltering amid junipers, cypresses and berberis is a Chusan palm, *Trachycarpus fortunei*, named for the Scottish explorer Robert Fortune, who plant-hunted in China in the mid-nineteenth century. The walls are cloaked in hydrangea, hops, solanum and other climbers, and though it has no herbaceous borders, the garden is noted for

Curling

Curling has long been one of the most popular winter pastimes in Scotland. Played on a rectangle of ice, the game is rather like boules, where two teams of four players each try to slide their stones closest to a central target. By the nineteenth century most large Scots estates had dedicated curling ponds, though frozen lochs, marshes and fire ponds could also be pressed into service. The word 'curling' derives from the Scots *curr*, which, like the English purr, describes the low growling sound that the rocks make while sliding over the ice; this noise also explains its common epithet, 'the Roaring Game'.

Though some describe curling as 'chess on ice' because of the strategy required, others think of it as 'housework on ice' because of the way players sweep the path ahead of their moving stones. The origins of the game are uncertain. While many believe it was imported by Flemish emigrants arriving in Scotland in the late sixteenth century, others trace it back further to Scotland's early sixteenth-century trading links with the Low Countries; certainly Pieter Bruegel the Elder painted several winter scenes in which Flemish peasants appear to be sliding rocks along frozen ponds.

Early on, the game was played with flat-bottomed river stones, but over time this was refined as heavy granite was found to be more effective. Today's curling stones, weighing up to 44 pounds, are made from hard igneous rock, one of the best sources of which is the blue-grey granite quarried from Ailsa Craig, a volcanic plug in the Firth of Clyde near **Culzean**. The oldest datable curling rock is from 1511, though the earliest curling club, founded in Kinross, wasn't established till 1688. Records from the Glasgow Assembly of Presbyterians attest to the game's early popularity with a case from 1638 in which a bishop of Orkney was accused of being 'a curler on the ice on the Sabbath!' In the eighteenth century the Scots formalized the rules of the game and in the nineteenth century they established the Royal Caledonian Curling Club as the governing body of the sport. Mass immigration during the Highland Clearances spread the game to all corners of the globe, and it remains extremely popular in countries such as Canada, where the climate ensures the requisite winter ice conditions.

Curling has been part of the Winter Olympics since 1998, but the increase in temperature over the past century has meant that Scottish lochs rarely freeze any more and the game was losing popularity. However, in 2002 the Scottish women's team galvanized the nation when they won a gold medal at the Winter Olympics. Suddenly curling attracted enormous interest on both sides of the border and it is now enjoying a comeback.

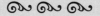

its spring carpet of crocuses and snowdrops. Initials inscribed in the trees attest to the popularity of the woodland walk, while a dog cemetery and a burn-side ice house provide atmospheric links with the past.

The grounds offer various entertainments, with a football pitch, mini train track, pitch and putt course, bandstand and tea room. They also contain an old curling pond. The origins of 'the Roaring Game' are lost in the mists of time, but most large Scots estates in the nineteenth century had dedicated curling ponds.

Culross Palace Garden (NTS)

Fife

T: (01383) 880359   E: information@nts.org.uk   W: www.nts.org.uk

Culross is a charming recreation of a seventeenth-century urban garden. The title 'palace', a long-standing misnomer, is a mis-translation of the Latin *palatium* or great hall. Although James VI visited on several occasions, Culross was never a royal residence, though it was the house of an affluent merchant, Sir George Bruce. Descended from Robert the Bruce, Sir George was granted the lease of local collieries and salt pans in the mid-sixteenth century, and after making a fortune exporting coal and salt to the Low Countries he used his wealth to build this elegant dwelling, complete with courtyard, stable block and garden.

No records exist of the original layout, but the NTS has reconstructed the garden to a typical seventeenth-century design. Within its ancient, enclosing walls, the steep slope has been divided into neat, geometric spaces reflecting the contemporary desire to assert man's domination over nature; a flowery meadow, turf benches, an apple arbour and masses of roses reveal an almost equal delight in the natural world. Bee boles are placed waist high in the walls, where the woven bee skeps could be easily maintained. Herb-edged, raised beds hold a selection of period vegetables, some of which – salsify, alexanders, skirret and Good King Henry – are quite unusual. The warm stone wall hosts a grape vine, an apricot *Prunus armeniaca* 'Peregrine' and a cherry *Prunus avium* 'Stella', as well as the ubiquitous medlar. Self-sown foxgloves thrust through the utilitarian beds, while pots of carnations – known as gillyflower because they flower in July – add colour and scent.

Culross Palace, Culross, Dumfermline, Fife KY12 8JH

Open garden: Apr to Sep, 10–6 or sunset if earlier; palace: Good Fri to 30 Sep, 12–5

Fee £8, conc. £5 (incl. palace); garden free when house closed

Centre of Culross, off A985

Willow hurdles, clay watering pots and paths of crushed cockle and mussel shells from the local beach give an air of authenticity, as does the compost heap, mischievously sited by the entrance gate. Old Scots Dumpies scratch about the orchard; wonderfully regal despite their name, these stalwart fowl were bred 900 years ago to provide meat and eggs while surviving the Scottish winter outdoors. Run on organic principles, this garden is a sheer delight; the only thing missing is a pig grubbing in the orchard.

Dawyck, Stobo,
Scottish Borders EH45 9JU

Dawyck

Open 1 to 28 Feb, 10–4;
1 to 31 Mar, 10–5;
1 Apr to 30 Sep, 10–6;
1 to 31 Oct, 10–5; 1 to 30
Nov, 10–4 (last admission
an hour before closing)

Fee £3.50, children £1

8m SW of Peebles on B712

Scottish Borders

T: (01721) 760254   E: dawyck@rbge.org.uk   W: www.rbgc.org.uk

Dawyck Botanical Gardens and Arboretum is one of the three specialist garden outposts of the **Royal Botanical Garden, Edinburgh**. An exposed hillside in one of the coldest parts of Scotland might seem an unlikely setting, but the cool, continental climate is particularly suited to species from the northern hemisphere and three centuries of planting have established Dawyck as one of the finest arboreta in the world. Though frosts can begin as early as September and can last as late as May, shelter belts mitigate the worst effects of the wind. While Dawyck was created by three families – the Veitches, Naesmyths and Balfours – its collection has been shaped by several of the world's greatest plant collectors.

The Veitches, who first settled the steep Tweed valley in 1491, were distant ancestors of the famous nineteenth-century nurseryman John Veitch. In 1650, when they planted a horse chestnut, *Aesculus hippocastanum*, from eastern Europe, the Veitches became the first arborists to introduce exotic trees to Scotland. At the end of the seventeenth century the Dawyck estate was bought by Sir James Naesmyth, a lawyer whose cruelty engendered the nickname 'the Deil o' Dawyck'. This devil was also a gardener who introduced new species from North America and Europe. His grandson, also Sir James, studied under the Swedish botanist Carl Linnaeus, inventor of the binomial system of plant naming which is still used today. Linnaeus is said to have been present

John Reid and The Scots Gard'ner

Little is known for certain about John Reid beyond the fact that he wrote *The Scots Gard'ner* (1683), Scotland's first garden book. He claimed to have been born near Niddrie Castle, 7 miles west of Edinburgh, and the preface to the third edition of the book states that he was gardener to Sir George Mackenzie of Rosehaugh on the Moray Firth; he is also thought to have worked as a garden boy at Hamilton Palace and later as a gardener at **Drummond**.

As well as providing invaluable information about how to garden in Scotland's bitter climate and rough topography, Reid's book also lays out the rules for creating formal pleasure gardens. Garden historians have long wondered where he trained; though his literary style is rather convoluted, his horticultural knowledge appears to exceed that which could have been gained from working in any of the Scottish gardens of the time. The fact that he advocates the uniquely Scots agricultural practice of run-rigging and, more crucially, that he makes no reference to the tender exotics which were fashionable in England at the time, militates against the suggestion that he gained his training at one of the grand English estates. Some suggest that since Reid shamelessly promotes James Sutherland in his book, he might have trained under Sutherland at the **Botanic Garden in Edinburgh**: 'If you would be further satisfied in the varieties of plants, consult the Learned and most Ingenious Mr James Sutherland's Catalogue Physic Gardener at Edinburgh.' Not surprisingly, Reid's book was offered for sale at the garden.

Though clearly extremely experienced, Reid is not particularly innovative; his advice on layout and design follows the practice common in Scotland at the time. He advocates a modest, formal, symmetrical layout, with all walks, avenues and hedges extending from the house, 'like the sun sending forth its beams': 'Make all the buildings and plantings ly so about the

in 1725 when Sir James planted Dawyck's European larches, *Larix decidua.*

Two generations later, in the 1830s, Dawyck acquired its classical features. When the existing house was destroyed by fire, Sir John Naesmyth commissioned an ornate gothic mansion with Italianate terraces, steps, bridges and urns all created by Italian masons imported for the task. Sir John is also credited with noticing an unusual upright sapling in a grove of ordinary beeches. He transplanted it beside the house, where it grew to over 60 feet high, and today this *Fagus sylvatica* 'Dawyck' is the most famous tree on the estate.

Sir John further embellished the estate with 2,000 acres of mixed woodland, but his most significant contribution to arboriculture was his sponsorship of some of the greatest plant-hunting expeditions of the nineteenth century. He supported house, as that the house may be the centre; all the walks, trees and hedges running to the house. Therefore, what ever you have on the one hand, make as much of the same form and in the same place, on the other.' He advised that the more utilitarian functions be located at the outer edge of the estate within an enclosing shelter belt of trees, while the entrance court-yard should be a simple design focusing on the main door: 'only one bordure at the wall, planted with laurels and other greens; one pathed or brick-walle in the middle leading to the middle of the front-house with a long grass-plot on each hand'. For the central pleasure gar-dens he advocates espaliered trees against the walls, evergreen shrubs clipped into geometric forms to punctuate the corners, gravel walks bisecting the space and grass plots flanked with potted plants or borders of flowers 'orderly intermixt, weeded, mow'd, rolled, and kept all clean and handsome'.

An early supporter of the practice of mixing vegetables, fruit and flowers, he wrote, 'The bordures of your kitchen-garden, round by the walkes, may be boxed with thyme, lavender, hyssop, rue etc, the next with parsley, straw-berries, violets, July-flowers etc, cherrie-gardens and physick-gardens with sweet-brier often cut, or box cut three times per annum, in April, June and August, remembering to cut their roots inside every second year that they exhaust not the strength or nourishment of the flowers or herbs. But that which I preferred for flower-gardens above all is dwarf-juniper, raised from seed and planted.'

Reid helpfully provided a plan at the beginning of the book, depicting a central house surrounded by a garden square, bisected by diagonal paths to create four triangular spaces. This inner area is, in turn, surrounded by orchards and woodlands. In 1683, the year his book was published, Reid emigrated with his family to the American colony of Perth Amboy in New Jersey, where, having been appointed Deputy Surveyor-General, he presumably made good use of his talents for layout and design.

various Veitch expeditions in East Africa and also subscribed to David Douglas's expeditions to the American North-West. Among Douglas's many discoveries, the Sitka spruce, *Picea sitchensis*, the western hemlock, *Tsuga heterophylla*, and the fir trees *Abies grandis* and *Abies procera* feature prominently at Dawyck. An enormous Douglas fir, *Pseudotsuga menziesii*, presiding in the Scrape Glen, was grown from a seed planted in 1835, a year after Douglas was tragically gored to death by a bull. Though its com-mon name commemorates the Scots plant-hunter, the tree's Latin name acknowledges the Scots botanist John Menzies, who first discovered it.

In 1897 the Dawyck estate was sold to the Balfour family. In the fashion of the time, the Balfours filled out the woodlands, under-planting with shrubs to create a denser, darker effect, and packed the meadows with – literally – tons of daffodils. In the early twentieth century Fred Balfour continued the plant-collecting tradition by subscribing to Ernest Wilson's Chinese expeditions, which produced, among many other treasures, the Dawyck cherry, *Prunus* x *dawyckensis*. Wilson also provided the seeds for various rhododendrons, acers, prunus and many other species whose native habitats in Sichuan and Yunnan are similar to Dawyck's rocky slopes and acid soil. Balfour corresponded with Wilson and was repaid with visits from the collector in 1911 and again in 1922. Inspired by Wilson's example, Balfour himself travelled to the American West, discovering in 1908 *Picea breweriana*, Brewer's Weeping Spruce. Over the years, through his own collecting and that of the plant-hunters he supported, Balfour amassed hundreds of hardy rhododendrons able to withstand Dawyck's bitter winters. In 1927 he was awarded the Victoria Medal of Honour for his contribution to arboriculture.

In 1968 a hurricane destroyed 50,000 of Dawyck's trees; the yews went down like ninepins, though the giant sequoias survived. In the aftermath of the storm the ornamental salmonberry, *Rubus spectabilis*, introduced as game cover at the beginning of the century, quickly invaded the clearings. Over the past few decades it has been replaced with the decorative but sterile *Rubus spectabilis* 'Flore Pleno'. More storms in 1973 further shaped the landscape, and in 1978 the 60-acre arboretum was separated from the estate and gifted to the nation.

While conifers are still the prime attraction, year-round interest is provided by spring snowdrops and daffodils; meconopsis and burn-side herbaceous plants give summer interest, while acers and sorbus provide autumn colour. The Heron Wood recalls the luckless quarry bred for falconry in one of James VI's favourite hunting grounds. The sport remained popular among the aristocracy until changes in agricultural practice reduced the noble falcon to a despised pest, rendering heronries a thing of the past. Today Dawyck's Heron Wood harbours the world's first cryptogram sanctuary. Established in 1993, it studies such 'lower plants' as ferns, fungi, mosses, mushrooms, horsetails, liverworts and lichen. Meaning 'hidden sex', the cryptogram reproduces by dispersing millions of microscopic spores via insects, animals and gusts of wind.

A two-hour signed walk takes in key trees, seasonal flowers, an azalea avenue, a rhododendron walk, a streamside walk, a rare-plant trail, a Swiss bridge and a dynamo pond which used to hold the water before it was piped downhill to generate electricity for the estate. Information plaques discreetly placed at ground level give details for those who want them without distracting those who prefer a pleasant, uninformed woodland stroll.

Drummond Castle

Drummond Castle,
Muthill, Perth and Kinross
PH5 2AA

Perth and Kinross

Open Easter weekend,
then May to Oct, 1–6
(last admission 5)

T: (01764) 681433   E: thegardens@drummondcastle.sol.co.uk
W: www.drummondcastlegardens.co.uk

Fee £4, children £1.50

2m S of Crieff on A822

For 500 years Drummond Castle gardens reflected the changes in Scottish history. As Royalists, the Drummond family fortunes were tied to those of the crown; indeed, the first Lord Drummond built his keep on land granted to him in the late fifteenth century. Set on a rocky south-facing outcrop, it had a river beyond and a wooded hill rising up the far side. The earliest indication of a garden is a 1508 note recording that Lord Drummond sent cherries to James IV, who was hunting in the Forest of Glen Artney nearby. The formal gardens were laid out by John Drummond, 2nd Earl of Perth – his brother, the 1st Earl, had earned the title by helping to secure peace with the Spanish in 1605. A mathematician living in France when he acquired the title in 1612, Drummond described the estate as small 'yet by the help of friends and honest mannagerie, it proved much better than expected'. Drummond went on to become Privy Councillor to James VI and then Charles I, and in 1630 he commissioned the King's master mason, John Mylne, to create a garden in the style of those he had known in France. Mylne designed a formal layout centred on an unusual obelisk sundial; the grandeur of the garden is indicated by the magnificence of this central piece, whose fifty faces indicate the time in as many capital cities.

In 1654 the castle was destroyed by the Parliamentarians and within four years it was said to have been engulfed in woodland. With the Restoration the estate was redeveloped and in 1674 the 4th Earl built a mansion beyond the keep, expanded the gardens and improved the policies. Appointed Lord Chancellor of Scotland in 1685, he still found time for agricultural improvements; though he planned an avenue of trees, four rows deep, leading from the estate to the city of Perth 20 miles away, this was never made. It is an indication, perhaps, of the Earl's horticultural perspicacity that he employed a gardener from Hamilton Palace, the young John Reid, who would go on to write *The Scots Gard'ner*, Scotland's first gardening manual.

In 1689, when James VII fled to France with the arrival of William and Mary, the Earl was imprisoned in Stirling Castle. Released to exile, he served the Scottish court in France and was created a duke for his loyalty. The King's exile coincided with a series of bad harvests and the ensuing hardship fuelled the Jacobite movement, which sought to restore James to the throne. After the Drummond family's involvement in the unsuccessful Jacobite uprisings, in 1746 the estates were annexed and the family didn't recover their land till 1785. By this time the fashion for formal gardens had passed, but the estate, nestled in a circle of surrounding hills, was well suited to the romantic taste. The policies were embellished in the landscape style, a pond was placed on the site of an abandoned settlement and the crumbling tower – said to have been ruined by the dowager countess in 1745 to prevent its being seized by the government – served as a picturesque eye-catcher with a suitably tragic history.

When the taste for formality returned in the early nineteenth century, Drummond's gardens were re-established, largely through the efforts of the factor, Lewis Kennedy, who had trained in France at Malmaison, home of the Empress Josephine. Under Kennedy's direction Drummond became one of the most important gardens in Scotland, reflecting the Scots baronial aesthetic in its celebration of the ancient past. As with many Victorian reconstructions, it was presented as a faithful reconstruction, though the inclusion of such contemporary elements as variegated evergreens, exotic plants and flowering shrubs reflected a romantic view of the austere seventeenth-century style.

While few records of the original garden remained, a military survey of the mid-eighteenth century indicated four grass plots symmetrically arranged on the plateau below the castle, with a broad central avenue leading southward to the kitchen garden. A popular song also indicated that the second duke's garden contained flowers and waterworks. These formal features were reinstated and embellished with statuary, urns and pools. The parterres were laid out in the form of the saltire – the Scottish flag – as part of the fashion for celebrating traditional Scots emblems. The venerable sundial at the heart of the design was set in a mosaic of black and white pebbles, suggesting the waves on the Drummond crest. The terracing, with its plantings of shrubs and exotic yuccas, resembles that designed by Charles Barry at **Dunrobin** several decades later. Indeed, Barry was invited to suggest alterations to the castle and, though these were never carried out, it is not unlikely that he would have been consulted about the garden at the same time. In the French fashion, the garden is extended into the landscape, with the central axis continuing as a wide avenue cut through wooded slopes beyond.

In the mid-nineteenth century Drummond's fortunes were once more touched by royalty when Queen Victoria paid a visit. While Albert went stalking in the Glen Artney Forest, Victoria recorded in her diary for Sunday 11 September 1842, 'We walked in the garden which is really very fine, with terraces, like an old French garden.' She also, apparently, planted several copper beeches, which flourish to this day. In 1901 and 1902 *Country Life* honoured Drummond Castle with several features, describing its garden as the finest in Britain. Once again blurring the distinction between restoration and recreation, the articles ignored the glaring white marble statues and exotic vegetation, concentrating on such features as the bastion walls and magnificent sundial to suggest this was the original garden of an ancient stronghold.

By 1918 tastes had changed again and Gertrude Jekyll complained of the 'sparkling spar' – white quartz which lined the garden paths. By the mid-twentieth century many of the parterres had been simplified for economic as well as aesthetic reasons. During the two world wars the gardens were neglected, but in the 1950s Phyllis Astor, wife of the 3rd Earl of Ancaster, revived the gardens once again. Stressing the original seventeenth-century structure, she preserved the ancient yew hedges and the Victorian copper beeches, thinned the overgrown shrubberies and emphasized the saltire pattern with borders of white-flowered *Anaphalis triplinervis* and a central cross of blue Hidcote lavender. Though undeniably a modern construct, Drummond today does convey some of the tranquillity and order of the original Scots Renaissance garden; nestled like some exotic jewel within the Lowland hills, it is an extraordinary amalgam of five centuries of horticultural fashion.

Falkland Palace Garden (NTS)

Fife

T: (01337) 857397   E: information@nts.org.uk   W: www.nts.org.uk

Falkland Palace has a long and romantic history, much of which is encoded in its gardens. Set beneath the twin 'paps of Fife', the estate provided solace for many a Stuart monarch and even the tragic Queen Mary spent several happy years here. Falkland was a royal retreat where kings would play tennis or practise archery on the rectangular range to the east of the palace. They also indulged in falconry and hunted deer and boar in the surrounding forests; indeed, records note that James IV transported local deer by litter to populate the royal hunting grounds at Holyrood in Edinburgh.

The current palace was built at the beginning of the sixteenth century on the ruins of a twelfth-century castle. Though designed in French Renaissance style, it was constructed of local sandstone, transported by sledge from the Lomonds nearby. The building was severely damaged in the Civil War, and by the end of the nineteenth century much of it was in ruins, providing a dramatic backdrop to the present garden. The rose garden sits in what was the earliest part of the castle, the north range. A 3-acre walled garden abutting the castle in the traditional Scots fashion dates to the twelfth century. The original enclosing wooden trellis was replaced, in the late sixteenth century, by a substantial stone wall, much of which remains today. The formal gardens were replanted in the early seventeenth century, but fell into decline when the court moved to London after the Act of Union. In 1887 the 3rd Marquess of Bute, Hereditary Keeper of the Palace, restored the gardens, adding specimen trees, shrubberies and ornamental areas. During the two world wars the grounds were dug up and used as potato fields and a forest nursery, but in 1947 the English designer Percy Cane was invited to redesign the garden. A darling of the social set, Cane was known for creating pre-war grandeur for post-war circumstances. He advocated such cunning, low-maintenance devices as bulking out herbaceous borders with shrubs and flowering trees, underplanting orchards with bulbs to decrease the need for borders and creating meadows with paths mown through them to replace high-maintenance lawns.

Falkland Palace, Falkland, Fife KY7 7BU

Open 1 Mar to 31 Oct, Mon–Sat 10–6, Sun 1–5.30

Fee garden: £5, conc. £3.50; palace and garden: £10, conc. £7

7m N of Kirkcaldy on A92 to A912, then 4m NE to Falkland

A great respecter of tradition, Cane set out to accentuate what remained of the palace while tracing the footprint of earlier, grander buildings. The old courtyard was turned into a formal flower garden, recalling the Renaissance grandeur of the palace. Stone steps lead down to a flagged terrace, at the end of which an ancient staircase descends to the lower lawn.

To emphasize the dramatic verticality of the palace, Cane planted Lawson cypresses outlining the plan of former buildings. The ruined walls create a picturesque backdrop for the dense herbaceous borders filled with delphiniums, lupins and roses. From the former archery court Cane created an elegant lawn, surrounded on three sides by herbaceous borders. In the fashion of the time, he embellished the lawn with island beds filled with cherry, philadelphus, weigela, ceanothus, cytisus and other flowering trees and shrubs. While the planting gives height, variety and interest, the curving lines of the beds provide a contrast to the straight rows of iris, delphinium and peony borders nearby. Several specimen trees – a purple sycamore and a cut-leaf beech, *Fagus laciniata* – lend an air of maturity to the still relatively young design.

To animate the end of the garden, Cane extended beyond the original 3-acre enclosure, creating a lily pool. A popular postwar feature, the pool recalls the stew ponds of medieval times while providing a reflective surface to magnify the ruins. There is also an orchard on the western edge of the garden, beyond which lies the royal tennis court. Built in 1539, this 'catch-spiel', as it was called, is the oldest functioning court in Britain and the only real-tennis court from the Stuart period to survive in Scotland. Originally played by hand, without the refinement of racquets, tennis was the most arduous of all ball games.

Although Cane's borders have been simplified over the decades, his other major Scottish commission, the garden at Monteviot, has been replaced, so Falkland provides a rare opportunity to appreciate the work of this discreet and underrated designer; it also offers a brilliant modern homage to the sixteenth-century style.

Floors Castle

....

Scottish Borders

T: (01573) 223333   E: marketing@floorscastle.com
W: www.floorscastle.com

Floors Castle gets its name, appropriately enough, from *fleurs*, and flowers abound in the enormous walled garden, which was built in 1857. It harbours greenhouses, a vinery and a peach house, herbaceous borders, annuals, orchards, soft-fruit cages and vegetables – not least among them the famous Kelsae onion, a large, heavy, pungent variety, introduced in the 1950s, which is traditionally sown on Christmas Day.

In 1907 the American heiress May Goelet, having recently married the 8th Duke of Roxburghe, spent over $600,000 to update both castle and garden in anticipation of a visit from the King. *Country Life* singled out the new 12-foot-deep borders in the walled garden for their 'barbaric splendour and generosity of bloom'. The lodges and wrought-iron gates were added in 1929 and the castle's gardeners were celebrated through the 1920s and 1930s, when society magazines depicted the glamorous reception rooms filled with exotic, home-grown flora.

In 1978 the walled garden was turned into a commercial nursery, though the ubiquitous tea room, gift shop and children's play area are discreetly integrated within its walls. Here, sub-divisions are cleverly created with espaliered fruit trees and rose-swagged chains. Entry to the walled garden is free, but visitors have to pay the 'house and garden fee' to visit the vast parks, woodlands, riverside walk or millennium parterre – a recent concoction in the French style made of box and *Euonymus fortunei* 'Emerald 'n Gold' depicting the intertwined initials of the present duke and duchess, with a double 'M' to indicate its date.

The castle itself, the largest inhabited house in Scotland, will be familiar to film-lovers as the setting for *Greystoke: The Legend of Tarzan, Lord of the Apes*. It presides over a glorious view of the River Tweed, with the Cheviot Hills beyond. Both Sir John Vanbrugh and William Adam have been credited with the original eighteenth-century design, though in the mid-nineteenth century the castle was remodelled out of all recognition. French prisoners of war built the great wall enclosing the park, and the holly tree which sits in its centre is said to mark the spot where

Floors Castle, Kelso,
Scottish Borders TD5 7SF

Open Easter weekend and
1 May to 28 Oct, 11–5
(last admission 4.30)

Fee grounds only: £3,
children free; house and
grounds: £6, children
£3.25

Off B6397, just W of Kelso

James II was killed in 1460 by a bursting cannon during the siege of Roxburghe. More recently the castle lawns were the setting for Prince Andrew's announcement of his ill-fated engagement to Sarah Ferguson.

Worth a minor detour, the local Kelso War Memorial Garden is a frequent winner of 'Best Kept Memorials', 'Beautiful Scotland in Bloom' and 'Britain in Bloom' competitions. A spreading yew is suitably sombre, while benches, flanked by 'The World Peace Rose Bed', address the delicate issue of war memorials in a peace-loving society. The site was donated in 1921 by the Duke of Roxburghe and abuts the ruins of the twelfth-century Tyronensian Abbey, an order whose monks were noted for their horticultural skills.

Greywalls

Greywalls, Muirfield, Gullane, East Lothian EH3 2EG

Open on certain days for Scotland's Gardens Scheme

Fee free to hotel guests

1m E of Gullare, off A198, signed

East Lothian

T: (01620) 842144   E: hotel@greywalls.co.uk   W: www.greywalls.co.uk

Greywalls is the only surviving Scottish work by the great design team of Edwin Lutyens and Gertrude Jekyll. Lutyens, a young architect, and Jekyll, a middle-aged garden designer, famously updated the eighteenth-century country-house style for the constraints of the twentieth century. Built in 1901 as a holiday home for MP the Hon. Alfred Lyttleton, Greywalls is magnificently sited by the ninth fairway of Muirfield golf course, overlooking the Firth of Forth. The eponymous walls are created by rattlebags stone drawn from a local quarry which was worked by monks in the Middle Ages.

While Scottish architect Robert Lorimer had to endure the indignity of being called 'the Scots Lutyens', Lutyens here seems to have taken his cue from Lorimer, employing a pared-down baronial style and following the old Scots tradition of placing the walled garden directly off the house. The distinctive north and south lodges by the front gate were originally footmen's bothies; each contains two rooms divided by a partition to accommodate eight manservants in total.

Visited by Edward VII before the First World War, Greywalls
still retains an air of Edwardian grandeur. The King himself is
immortalized in the King's Loo, discreetly tucked away in the
garden, which today offers extra accommodation. In 1911 the
nursery wing on the west side was added by Robert Lorimer.
In 1924 the estate was bought by the Weaver family, which,
just after the Second World War, anticipating the market for
luxurious weekend retreats, turned it into one of Britain's first
country-house hotels.

Although the region has less rainfall than the south of France
it is subject to brutal north-east winds. To combat these, Lutyens
created an enclosed garden with massive walls and sheltered
the entrance courtyard with elegant, sloping wings. On a visit
between the wars, he was distressed to find his austere entrance
filled with garish flower beds which distracted 'from my beautiful, favourite house'; this aberration was duly amended and the
entrance court has been simply laid to lawn ever since. The
exposed north façade of the house has a sunken lawn to provide
shelter without obstructing the views over the golf course and
the sea beyond.

Despite changes in planting over the century, the walled garden still exhibits Jekyll's subtle appreciation of colour, texture
and form. Its high stone walls are fronted by deep herbaceous
borders, lined with stone and flanked by grassy paths. The original rose garden, nestling next to the house to maximize heat
and minimize wind, was recently replanted with herbaceous
beds when the roses succumbed to chronic disease. Today
vibrant orange poppies predominate in the early summer,
though a more subdued palette of pinks and blues prevails
through spring and autumn. In the north-east corner a simple
pavilion, known as the 'tea room', offers sheltered views. The
south garden beyond combines pleasure and utility with its
mixture of orchards, lawns and planting beds.

Deviating from tradition, Lutyens created a raised *claire-voie*
in the southernmost wall to frame the distant Lothian Hills.
Though Scottish designers tended to rely on windows in garden
pavilions to provide views of the landscape beyond, Lutyens
might have found his inspiration in the seventeenth-century
claire-voie at **Kinross** along the Forth. Greywall's *claire-voie* is
sited so that visitors can appreciate its framed views from the
shelter of the rose garden – or, indeed, from the comfort of the
sitting room.

The garden is open to the public several times a year for the Scotland's Gardens Scheme; for those visiting at other times, it is well worth the price of a cup of tea to see this unusual Scottish manifestation of the English country-house style.

Harmony Garden,
St Mary's Road, Melrose,
Scottish Borders TD6 9LJ

Open Good Fri to 30 Sep,
Mon–Sat 10–5, Sun 1–5

Fee £3, conc. 2

Off A609 in Melrose,
opposite the Abbey

Harmony Garden (NTS)

Scottish Borders

T: (01721) 722502 E: information@nts.org.uk W: www.nts.org.uk

Harmony Garden was named after the Jamaican allspice plantation where local joiner James Waugh made his fortune. In 1807 he retired to his home town, built an austere stone house and surrounded it with a 2-acre walled garden. Into this he retreated, earning the name 'Melancholy Jacques', as he emerged only for the local hunt. In 1996 Harmony Garden was donated to the National Trust for Scotland; the villa is closed to the public and the yew hedge in the north-west corner screens off part of the garden for the use of the tenants.

A gold border at the back of the villa is a typical 1960s feature, planted to celebrate a golden-wedding anniversary. To the west the shadow of a sunken lawn suggests Victorian parterres, Edwardian tennis courts or some earlier curling pond – most likely the latter, as a previous owner had been president of the Melrose Curling Association. The hazel woodland beyond is a sea of bluebells in late spring. To the east are dense borders filled with herbaceous plants and shrubs, indicative of post-war, low-maintenance planting. Yew hedging and Scots briar roses outline the original turning circle in front of the villa. This was replaced in the early twentieth century by a magnificent double border flanking a path leading from the main entrance down the lawn to the trees at the bottom of the garden. Like many such features, this border was grassed over during a post-war economy drive.

Conceding to the modern desire for year-round interest, the trust has under-planted the rhododendron bed by the garden gate with herbaceous perennials. Stately conifers at the end of the lawn provide a windbreak, while the grass is planted with thousands of spring bulbs. Beyond the eastern border lies an impressive fruit and vegetable garden, which also hosts such cutting flowers as sweet peas, penstemon and phlox.

The garden offers spectacular views of the Eildon Hills and the nearby twelfth-century Melrose Abbey, which is reputed to house the heart of Robert the Bruce. Harmony Garden is paired with **Priorwood**, also owned by the National Trust (one ticket, purchased at Priorwood, provides entry to both properties; payment for Harmony alone is via an honesty box at the front gate).

Hill of Tarvit (NTS)

Fife

T: (01334) 653127 E: hilloftarvit@nts.org.uk W: www.nts.org.uk

Hill of Tarvit, Cupar, Fife
KY15 5PB

Open estate: all year, 9.30–sunset; house: Good Fri to 30 Sep and first weekend in Oct, 1–5

Fee estate: free; house: £8, conc. £5

2½m S of Cupar, off A916

Hill of Tarvit is a story of family tragedy and horticultural loss. Created in 1906 by Dundee financier Frederick Sharp, it was inhabited by only one generation. This spared it the updating and remodelling of subsequent owners, leaving the estate a perfect example of early twentieth-century Scottish horticultural taste.

The Sharp family, who liked to proclaim that they were raised from the mud of the River Tay, made their fortune manufacturing jute during Scotland's early twentieth-century industrial revolution. In 1905, following the fashion of the day, Frederick Sharp bought himself a rural estate, conveniently sited between his workplace in Dundee and his golf course in St Andrews. Though planned as a country-house retreat, Hill of Tarvit was primarily designed to display Sharp's magnificent collection of Old Master paintings, Flemish tapestries, Chinese porcelain and French furniture.

The young Robert Lorimer, who had established a reputation for combining sophistication with comfort, was commissioned to redesign the house at the heart of the 1,500-acre estate. Despite his devotion to Scottish tradition, Lorimer demolished the seventeenth-century hall – originally designed by Sir William Bruce (see **Kinross House**) – and put in its place an elegant Italianate villa. Perhaps it was this act of architectural vandalism which provoked Sharp to change the name from Wemyss Hall to Hill of Tarvit – *tarvit* from *tarff*, meaning 'a place of bulls'. The name also recalls Scotstarvit Tower, an ancient keep within the grounds.

The house is sited near the top of a hill overlooking the Fife countryside; though Fife derives from the Danish for 'wooded country', the woods had long gone, leaving a landscape of rolling hills. To emphasize the magnificent views, Lorimer moved the main entrance from the south to the west side of the house and banished all colour from the new south front, creating a green sweep of lawns and terraces with French windows on to the garden from the ground-floor public rooms.

The south lawn has a simple, French formality – typical of traditional Scots manor houses. A niche statue of Ceres, with her overflowing cornucopia, presides over the garden entrance. Though a classical image of rural abundance, Ceres is also the ancient Gaelic for 'a town to the west' – Cupar, the local town, being west of St Andrews. The south terrace is narrower than might be expected, as it was created from the former turning circle. A stone staircase leads through the impressive, 420-foot-long grass terrace to the lowest lawn. Originally a tennis court and croquet lawn, this large plateau is guarded by a charming pair of toothless stone lions, whose gaze directs the eye to the surrounding hills – the most prominent of which used to be Frederick Sharp's private nine-hole golf course. The enclosing circular yew hedge and bastion hedges which break up the high supporting walls were later additions, though they harmonize with the architectural austerity of Lorimer's original plan.

To fulfil his client's demand for flowers, Lorimer designed a rose garden round a stone basin, sunk into the terrace so its colours wouldn't spoil the green sweep. Invisible from the main approach, it offers a gentle surprise to visitors strolling along the garden terrace. The rose garden is balanced by a small enclosure off the dining room, also surrounding a stone basin; a third basin is off the smoking room. Though all three basins were designed by Lorimer, they resemble the venerable Italian well-heads which colonized Edwardian gardens when Venice's municipal authorities provided mains water in the 1890s releasing a slew of ancient well-heads for discerning antiquarians.

The gardens to the north of the house were designed by Sharp himself, while a small summer house, reminiscent of a Renaissance banqueting hall, nestles in the north-east corner. Incorporated into the wall at the top of the garden is an unusually ornate gate by Thomas Hadden of Edinburgh. Now virtually obscured by the overgrown woodland beyond, its grandeur suggests an earlier intention to develop the area.

The remains of a water garden, designed by Frederick's son, Hugh, in the 1930s, lie to the east of the main garden. These were discovered recently when the gardener, Peter Christopher, noticed expensive glacial-washed stones and lead pipes in several woodland springs. Exploring further, he uncovered exotic woodland plantings such as North American trilliums and dog-toothed violets. The real treat, however, was the discovery of some rarely seen species such as *Rhododendron yunnanense*. One of the oldest of its type in this country, it was introduced in the 1930s by Frank Kingdon-Ward and its presence attests to the Sharps' keen interest in horticulture in general and rhododendrons in particular.

Sadly, the Sharp dynasty expired after only one generation at Hill of Tarvit. In 1932 Frederick died, leaving the estate to his only son. In 1937 Hugh was killed in a train crash en route to visit his fiancée, after her insistence that he travel by rail because a severe snowstorm was forecast. His mother and sister, devastated by his death, created a massive pyre in which they burned Hugh's effects, including many important estate maps, plans, records and other documents which might have given some idea of the design and planting of the water garden. In 1946 Mrs Sharp died; two years later her daughter followed. The house and garden, with an endowment, were left to the National Trust for Scotland and today the Sharps' impressive library of botanical books is housed at **Threave**, the NTS's gardening school.

Although it is one of the most modern estates to be accepted by the National Trust, Hill of Tarvit demonstrates the unique Scottish marriage of cosmopolitan influences – the formal French south front, the elegant Edwardian rose garden, the Elizabethan summer house. While two gardeners now do the work originally done by seven, the grounds are well maintained and provide an interesting comparison with Lorimer's more intimate **Kellie Castle** nearby.

ટ્સ ટ્સ ટ્સ

The Hirsel, Coldstream,
Scottish Borders TD12 4LP

The Hirsel

Open all year,
dawn–sunset

Scottish Borders

Fee free; parking £2 per
car

T: (01890) 882834 W: www.hirselcountrypark.co.uk

Just W of Coldstream on
A697

The word *hirsel,* meaning 'sheepfold', evokes an image of pastoral tranquillity which is fully realized in this glorious piece of Borders landscape. The former home of Sir Alec Douglas-Home, who was Conservative prime minister from 1963 to 1964, The Hirsel has been in the Home family since the early seventeenth century. Today its 3,000 acres are largely turned to farming and forestry, though a portion of the estate has been made into a golf course – a common fate for large parklands, and not such a bad fate, considering the alternatives. The elegant stable block now houses craft workshops and the ubiquitous gift shop and café, as well as a sturdy old *doocot,* carefully sited where staff could prevent irate farmers from attacking the thieving birds, which routinely destroyed their crops.

In the early nineteenth century J. C. Loudon noted that the garden of The Hirsel contained a fine tulip tree, *Liriodendron tulipifera.* A century later Sir Herbert Maxwell noted that the tree, though decaying, was still flowering well. What he did not mention was that it had been decapitated in the great storm of 1880, which left its profile ignobly truncated. Remarkably, the tree still survives in the walled garden and it still flowers. As it was reputed to be 100 years old in Loudon's day, this must be among Britain's oldest tulip trees, since the species was not introduced to the country until the mid-seventeenth century. Though the garden is no longer open to the public, the woods and parkland are, and they offer a paradise for bird and birdwatcher alike.

Situated above the River Tweed, the 27-acre Hirsel Lake provides refuge for water birds disturbed by activity on the Tweed. Of particular interest are the many swans, which still seem exotic even though the species has been in this country since the Crusaders first brought them back from the East. The trout-filled Leet, a tributary of the Tweed, is home to kingfisher and goosander as well as sandpiper, wagtail and dipper. Dundock Wood, to the south, houses woodpeckers, flycatchers, warblers and rare marsh tits. Planted mainly with oak, beech and ash, Dundock is famous for its fine hybrid rhododendrons, which shelter amid more common *R. ponticum* in the woodland glades.

In early spring the grounds are covered in consoling aconites; as Gerard claimed in his *Herball* (1597): 'yea, the colder the weather is, and the deeper that the snow is, the fairer and larger is the flower.' Snowdrops and daffodils follow, then in early summer the rhododendrons come into their own and in autumn the deciduous woods blaze with colour.

Inveresk Lodge

East Lothian

T: (0131) 665 1855   E: information@nts.org.uk   W: www.nts.org.uk

Inveresk Lodge is believed to have been built by the Cistercians of Newbattle Abbey as a resting point on the journey to the port of Musselburgh. Gaelic for 'the confluence of the water', Inveresk sits above the River Esk, overlooking the Pentland Hills. Though not open to the public, the lodge, dated 1683, provides an atmospheric backdrop to the 2-acre walled garden. In the late eighteenth century the estate was purchased by James Wedderburn, who made his fortune in the Caribbean, trading slaves, coffee, sugar and tobacco. On his return to Scotland, Wedderburn spurned his mulatto son, Robert, who subsequently became a famous Scots abolitionist and lived to see the banning of the West Indian slave trade.

The garden was redesigned in Victorian and again in Edwardian times. In the early twentieth century it was maintained by four gardeners, but during the Second World War large parts were neglected, while the rest was turned over to vegetable cultivation. When the NTS acquired the property in 1959, they retained significant historical features but simplified the layout so the property could be maintained by a single gardener.

Despite its chequered history Inveresk has enormous charm and variety. A small entrance courtyard opens on to a croquet lawn, recalling the bowling green of Tudor times; terraced walks beside the old stone walls and a seventeenth-century stone sundial on the upper lawn reinforce the sense of age. More recent features include island beds and an elegant Victorian glasshouse which hosts a grape vine – rather lost amid exotic climbers, tree ferns and an aviary filled with cheerful birds. It also holds the national collection of tropaeolums, that cheerful, pungent climb-

Inveresk Lodge,
24 Inveresk Village,
Musselburgh, East Lothian
EH21 6BQ

Open all year, 10–6 or sunset if earlier

Fee £3, conc. £2

6m E of Edinburgh on A1, then A6124 towards Musselburgh

ing herb whose best-known manifestation is the popular nasturtium. Beyond the greenhouse, a shrub rose border designed in the 1960s by Graham Stuart Thomas has recently been replanted with tender shrubs which flourish in the sandy loam.

The garden, extending down several levels, is enhanced by elegant garden gates, a simple pavilion, an enormous stone urn, a 1930s blue wooden bench, a 1960s wheelbarrow bench and a contemporary swinging seat. The upper terrace is lined with a double avenue of junipers. Below it lie a lawn studded with trees and a vibrant September border filled with autumn-flowering plants. To the east is a white border backed by a dark-red hedge of *Prunus cerasifera* 'Nigra'. This deciduous tree can grow up to 30 feet tall, but if kept firmly clipped it makes a dense and dramatic hedge; it was particularly popular in the early decades of the twentieth century.

In the less formal area beyond, a spring border embellishes a circular lawn, while a blue border above adds further interest. Steps from the lawn descend to a lower walk, which leads eastwards into a woodland. Inveresk has some of the lowest rainfall in Scotland; this, coupled with unusually high stone walls and a south-facing aspect, creates a warm microclimate in which tender plants thrive.

Kailzie, Peebles, Scottish Borders EH45 9TH

Open walled and wild gardens and woodland walks: all year, dawn to dusk; walled garden: end Mar to end Sep, 11–5.30

Fee £2–£3 depending on season

2m east of Peebles on B7062

Kailzie

Scottish Borders

T: (01721) 720007   E: info@kailzie.com   W: www.kailziegardens.com

Kailzie is one of the few large Scottish estates still in private ownership; the current layout and management provide an interesting example of twentieth-century strategies for survival. Kailzie, pronounced 'kailie', means 'wooded glen'. The garden encompasses 18 acres of wild and formal gardens – quite a feat considering that Peeblesshire is the highest county in Scotland, with frosts recorded in every month of the year, and the estate itself is 700 feet above sea level and very exposed to bitter winter storms.

The Georgian mansion was de-roofed in 1962, when a particularly short-sighted piece of legislation gave tax exemption

to roofless buildings. Inevitably, along with many other architectural treasures, the mansion crumbled and had to be torn
down. Nonetheless the stable block from 1811 remains, as do an
early *doocot* and an impressive walled garden.

During the Second World War the garden was grassed over
and by the 1960s, when the present owner, Lady Buchan-
Hepburn, took over, all records relating to the pre-war garden
had been lost, leaving her free to design without the pressure of
precedent. Greenhouses are crucial, as the growing season is so
short that pots can't be put out till June and must be brought in
by September. Kailzie's elegant Regency greenhouses contain a
range of exotic conservatory plants – camellias, schizanthus,
fuchsias, begonias and some unusual geraniums, including Els,
Arctic Star and Stella. Fat figs, grapes and a delicate plumbago
fight for space within, while espaliered fruit trees vie with roses
for the wall outside.

Kailzie exhibits many of the horticultural features which
evolved in the straitened post-war years to suggest the leisurely
country-house style: island beds are planted with low-maintenance flowering shrubs such as *Rhus continus*, *Viburnum burk-
woodii*, spiraea and cornus; herbaceous borders are bulked out
with a copper beech hedge behind; grass paths replace stone
walks, lawns replace elaborate parterres, and bulbs are planted
in the woods to provide low-maintenance floral colour. The garden is maintained with labour-saving machinery and a heavy
reliance on mulching. Three gardeners now manage an estate
that employed twenty-two before the last war. In 1977 the garden
was opened to the public; in the early 1980s, to extend the season, a laburnum walk was added, followed by a formal rose garden, the provision of year-round interest being one of the
distinguishing features of late twentieth-century garden design.

Over the years the estate has had to diversify to survive. A gift
shop, a café and an art gallery were put into the steadings. An
experiment in exotic birds was thwarted when visitors insisted
on shoving fingers, junk food and cigarette butts into the
aviaries. Recently, in an effort to attract local visitors and ensure
repeat visits, a putting range, a beauty parlour and a trout pond
were added.

The woodland walks are impressive all the year round.
A Wellingtonia presides over the south corner, while the
18-foot-high garden wall is dwarfed by the Kailzie larch. A gift
from Sir James Naesmyth of **Dawyck**, this *Larix decidua*,

planted in 1725, is said to be the largest in Scotland. Snowdrops flourish in early spring and, because of the long, cold season, remain in flower for up to ten weeks, creating a visual link with the distant snow-capped Leithen Hills.

A recent planting of *Primula pulverulenta* provides bright spring colour along the burn, while in summer the bog planting includes the huge, dramatic leaves of *Gunnera manicata*. The burn attracts many wild birds – herons, oyster catchers and kingfishers; the nearby moors also draw curlews, lapwings, larks and cuckoos, while woodcock, pheasants, grouse and partridge nest in the undergrowth, making Kailzie a magnet for ornithologists as well as horticulturists.

Kellie Castle, Pittenweem, Fife KY10 2RF

Kellie Castle (NTS)

Open garden: all year, 9.30–5.30; castle: Good Fri to Easter Mon and 1 May to 30 Sep, 1–5

Fife

Fee garden: £3, conc. £2; castle and garden: £8, conc. £5 (incl. castle)

T: (01333) 720271   E: information@nts.org.uk   W: www.nts.org.uk

3m NW of Pittenweem on B9171

Kellie Castle has one of the most romantic gardens in the whole of Scotland, perfectly fulfilling Sir Robert Lorimer's dictum that a garden should be 'a sanctuary, a chamber roofed by heaven'. Indeed, Kellie was Lorimer's training ground, instilling in him a love of the old Scots style which prevailed before Renaissance grandeur superseded its simple charm.

Though parts of the north tower date back to the fourteenth century, the east tower is inscribed with the date 1573 and the initials of Margaret Hay, to whom the estate was given as a dowry by her husband, the 4th Lord Oliphant. Probably built for Hay herself, the tower looks out to the Firth of Forth. There might have been a garden here in her time, but the current walls are four centuries old, suggesting that the present form was not established until the seventeenth century. An old print indicates that there was once a formal garden round the castle, but that was long gone by 1877, when Professor James Lorimer acquired the derelict property and inscribed, in Latin, over the entrance: 'This dwelling, from which the crows and owls have been evicted, has been devoted to honourable repose from labour.' The rooks' cries prevail to this day and a century ago Gertrude Jekyll noted of the rookery in the western glen, 'When strong winds blow in early spring the nests in the swaying treetops come almost within hand reach of the turret windows.'

In 1880 the sixteen-year-old Robert Lorimer – who later read Greek, Humanities and Fine Arts before becoming an architect – laid out the grounds. He once wrote, 'I always think the ideal plan is to have the park, with the sheep or beasts grazing in it, coming right under the windows at one side of the house, and the gardens attached to the house at the other side.' At Kellie, he cut paths through the surrounding woods and under-planted an old lime avenue with daffodils and other spring-flowering bulbs. The rectangular bowling green along the garden wall was left as a simple lawn. The garden itself abuts the north side of the castle, precluding any direct sunlight. Nonetheless the 1½-acre space within is sheltered and serene, and so romantic that Victorian novelist Mrs Oliphant used it as the setting for her story *Katy Stewart*.

In his plan for the walled garden Lorimer copied the old Scots style, having fruit, flowers and vegetables all jumbled together. Abutting the wall in the north-west he designed a traditional gardener's shed which today houses exhibitions on the garden and related subjects. This single, square room has a ladder leading to the loft and a window facing out of the garden to the countryside beyond – an unusual feature which is also found in the eighteenth-century potting shed at **Geilston**. The ancient walls are lined with bee boles, while rhubarb forcers and an old armillary sphere add to the medieval air. Luxury is provided by the intoxicating scent of the honeysuckle, peonies, sweet peas and sweet william. Jekyll applauded Kellie's use of tall, sturdy plants, praising the old Scottish gardens for escaping 'that murderously overwhelming wave of fashion for tender bedding plants alone, that wrought such havoc throughout England'. She also noted appreciatively the briar roses, which were planted with other 'strong-growing' plants. Certainly tough shrub roses feature, as do hollyhocks, pinks, penstemon and erigeron – whose vulgar name, 'fleabane', explains its popularity in cottage gardens. Grass paths subdivide the space, arches sag beneath 'Dorothy Perkins' ramblers, fan-trained fruit trees spread across the walls, box-edged herbaceous beds simmer with summer colour and simple borders of catmint seethe with butterflies and bees.

Lorimer's love of 'a garden within a garden' is demonstrated in two enclosures on the south wall, a yew room and a secret garden, known variously as 'Robin's Corner', after its designer, or 'Cupid's Corner', after a sculpture which was later vandalized and removed. Happily the amorous god has been replaced by a stone basin, carved by the architect's son Hew, who, after the death of his uncle John, moved in and with his green-fingered wife restored the neglected castle and garden. A sculptor and artist, Hew studied with Eric Gill, whose influence is evident in the monumental simplicity of many of his pieces. Hew also created the oriental green bench at the head of the main walk and the corner seat in Robin's Corner. His studio, in the old coach house, has recently been turned into a gallery space.

In 1955 Hew reduced the amount of ground under cultivation by turning part of the south garden to lawn and orchards. In 1970, when the National Trust bought the estate, they undertook some restoration based on George Ellwood's watercolour illustration and Gertrude Jekyll's descriptions in *Some English Gardens* (1904). These, plus a 1906 feature on Kellie Castle in *Country Life*, both suggest that the garden is at its best in late summer, but at any time of year Kellie Castle is a little Eden, fulfilling Sir Robert Lorimer's desire that the garden be 'a little pleasaunce of the soul, by whose wicket the world can be shut out from us...'

Kinross House Garden

Kinross House, Kinross, Perth and Kinross KY13 8ET

Open Apr to Sep, 10–7; no dogs

Fee £3, children free

Signed from Kinross, junction 6 on M90

Perth and Kinross

T: (01577) 862900   E: jm@kinrosshouse.com   W: www.kinrosshouse.com

With its dominant axis, symmetrical layout, clipped hedges, simple topiary, spacious lawns and fine stonework, Kinross House Garden exemplifies the Scots adaptation of the French horticultural style. In 1675 the estate was bought by the architect Sir William Bruce, famous for designing, among other things, the seventeenth-century gardens at Holyrood Palace. One of many Scots Royalists who served Charles II in exile, Bruce returned to Scotland when the Commonwealth ended, and began promoting the French formal style in architecture and horticulture.

Undaunted by the damp, low-lying site – originally a marsh and subject to occasional flooding – Bruce designed himself an

The Auld Alliance

The old alliance between Scotland and France dates to 1295, when the two countries joined forces to curtail English expansion. Though primarily a military alliance, the treaty encouraged an exchange of scholarship, culture and trade, introducing French manners, cuisine, language and law, as well as French plants and horticulture, to the northern nation. Until the Reformation France was Scotland's traditional ally, the two countries being united by their adherence to the Church of Rome. In the sixteenth century Mary of Guise (1515–60) probably had a profound effect on Scots horticulture – as she had on Scots history. Rejecting a marriage proposal from the English king Henry VIII, she chose instead to marry Scotland's Catholic king, James V. Her previous husband, the Duc de Longueville, was famous for having introduced many foreign plants to France and she might well have been the major force behind the King's Knot, a formal garden created at the new palace at Stirling. With its long, rectangular shape, geometric sub-divisions and terraced octagonal mount, it reflects the French preoccupations with geometry, symmetry and earthworks. Though no written records remain, the garden's outline can still be seen from the castle walls in the flat plateau to the west.

When James V died several days after their daughter's birth, Mary of Guise pushed for a Catholic alliance for the infant, also named Mary. Even after an engagement had been agreed to Prince Edward (later Edward VI) of England, she secretly negotiated to marry her daughter to the French dauphin. This betrayal aggravated the civil war with England, during which Mary Stuart (who assumed the French rather than the Scots spelling of her name) was sent to France, where she was raised and duly married in the French court. The dauphin became king in 1559; a year later he died and in 1561 his widow returned to Scotland to assume her rightful place as Queen of Scots till her tumultuous reign ended in forced abdication six years later.

F. Marian McNeill, in *The Scots Kitchen* (1929), suggests that the sorrel which flourished in the neighbourhood of Craigmillar Castle outside Edinburgh was introduced by the courtiers

elegant manor house. Unusually, the gardens appear to have been laid out before the building; the house, which took seven years to erect, was completed in 1692, while a 1688 letter to Bruce from Sir Charles Lyttleton claims, 'Lady Lauderdale's gardens at Ham are but a wilderness compared to yours.'

Bruce's loyalty ensured him a knighthood in 1668, and thirteen years later he was appointed the King's Surveyor. It was this position that allowed him to purchase the fine stonework and statuary found throughout the garden; indeed, the whole 4-acre plot is surrounded by a massive stone wall surmounted by impressive statuary. Laid out in an oblong twice as long as it is wide, the space is divided by the house to create a large, open forecourt and a rear pleasure garden. With its central position of Mary of Guise, while the *Archangelica officinalis*, then used in confectionery, had been introduced by Mary Stuart on her return from France.

In the 1630s John Drummond created the formal garden at **Drummond Castle**, inspired by the gardens of his French estates. Horticulture played a prominent role during the Commonwealth, when the 1st Lord Belhaven, an ardent Royalist renowned for his formal garden at Beil, disguised himself as a labourer and used his horticultural prowess to secure work at Kew; thus enabling him to transport secret letters to the exiled king while officially purchasing bulbs in Holland.

The French influence was particularly strong after the Restoration, when Royalists, many of whom had joined the King in exile, embellished their estates with allées, parterres and statuary in the French fashion. Sir William Bruce, having secretly visited Charles II in exile, acquired a taste for continental formality which he later expressed in his own gardens at **Balcaskie** and **Kinross**, in the gardens he designed for the restored King at Holyrood Palace, and at **Pitmedden**, which he is thought to have influenced, if not actually designed. The grand French gardens at **Drumlanrig** were created by another Royalist family and even **Traquair**, though now laid largely to grass, reveals the vestiges of an earlier French formality.

In the eighteenth century, after the union with England, many pragmatic Scotsmen embraced the English style, redesigning their houses with a Palladian classicism and reshaping their gardens into landscape-style parks. Others, such as the Arbuthnotts at **Arbuthnott House**, retained their formal gardens but incorporated Union Jack motifs. The enduring taste for French formality was demonstrated in such grand estates as **Castle Kennedy**, designed in the 1730s with formal ponds, parterres and allées, and **Blair**, with its radiating avenues and wilderness. In the nineteenth century Sir Charles Barry's grandiose design for **Dunrobin** was an unashamed homage to Versailles. In the twentieth century horticultural styles became more diverse but the avant-garde **Little Sparta**, strongly influenced by French philosophy and politics, indicates that 800 years after the treaty was signed, the old alliance persists in Scotland's horticulture.

and imposing architecture, the manor house dominates the estate. It was described by Daniel Defoe as 'the most beautiful and regular piece of architecture in Scotland', while the contemporary historian Sir Robert Sibbald declared it 'unsurpassed'.

The entrance court is flanked by two small gardens, enclosed in high hedges with charming ogee-roofed pavilions overlooking the lawns behind. A long tree-lined avenue cutting across the parkland links the house to the town of Kinross through what Bruce's builder tantalizingly described as a 'great gate of curious architecture' – now just two fragmentary pillars.

The pleasure garden behind is a large, open lawn, embellished with specimen trees and outlined with deep herbaceous borders sectioned by buttressing hedges. A yew-enclosed rose garden surrounds the central fountain, while two classical pavilions provide shelter from the elements. An anachronistic rhododendron walk, added in the 1920s, provides a slash of colour across the centre of the austere space.

The dominant axis bisects the property, leading from the town, through park, forecourt, mansion and pleasure garden, to terminate in the Fish Gate. Overlooking Loch Leven just beyond the enclosing wall, the Fish Gate is named for the carved stone basket at its centre displaying the seven types of fish in the loch: carp, bream, perch, pike, catfish, bull trout and red trout. Essentially a *claire-voie*, the Fish Gate frames a picturesque view of the ruins of Loch Leven Castle. This poignant spot figures prominently in the Scots imagination, as it was while imprisoned in the island castle in 1567 that Mary Queen of Scots was forced to abdicate in favour of her infant son, James VI. Escaping the following spring, Mary made her way south and threw herself on the mercy of her cousin, Elizabeth I, who finally found her too much of a threat and had her executed on a charge of treason.

In the nineteenth century Kinross House was abandoned – a fact lamented by the Edwardian designer Inigo Triggs, who described it, in 1902, as having 'a very desolate and ruinous aspect'. Thus spared the excesses of Victorian remodelling, house and garden were sympathetically restored in the twentieth century and continue to be exquisitely maintained.

Landform Ueda

Edinburgh

T: (0131) 624 6200 E: enquiries@nationalgalleries.org
W: www.nationalgalleries.org

Scottish National Gallery of Modern Art
75 Belford Road,
Edinburgh EH4 3DR

Open all year, 10–5

Fee free

NW of city centre

Land art, horticulture and sculpture combine in this distinctive, spiralling grass mound designed by American architectural historian Charles Jencks. Recalling the Snail Mounds and Slug Lakes of Jencks's Garden of Cosmic Speculation at **Portrack** in Dumfries and Galloway, Landform Ueda rises 23 feet over three adjacent crescent-shaped pools. Essentially a series of overlapping curves, it is apparently based on chaos theory. More precisely, it is inspired by the rhythmical patterns in nature: the swirl of air currents, rock curls in mountains, sea waves and their effect on sand. The landform is named after a Japanese scientist who studied the phenomenon of nature's similar but non-repetitive patterns.

For those of a less scientific bent, the landform evokes ancient ziggurats, medieval mounts, eighteenth-century earthworks and contemporary land art. An inscription in the terrace, *Festina lente* – Make haste slowly – is a wry horticultural allusion: an appropriate caution for those attempting the slippery ascent, it also evokes the classical landscapes of Renaissance Italy, being the motto of Cosimo de' Medici, whose Boboli Gardens in Florence are the foundation of western horticultural traditions.

A series of mown paths invite the viewer to engage directly with the work, ascending to the top, where views over the city link the gallery to its sister institution across the road and to the urban skyscape beyond. A favourite of boisterous children and strolling adults, Landform Ueda gained the gallery a Gulbenkian Award in 2004.

Lawhead Croft

West Lothian

Lawhead Croft, Tarbrax, West Calder, West Lothian EH55 8LW

Open Jun to Sep, any reasonable time

Fee £2, children 20p

6m NE of Carnwath, off A70, left towards Tarbrax down dirt track

Over the past thirty years Sue and Hector Riddle have transformed the bleak, open fields round their cottage into an intriguing labyrinth of garden rooms. *Law* is old Scots for 'a conical hill', but whatever feature gave this croft its name is no longer discernible. A rusty cowbell on a chain secures the entrance gate, laundry flaps in the trees nearby and a wee pond by the house is guarded by a bronze frog and a cement owl. Bitter winds, freak June frosts, shallow, dry soil and greedy birds are just a few of the forces they have to contend with. Apple trees succumb to canker in the damp and plums have to be netted against thieving finches, but several greenhouses ensure a plentiful supply of grapes, figs and peaches, while a rich crop of strawberries is cultivated in plastic milk cartons.

High beech hedges provide an outer layer of shelter, while interior hedges of yew create many separate enclosures, each with a different mood. This is a plants person's garden, with such rarities as the June-flowering Nepalese lily *Notholirion bulbiferum* cosseted within a willow chamber and several enclosures devoted solely to bonsai. Formal elements include a circle of clematis towers and an ingenious column created by stacking drum-shaped terracotta pots. A formal pool in a square room balances an informal pond planted with bulrushes; tight herb parterres vie with annual borders littered with self-seeded intruders. A novel arcade of interwoven larches graces a classical space, while a pair of bent larches acts as a living handrail along the wilderness walk. Rustic benches are fashioned from gnarled rhododendron stems and a cement Loch Ness monster provides a seating circle. Homemade artworks are dotted about, the most intriguing perhaps the moth made of old spectacles. As soon becomes obvious, this quirky garden is full of wit and ingenuity.

Little Sparta

South Lanarkshire

T: (01556) 640244   E: info@littlesparta.org   W: www.littlesparta.co.uk

Deep in the Pentland Hills, up a long, winding cart track, the late Ian Hamilton Finlay created one of the most significant gardens of the twentieth century. Though regularly cited in discussions of avant-garde art, horticulture and landscape design, Little Sparta has also been compared with the medieval *hortus conclusus*, the Renaissance sculpture gallery and the eighteenth-century landscape park; indeed, some question whether it is a garden at all.

Finlay first came to prominence in the 1960s as a controversial publisher, poet and artist. He was one of the early exponents of concrete poetry – a combination of art and literature where the meaning of a word is altered by its placement on the page. From 1966 he began translating concrete poetry into garden art, embellishing his isolated croft with inscriptions on stone, ceramics and wood. Plants are incidental and the bleak moorland landscape simply provides the backdrop for an exploration of complex philosophical notions. For visitors hoping to understand this extraordinary garden, it is worth examining some of the ideas behind it.

Little Sparta, Dunsyre, South Lanarkshire ML11 8NG

Open 3 Jun to 30 Sep, Fri and Sun, 2.30–5; no young children or dogs

Fee £10

Turn off A721 at Newbiggin, up farm track 1m W of Dunsyre, signed

Though there is no particular symbolic programme, classical mythology, military conflict and landscape painting are major inspirations, while nautical imagery links the landscape to the distant sea. Apollo, Greek god of arts, archery and divination, is the guiding spirit of the place and Finlay transformed an old stone cow byre into a Temple of Apollo by painting Greek columns on its façade. The lintel inscription, TO APOLLO, HIS MUSIC, HIS MISSILES, HIS MUSES, recalls a long-running battle with the local council when Finlay refused to pay commercial taxes, claiming that his Temple art gallery was a religious site. Though he lost the battle, and many of his artworks were impounded, this conflict galvanized the artist to transform his garden into a celebration of the ideals of the past while decrying the superficiality of contemporary life. Identifying himself with the disciplined Greek city-state Sparta in its battles against the decadent Athenians, Finlay changed the name of his small-holding from Stonypath to Little Sparta.

A Roman *lararium* – a shrine to the household gods – displays a model of Apollo carrying a machine gun. Elsewhere a gilded head of Apollo bears the inscription APOLLON TERRORISTE, referring to the eighteenth-century Louis de Saint-Just, who was one of the most zealous advocates of the Terror during the French Revolution. At the edge of the garden Saint-Just is evoked once more in an installation of eleven large stones inscribed with his proclamation THE PRESENT ORDER IS THE DISORDER OF THE FUTURE.

A plaque inscribed L'ILE DE PEUPLIERS commemorates Jean-Jacques Rousseau, whose championing of justice, liberty and equality inspired the Republicans before he died and was buried on a poplar-filled island on the estate of his admirer the Marquis de Girardin. Among other heroes of the French Revolution, Maximilien Robespierre is commemorated with a watering can bearing the dates of his life, a whimsical contrivance recalling the fact that Robespierre was executed on the day known as *Arrosoir* (French for 'watering can') in the short-lived Republican calendar. George Couthon, another guillotined Jacobin, is honoured with a broken section of serpentine column – a fitting memorial to a man whose body was twisted by paralysis.

A model of an aircraft carrier doubles as a bird bath in the Roman Garden, where a collection of stone ships recalls the *naumachie* or mock naval battles of the classical world. Rising from the side of Loch Eck, a large black stone inscribed NUCLEAR SAIL suggests the conning tower of a nuclear submarine, while its colour refers to the black sail which signals a death at sea. In a landscape haunted with nautical allusions, a stone plaque at the boundary of the garden reads MARE NOSTRUM – our sea – the Romans' name for the Mediterranean. A wooden bench below is inscribed THE SEA'S WAVES, THE WAVES' SHEAVES, THE SEA'S NAVES. The rhythm and repetition of the words suggest the movement of waves, the juxtaposing of 'waves' and 'sheaves' establishes the similarity between seas and hills, while the final line equates the valley with a church nave, introducing a spiritual element to the garden. In a clever piece of wordplay the final 'naves', from the Latin *navis*, or ship, suggests that the garden itself is a ship in the sea of the surrounding hills.

Elsewhere a sweep of grass, reminiscent of English parkland, contains stone blocks, floating like vessels through the green, each inscribed with the word 'wave' in a different language: WAVE, VAGUE, WOGE, ONDA, UNDAM – the vowels move through the inscription with the rhythm of a wave. Facing west to catch the evening sun, a small weathered wooden board is carved with a simple sail and the words EVENING WILL COME / THEY WILL SEW THE BLUE SAIL, suggesting the end of day, when sailors repair their sails and old men prepare for the afterlife.

Landscape painting is another inspiration. Little Sparta is aligned with Eden in a woodland setting where a stone hanging from a branch is inscribed with Albrecht Dürer's monograph, as depicted in Dürer's own painting *The Fall of Man*. A more contrived artistic style is evoked by a wooden fence leaning into Loch Eck; carved with the single word PICTURESQUE, it recalls the horticultural style which incorporated such elements as rotting trees and ruined buildings. In contrast, a peaceful waterside site with an obelisk inscribed IL RIPOSO DE CLAUDIO pays homage to Claude's paintings, which inspired the natural movement in English landscape design.

The classical world is intriguingly evoked in a surrealist, sheet-metal cutout of Apollo chasing Daphnis. Drawn from Ovid's story of metamorphosis and inspired by Bernini's sculpture of the pair, this shadow-board combines classical art and contemporary cartoon.

The garden also has less arcane allusions. A tablet inscribed BRING BACK THE BIRCH exhorts the return of Scotland's native birch trees. A simple bridge of parallel planks is inscribed, in each direction, THAT WHICH JOINS AND THAT WHICH DIVIDES

IS ONE AND THE SAME. A sheepfold carrying the inscription ECLOGUE: FOLDING THE LAST SHEEP is a fitting end to a tour of the garden, an eclogue being a short pastoral poem, a form often used by Finlay's favourite poet, Virgil.

Malleny Garden (NTS)

Malleny, Balerno, Edinburgh EH14 7AF

Open all year, 10–6 or sunset if earlier; no dogs

Fee £3, conc. £2

Off A70 in Balerno, 6m W of Edinburgh city centre

Edinburgh

T: (0131) 449 2283   E: information@nts.org.uk   W: www.nts.org.uk

The frontispiece of Sir Herbert Maxwell's 1911 *Scottish Gardens* features an illustration of Malleny: a nostalgic watercolour of summer flowers, clipped yew, picturesque doves and a poignant sundial. Maxwell regretted that the growth of Edinburgh had engulfed the country seat in suburbia, but assured his reader that Malleny remains 'delightfully secluded, screened by woodland containing some magnificent sycamores'. Nearly a century later these words remain true and the screening woods have been enhanced to create a woodland walk with year-round interest – a crucial requirement of today's public gardens.

Malleny consists of a 3-acre walled garden, one wall of which was removed in Georgian times when the forecourt of the house was extended to accommodate new rooms. A late nineteenth-century tenant, Sir Thomas Carmichael, filled the space with weird metal creatures of his own creation, while his wife, Lady Gibson-Carmichael, draped the clipped yews with flowers. Sadly nothing survives of this eccentric exuberance, but the garden does feature four large yews reputed to have been planted in 1610. Together with a further eight, which were removed in the 1960s, these were known as the Twelve Apostles.

Former parterres have been laid largely to lawn with charming borders surrounding; peonies, alliums, geraniums and weigela provide a delicate palette of pinks and blues. Beyond a clipped yew arch is a neat potager with raised beds and the enticing sound of the Bavelaw Burn running beyond the high stone wall. An ancient deodar presides over the garden and two greenhouses display a range of geraniums. The enclosure is particularly pleasant in midsummer, when the roses are at their height. Malleny holds a national collection of nineteenth-century shrub roses. Such delights as the Bourbons 'Mme Ernst Calvat', introduced *c.* 1888, 'Bourbon Queen', *c.* 1884, and *Rosa centifolia* 'Fantin Latour', *c.* 1900, recall that the French were the main rose breeders in Europe, working from the eighteenth century to perfect the *R. gallica* imports then pouring in from the Orient.

Manderston

Scottish Borders

T: (01361) 883450 or 882636   E: palmer@manderston.co.uk
W: www.manderston.co.uk

Manderston, Scotland's most impressive country house, has been described as 'the swansong of the great classical house'. The original manor was built in 1790, inspired by Robert Adam's Kedleston Hall, though both house and gardens were extensively remodelled over the years. Familiar to many from the Channel 4/PBS television series *The Edwardian Country House*, today it combines Georgian elegance with Edwardian efficiency. In 1893, when the owner, Sir James Miller, married the Hon. Eveline Curzon, he commissioned the Scottish architect John Kinross to create the chalet-style boathouse as a present for his bride. Keen to impress his father-in-law, Sir James then commissioned the elegant stables with marbled panels, teak walls and tiled troughs. In 1901, having returned from the Boer Wars, he once again engaged Kinross to modernize the façade of the house and update the interior. A silver staircase, based on Mme Pompadour's staircase at the Petit Trianon, was just one of the dazzling features of this lavish remodelling.

As money was no object – Miller's ancestors had made a fortune trading hemp and herrings with the Russians – Kinross also helped Sir James landscape the 56-acre estate. To the south, with its views over the Cheviot Hills, Kinross added four formal terraces planted in the Edwardian style with topiary, pools, parterres and masses of roses climbing the retaining walls. These are further embellished with statuary supplied by the infamous art dealer Lord Duveen. The terraces descend to a serpentine lake over which a chinoiserie bridge-cum-dam leads

Manderston, Duns,
Scottish Borders TD11 3PP

Open garden: 10 May to
30 Sep, Sun and Thurs,
and Bank Holiday Mon
in May and Aug,
11.30–sunset;
house: 1.30–5
(last admission 4.15)

Fee gardens: £4.50,
children £2;
house and gardens: £8,
children £4.50

2m E of Duns on A6105

to an informally planted island. Developed in the 1950s, this woodland garden features rare azaleas and rhododendrons.

The gardens on the east front are more austere. An imposing wrought-iron gate opens on to a rectangular croquet lawn flanked by four massive stone vases, while an impressive copper beech presides over the whole ensemble. Happily Kinross left the sweeping grounds to the north virtually untouched; today it is one of the few such parklands to survive in Scotland. A magnificent *Cedrus atlantica glauca*, planted in 1937 to commemorate the coronation of George VI, holds its own among the specimen trees – many from the original eighteenth-century garden. In spring the parkland is a sea of bluebells.

The north lawn leads to a formal walled garden, entered through magnificent gates, the tops of which were gilded to catch the evening sun. Within is a kaleidoscope of colour and scent, the sheer opulence of which leaves one gasping for good Scots austerity. A fantastical gardener's cottage, built like a miniature feudal castle, demonstrates the early twentieth-century penchant for evocations of Scotland's baronial past. At its height Manderston employed over 100 maintenance staff; today it manages with eight.

Mellerstain

Mellerstain, Gordon,
Scottish Borders TD3 6LG

Open Good Fri to Easter
Mon, 11.30–5.30; May, Jun
and Sep, Bank Holiday
Mon, Wed and Sun,
11.30–5.30;
Jul and Aug, Mon, Wed,
Thurs and Sun,
11.30–5.30; Oct, Sun,
11.30–5.30

Fee £3.50, children free

6m NW of Kelso, off A6089

Scottish Borders

T: (01573) 410225 E: enquiries@mellerstain.com W: www.mellerstain.com

Mellerstain's history reads like a Walter Scott novel. The name first appears in 1451, when the lands of Mellerstain, with their spectacular views across the Cheviot Hills, were granted by James II to Patrick Halliburton. Two centuries later, in 1642, the estate was granted by Royal Charter to George Baillie, the son of a prosperous Edinburgh merchant. He died four years later during the Civil War and his son Robert was executed for Royalist sympathies. Robert's son George fled to Holland, where he became an officer in the Prince of Orange's Horse Guards, and when the Prince became William III of England, Baillie's estate was restored to him.

Baillie's wife, Lady Grisell Baillie, was beloved by Royalists for having, at the age of twelve, courageously carried messages to George's father during his imprisonment. Beautiful and accomplished, as all true heroines must be, she kept a household book which has survived as a classic of social history. In 1725 the Baillies commissioned William Adam, father of the more famous Robert, to design their new mansion. Inspired, no doubt, by his years of continental exile, Baillie had the surrounding gardens laid out in the formal Dutch style. Unlike the endless vistas of grand French designs, the smaller scale of Dutch estates created static, inward-looking gardens, more suited to the Scottish topography and temperament. At Mellerstain a natural lake, an offshoot of the River Eden, was canalized into a formal canal measuring 1,200 by 400 feet. In keeping with the Dutch style, this was surrounded by raised grass walks lined with classical statues.

When George died in 1738, only two wings of the house were complete. The central part was not built until the 1760s, when another George Baillie, having succeeded to the estate, employed Robert Adam to complete the house in the new classical taste. Much of its magnificent interior remains untouched, and among the paintings on display are works by Van Dyck, Gainsborough and Ramsay. It is tempting to believe that the portrait of Lady Grisell Baillie in the front hall depicts Mellerstain in the background, but the formal terraces and fountain did not come about till the twentieth century. Indeed, throughout the eighteenth and nineteenth centuries Mellerstain was moored in a sea of parkland, with grass sweeping up to the house in the fashion of the time. It was not till 1909 that the formalist Sir Reginald Blomfield was called in to link the grand house to the canal beyond.

Blomfield envisioned a grand design with terraces, bastion walls, loggias, a crypto-porticus, parterres and water works; his original scheme even included an immense grass hemisphere cut into the bottom of the hill overlooking the water. Much of this plan was abandoned because, as he explained it in his *Memoirs*, 'it would have required the resources of Louis XIV to carry out the whole of my design'. Nonetheless there are still an elaborate parterre, several bastion walls, balustrades and a grand staircase with a recessed oval fish pond, all in golden Black Pasture stone.

A long grass walk fronts the house; legend has it that as a birthday surprise for her husband, Lady Haddington, the present Earl's mother, had the existing gravel walk grassed overnight.

As field turf was used and the path was laid in haste, the outline of the earlier walk is still visible in dry weather. The lower terrace was laid out by Blomfield with palmate box work and scroll beds planted with red and yellow roses, under-planted with *Nepeta* 'Six Hills Giant' and the more delicate compact cross *N. fassenii*.

Blomfield demonstrated more restraint as he moved away from the house. Despite his reputation for strict formality, he restored the canal to its original shape as a lake, which he then surrounded with woodland, creating a gradual transition from formal garden to natural landscape. Plantings of *Sambucus nigra* 'Black Lace' and 'Black Beauty', *Sorbus hupehensis* 'Pink Pagoda', *Betula utilis* var. *jacquemontii* and decorative willows and alders have recently been added to increase shelter and interest.

A woodland walk meanders from the east gate into the parkland, past an old ornamental pool and into a glen where a ruined tower and crumbling walls indicate the site of the old laundry. Deep in the undergrowth are the remains of the old walled garden. Sadly there are no plans to restore this, as it is cheaper to purchase produce from the local supermarket. The path emerges on to a simple stone terrace – a landing stage for the lake. Blomfield ingeniously used the infill from the initial expanding of the lake to create the terraces. However, a decade ago, when the lake was last dredged, two ancient steam engines laboured for days hauling up silt, which was simply deposited in a distant lagoon.

Today the gardening is done by one full-time gardener and a groundsman. Even at its most extravagant, however, Mellerstain was never heavily planted and employed only six gardeners; formal stone work, clipped hedges and an immaculate lawn have always been its major features. Beyond an ornate woodland gate a rhododendron walk wanders off to the west, where visitors are serenaded by the Earl's prize turkeys, hidden in the trees beyond. To the front, the park is planted with oak, beech and some magnificent sycamore – it is a rare treat to see parkland untainted by nineteenth-century coniferous imports. Hidden in the trees, surrounded by its own cottage garden, is a thatched Victorian tea hut, probably originally a dovecot.

One of the secret delights of Mellerstain is an architectural folly, created in 1731, on a distant hill overlooking the lake. When viewed from the main terrace this massive, free-standing wall appears to be a gothic castle. Named the 'Hundy Mundy' after *Huni Mundias*, a Pictish princess who lived on the hill, it is now almost hidden in trees, though in its time it would have been visible for miles around.

Mertoun

Scottish Borders

T: (01835) 823236   W: www.discovertheborders.co.uk

Mertoun – said to derive its name from a long-forgotten village in the nearby mere, hence 'mere-town' – is one of Scotland's great horticultural treasures. Its owners make no efforts to promote it, it follows no horticultural fads, its few herbaceous borders are not noteworthy, and yet it is this very lack of showiness that makes Mertoun so delightful. The major feature of the estate is a magnificent 3-acre walled garden dating from the seventeenth century, immaculately maintained and overflowing with fruit, flowers and vegetables. Its peach and fig houses are still producing enviable fruit, while the flower beds and floral greenhouses provide glorious displays for the 'big hoose' and the local church. An unusual mushroom house by the lower gate has the names of generations of gardeners inscribed on the back of the door. The current gardener laments the fact that the estate no longer keeps cattle, as there will soon be a paucity of rotted manure to keep his strawberries fertilized.

An orchard within the walled garden contains, among its ancient and now neglected trees, a picturesque Siberian crab apple. At a time when staff are paid in cash rather than produce, much of the garden's riches go unused, except by wildlife; indeed, after the first frost the orchard is often awash with hungry birds. In the midst of the garden sits the original Mertoun House of 1677. Now the gardener's cottage, this delightful stepped-roof dwelling was superseded in 1703 by the current manor house, built in the Palladian style by Sir William Bruce a dignified distance from the walled garden.

Remarkably, the new house was sited sidelong to the glorious views sweeping down to the Tweed. Two elegant stone foxes preside over the rear steps, which descend to a simple lawn, planted with spring bulbs and the Himalayan poppy, *Meconopsis*

Mertoun, St Boswells, Melrose, Scottish Borders TD6 OEA

Open 1 Apr to 30 Sep, Mon, Fri, Sat and Sun, 2–6, or by appointment (last admission 5.30)

Fee £2.50, children 50p

2m NE of St Boswells on B6404

The Burry Man

For more than three centuries the intriguing character of the Burry Man has appeared on the second Friday of August as part of South Queensferry's annual 'Ferry Fair'. Each year a townsman, chosen by the local council, dons a flannel body-costume which is then covered with burs and embellished with flowers. With two flower-draped staffs to help support the weight of his costume, the Burry Man processes through the streets from dawn until dusk, stopping in each of the town's pubs to be served a glass of whisky – which he is only able to drink through a straw.

Though the event has been conducted since 1687, its origins probably lie in pagan ritual, a local version of the Green Man fertility figure or a scapegoat character who paraded through the town, absorbing evil spirits before being sacrificed or banished.

The eponymous burs, members of the daisy family, are *Arctium lappa* and *Arctium minus* – Britain's two native burdock species, which flourish in Midlothian's shale wastelands. The thistle-like flowers dry, creating the burs whose deep hooks catch the fur of passing beasts to ensure the wide dispersal of their seeds. In the past burdock roots were used to create skin ointment, while young stems were eaten raw or boiled, though they have a mild laxative effect.

sheldonii – recently chosen as Edinburgh's floral emblem. A generation ago the previous Duke and Duchess of Sutherland added an ornamental pond which is now backed with deep herbaceous borders and red oaks brought from Kew as acorns.

The real pride of Mertoun is the arboretum and woodland. Scots pines, which were planted in masses to protect the more delicate ornamentals, are slowly being removed as the specimens mature. An earlier incumbent had a penchant for drooping boughs, and one of the prizes of the arboretum is an enormous weeping elm, at least a century old, whose bizarrely contorted branches stretch to a circumference of 25 feet. Other treasures are a glaucous hemlock, several *Cedrus atlantica* and a magnificent *Sequoia sempervirens*. Recent additions include an ironwood tree, *Parrotia persica*; with its dramatic peeling bark and splendid autumn colouring, this shrubby tree manages to flourish far from its native habitat in Iran. There is also an *Araucaria araucana* which would puzzle any monkey. Azaleas are a favourite and in the first week of June, when the glen is ablaze, the scent is overpowering.

In the early twentieth century, herbaceous borders used to stretch along the woodland path, but during the wartime labour shortages these were grassed over. More lamentable is the loss of the carpet of phloxes, edged with deep-blue *Gentiana acaulis*, which used to grace the dell by the *doocot*. While the date-stone of 1576 may have been reused from another structure, the dove-cot's beehive construction places it in the sixteenth-century tradition. So named because of the resemblance to bee skeps, the circular, stone walls of this type of construction were raised in stages, each marked with a rat course, or projecting ledge, to deter vermin from scaling the walls.

The main approach to Mertoun winds along a serpentine drive, flanked by mature birches. In the eighteenth-century fashion, this overlooks open parkland, separated from the house by an elegant, curved ha-ha restored fifty years ago with stones from demolished wings of the house. Before the war Mertoun supported thirty gardeners; after the war that number was reduced to seventeen. Today the 26 acres of garden are maintained by a staff of three, while two foresters oversee the 6,000-acre estate. Despite such economies, the grounds are enchanting.

Monteviot

Scottish Borders

T: (01835) 830704   W: www.discovertheborders.co.uk

Monteviot, Jedburgh,
Scottish Borders TD8 6TJ

Open 1 Apr to 31 Oct, 12–5

Fee £2.50, children free

3m NE of Jedburgh, turn
right off A68 towards
Nisbet on B6400, second
on right

Monteviot demonstrates several centuries of horticultural evolution. Mount Teviot, as it was originally named, sits on a hill overlooking the River Teviot. A fishing lodge in the early 1700s, it was transformed later in the century into a classic Palladian villa. In 1877 a massive sandstone terrace was built between the house and the river and a gravel walk was added running the length of the house. A small herb garden, centred round an old sundial, is set into a sheltered courtyard. Yew hedges partially enclose the walk on one side, while the other is lined with pink shrub roses. Recent planting includes a sorbus-lined avenue linking the two terraces, and a bed by the east stairway filled with azaleas and backed by several *Prunus pissardii nigra.*

In the 1960s the grounds were redesigned by Percy Cane, a fashionable English designer who had recently restored **Falkland Palace Garden**. In *The Creative Art of Garden Design* Cane explained that before his improvements the lawn was too steep, giving 'the uncomfortable feeling that the terrace was not adequately supported'. He added a lower terrace which leads through a high stone wall to a charming rose garden with glorious river views. Invisible from the main house, the garden is sheltered on the sides by deep yew hedges. Simply arranged rectangular box-edged rose beds are filled with floribundas, hybrid teas and shrub roses, while carved stone benches suggest the country-house elegance at which Cane excelled, creating an atmosphere of Edwardian opulence for post-war budgets.

The rose garden leads on to the river garden, created in the meadow between a semicircular nineteenth-century 'preservative wall' for growing peaches and a landing stage on the river. In the past 100 years this area has seen four different gardeners, designs, colour palettes and moods. Photos from the 1920s show an exuberant avenue of herbaceous flowers leading down the open field to the river. Monteviot suffered during the two world wars, and in the 1960s, when Cane was commissioned to help restore it, he created an air of Italian formality with a flower-lined avenue of *Prunus sargentii* – chosen for its autumn colours and upright habit. A generation later the present Lord Ancram, preferring informal curves, instructed his gardener to remove Cane's trees and reshape the borders into island beds to create a more casual effect. Twenty years on, the current gardener has bulked out Cane's remaining lilacs, deutzias, shrub roses, Himalayan birches and ironwood *Parrotia persica* with that contemporary favourite, low-maintenance grasses. To satisfy modern expectations, he has also added spring- and autumn-flowering plants to extend the season of interest, hot-coloured flowers to contrast with the subtle pastels of his predecessors and architectural plants to arrest the eye.

Monteviot's grounds also contain a laburnum arch, planted as a millennium project, and an oriental water garden. Established several years ago in the old curling pond, this features spring-fed pools, elegant bridges and aquatic and bog planting. As winters are rarely cold enough now to freeze Scotland's ponds, outdoor curling has become one of the lesser-known casualties of climate change.

The arboretum, planted in the 1840s, was damaged by the storms of 1973, which destroyed many of the specimen trees, including the Macedonian pines for which it was renowned. It still boasts a noble fir, *Abies procera*, and a Douglas fir, *Pseudotsuga menziesii*, which rises 133 feet, towering above the other species. In the past five years more than 200 trees have been added to the arboretum, among them a collection of Mexican and Californian oaks, including the red oak, *Quercus rubra*. Traditionally used in charcoal making, house building and furniture, oak was also valued for tannin, which was extracted from its bark and used in leather curing. Over-zealous cutting and irresponsible grazing by sheep have led to the tree's decline in Scotland.

Where many gardens are simply maintained, Monteviot is pursuing new horticultural challenges with the construction of a new dene garden; concentrating on foliage, this area features such plants as eryngium, hostas, pulmonaria, ferns, hemerocallis and heuchera. Care has been taken to provide disabled access, an obligation as well as a politeness in modern times. A small commercial nursery tempts, but thankfully, so far, there is neither café nor gift shop. The pleasures of Monteviot are complemented by such whimsical elements as a nineteenth-century bell tower, a pet cemetery and a 150-foot Wellington Monument – a Doric column, erected in 1817 to commemorate Napoleon's defeat at the Battle of Waterloo.

Netherbyres

Scottish Borders

T: (01890) 750337

As Netherbyres sits on an exposed piece of low-lying land, its walled garden provides a sheltered enclave from the biting winds of the North Sea. Though the estate appears on maps as early as 1645, the 1½-acre walled garden wasn't created till 1740. Designed by a renowned mathematician, William Crow, its unusual elliptical shape contravened traditional wisdom; James Justice's *The Scots Gardener's Director* (1754) counselled against curved walls, as he felt they would trap the frost. Nonetheless Crow was savvy enough to line the stone walls with heat-

Netherbyres, Eyemouth,
Scottish Borders TD14 5SE

Open Apr to Sep by appointment

Fee £2 (£3 in July), children £1

¼m from Eyemouth on A1107

retaining bricks. Of Dutch origin, these probably came as ballast from Holland, with which the nearby town of Eyemouth had a lively export trade. A change in the style of bricks towards the top of the wall indicates that it was once lower on the side facing the house; possibly this was to allow the garden to be seen from the main terrace. In traditional English fashion, the walled garden is located far from the house, which is now run by the Gardeners' Royal Benevolent Society as a home for retired gardeners. An Ordnance Survey map records that in 1856 a formal layout of fountain, paths and mature trees spread out in front of the house, though today this area has been given over to parkland.

When the old house was separated from the estate, a new dwelling was built inside the walled garden on the site of Victorian greenhouses. Though traditionally Scots gardens combined produce with flowers, at Netherbyres a yew hedge screens the pleasure garden from the utilitarian orchard and vegetable beds, with emblematic thistles and roses marking the passage through the hedge. The pleasure garden is quartered with rose borders – one bed particularly favoured by bees is stuffed with delicious pink 'Fragrant Cloud', 'Lilli Marlene' and 'Ingrid Bergman' roses, under-planted with nepeta. Island beds ornament the lawn, herbaceous borders vibrate with butterflies and a charming gazebo, surrounded with delicate fuchsias, flanks the main axis. A carved stone owl presides from the roof of the modern house, while its twin glares from the ancient gatepost amid clouds of jasmine. Though occasionally the sound of traffic competes with the cooing of doves, this pleasure garden demonstrates what an oasis of calm the old walled Scots enclosure can be.

Newhall, Carlops,
Midlothian EH26 9LY

Open walled garden:
Apr to Oct, Wed 2–5:
glen walks: all year,
Tues–Thurs 1–5

Fee £2.50, children free

On the A702 1m E of
Carlops

Newhall

Midlothian

Tel (01968) 660252

Newhall offers a magnificent 2-acre walled garden and glorious glen walks. The site of an old monastic estate, the name Newhall is thought to refer to a house constructed in the thirteenth century, when sheep farming was beginning to replace the ancient game and timber preserves in the region. The present house dates from the eighteenth century, when it was built as a weekend home for a family of Edinburgh advocates, the Forbeses. Newhall soon became a literary and artistic retreat for such luminaries as the poet Allan Ramsay, whose most famous poem, 'The Gentle Shepherd', was inspired by the surrounding countryside. Ramsay's son, the painter Allan Ramsay, did a portrait of the subsequent owner, Robert Brown.

Brown settled in Newhall, giving up his legal career to live as a country gentleman. In the tradition of enlightened estate management, he built the nearby village of Carlops to house his workers, then introduced cotton weaving to give them employment. He also expanded the estate, incorporating the latest agricultural improvements, created the walled garden and capitalized on the literary heritage of the place by placing mementoes of 'The Gentle Shepherd' round the glen. Today, with one part-time gardener, Trish Kennedy is attempting to maintain the traditional walled garden and the wider informal landscape.

Between the walled garden and the farm steadings is a little Victorian pond with a cascade known as 'Fairy's Lin' – the lin could derive from the Gaelic *linne*, 'a pool', or the Old English *hlynh*, 'a waterfall'. The walled garden is laid out in a cruciform shape, with beech hedges creating internal divisions. A Coade-stone statue of an eighteenth-century gentleman – known as Adam because he was the first delver – presides from a heady bed of roses, lilies and nicotiana. Silk ribbons and stitched buttonholes suggest the statue is more than a generic gentleman – some believe it depicts Robert Brown, the garden's creator. The sundial beyond, dated 1703, predates the garden by nearly a century and its plinth is even older.

In one quadrant vegetables line up in ordered ranks behind delightful Victorian ironwork plant markers. Other treats are a heated melon pit, a recently renovated peach house and an old greenhouse hosting what is reputed to be the oldest vine in Scotland. The herbaceous borders, at their best in July, are filled with old varieties, while the corner peony bed holds such delights as the charming purple-pink single *veitchii* and the modern favourite 'Molly-the-witch'. A phlox border recalls how popular this flower once was in Scottish gardens – witness the late and much-lamented phlox meadow at **Mertoun**. *Rosa moyesii* flourishes around the edges, its nondescript flowers giving way to glowing, elongated red hips which provide welcome colour in autumn.

The lower half of the garden is laid to lawn, with a pond and island beds, in the fashion of the 1950s. There is also an unusual shade garden, enclosed by a bamboo grove and several dry-stone walls; while primulas multiply in the grass, alchemilla and cat-mint flourish in the wall. The south gates are flanked by magnificent sequoia trees and topped by eighteenth-century stone busts of Pan and his mother, Pastora. Exiting through these gates, visitors can pick up the glen walks, a series of romantic paths set out in the early nineteenth century. At the footbridge is a plaque inscribed with lines from the Prologue of Ramsay's 'The Gentle Shepherd'. Following the river, past the Washing Green – a flat meadow used for drying laundry – is a second plaque, quoting two laundry lasses from the poem.

Newhall itself, with nostalgic gothic turret and baronial tower, is set on a bank jutting into the glen. A sundial, dated 1810, provides a focal point for the front lawn, its eight tapering panels inscribed with extracts from the ubiquitous 'Gentle Shepherd'. A pair of recently beheaded stone foxes guards the point, while a pair of exotic elephant statues from **Pollok House** flanks steps to the side. Hidden in the shrubbery is Hew Lorimer's sculpture of St Fiacre – patron saint of gardeners – depicted in monk's habit in deference to the monastic origins of the site. Having been brought up at **Kellie Castle** with its magnificent walled garden, Hew must have felt some affinity with the subject of his sculpture.

Paxton House

Paxton House, Berwick upon Tweed, Scottish Borders TD15 1SZ

Scottish Borders

T: (01289) 386291 E: info@paxtonhouse.com W: www.paxtonhouse.com

Open garden: 1 Apr to 31 Oct, 10–sunset; house: 1 Apr to 31 Oct, 10–5

Fee garden: £3, children £1.50; house and garden: adult £6, children £3

On B6461, 3m from the A1 Berwick upon Tweed bypass

One of the finest Palladian houses in Scotland, Paxton was designed in 1758 by John and James Adam. Its grounds were landscaped by Robert Robinson at about the same time, though the croquet lawn, lily garden and several herbaceous borders are Victorian additions. A charming triple-arched stone bridge on the entrance drive sets the scene for 80 acres of woodland parks, riverside walks and designed gardens.

Though dependent on tourism, Paxton is refreshingly uncommercial; its reception area is discreetly housed in the stable yard, while the playground is hidden in a glen. An intriguing 'squirrel hide' is consistent with Paxton's ecological approach to estate management. Since indigenous red squirrels are being overrun by the larger grey squirrels introduced from North America a century ago, Paxton is replacing older trees with Scots pine, larch, rowan and hazel to provide the endangered squirrels with their preferred habitat. The woodlands also harbour hare and deer, while a bird hide on the river promises seals, cormorants, herons and mute swans.

At the *sheil* or fishing station, housed in a nineteenth-century boathouse, a bird-besmirched boat adds a note of authenticity, while poignant photographs trace the history of salmon fishing on the Tweed. The frequency of the word *stell*, meaning 'fishtrap', at the end of local place-names indicates the importance of fishing in the area; indeed, ancient stone carvings reveal that fishing has taken place on this stretch of river for thousands of years.

Fish were one of the few features of the region to find favour with the intrepid seventeenth-century traveller Celia Fiennes, who complained, 'all here about which are called Borderers seem to be a very poor people which I impute to their sloth...I see little that they are employed besides fishing which makes provision plentiful...', and later, unable to eat the 'clapt oat bread', she bought fish, 'which was full cheape enough nine pence for 2 pieces of salmon half a one neer a yard long and a very large trout of amber colour...'

Throughout the seventeenth century the Dutch were great exploiters of Scots fish, focusing on the Firth of Forth, with its eel, skate, herring, flounder, mackerel, lobster and crab; in fact, there is an old saying that Amsterdam was built on Scottish herring bones. By the eighteenth century the Scots had begun to develop their own fisheries, preserving fish in salt and shipping it to London's Billingsgate Market. A small fish-store at Paxton, cut into the river bank, provided a cool, damp cavern for holding the catch until it could be taken by boat to Berwick and sold on. At that time, when it was common to land 750 salmon in a single cast of the nets, terms of employment would specify that staff could not be fed the ubiquitous fish more than twice a week!

In 1788 ice replaced salt as the preferred preservative. As round salt barrels gave way to flat ice boxes, commercial ice houses sprang up around Berwick to supply the salmon trade. Though local ponds provided most of the ice, in warm winters it could be imported from Norway. Further along the shallow, meandering river, a stone alcove displays a 6-foot-high tide mark with the inscription 'Flood 1772'.

A woodland walk rises up from the river, past magnificent oak and chestnut trees. Nestled in the forest is a recent 'Well Garden', with streams cascading from an old well, surrounded by viburnums, saxifrages, euphorbias, hellebores and rhododendrons. Round a corner the unsuspecting viewer comes upon *Entrances* (Julia Hilton, 1993). A surreal folly, this intriguing construction comprises two tall concertina walls of carved and glazed brick, inspired, apparently, by an opening bud. Whatever one thinks of the artistic merit, its presence demonstrates an admirable patronage of contemporary art.

Priorwood (NTS)

Priorwood, Melrose,
Scottish Borders TD6 9PZ

Open Good Fri to 24 Dec,
Mon–Sat, 10–5; Sun 1–5

Fee £3, conc. £2

Off A609 in Melrose,
beside the Abbey

Scottish Borders

T: (01896) 822493   E: priorwooddriedflowers@nts.org.uk
W: www.ngs.org.uk

Built within the precinct of Melrose Abbey, the 6-acre walled garden of Priorwood was first cultivated by the abbey monks in the twelfth century. Some 700 years later it became the kitchen garden of the newly built Priorwood House, which is now separated from the grounds and used as a youth hostel. While the eastern edge of the garden is bounded by dense woodland, a change in the colour of the brickwork on the three remaining sides shows where the eighteenth-century wall was heightened in 1904; the decorative, half-moon ironwork added at that time has been attributed to Edwin Lutyens.

In the middle of the twentieth century Priorwood's garden operated as a commercial nursery, but after the Second World War, with the rise in imports and large-scale farming, such a small enterprise became unprofitable and was abandoned. In 1974 a planning application to replace the garden with a car park galvanized local residents and, after convincing the National Trust for Scotland to purchase the garden, volunteers began a dried-flower business to help finance the project. The gardener's cottage, dated 1820, was restored and turned into a gift shop, and as the business became more successful, new sheds were added for drying and demonstration. Today courses are offered in flower arranging, while visitors can explore the history of flower drying, from ancient Egyptian times, when sand was used to dry the rose petals that lined the tombs, through to Victorian times, when borax was used to dry flowers for winter bouquets. This area is worth visiting for its heady scents alone: the hay-like odour of delicate grasses, hydrangeas and poppies hanging in the 'air drying' room contrasts with the burnt-sugar smell of the more robust buds in the 'desiccants and hot air' room.

The visitors' entrance to Priorwood opens directly into the working garden. Although no historic plan existed to guide the garden's restoration, a Victorian air pervades. A long herbaceous border is informally planted with such useful specimens as *Rodgersia pinnata*, whose elegant burgundy leaves are used in dried arrangements, as are the black seed-heads of *Papaver somniferum*. Monarda, gypsophila, delphiniums and astrantia are all grown for their flowers, which maintain their shape and colour when dried, while the adjacent herb garden provides scented stuff for sachets and potpourri. The gardens are filled out with annual beds, while a grass bed in the north-west corner nods to current horticultural fashion. Roses throughout provide colour and scent, while such architectural plants as *Corylus avellana* 'Contorta' furnish contemporary and oriental bouquets.

While the dried flower business takes up the eastern third of the garden, the rest is given over to meadow, orchard and wild flowers. As time and finances permit, the southern woodland is also being developed; hydrangea, laurel, ivy and fern under-planting gives a dense, Victorian feel, while serpentine paths allow visitors to contrast the romance of the wilderness with the productivity of the garden.

Picnic tables are provided in the family-friendly orchard, where an abstract bronze of three doves by David Annan commemorates Jill Currie, who led the campaign to preserve the garden. Since 1981 the area has been developed as an apple orchard, illustrating the history of the apple in Britain since Roman times. As monks were the main horticulturists, the dissolution of the monasteries in the mid-sixteenth century had a detrimental effect on Scottish gardens. In any case, fruit was not a major part of the Scots diet before the eighteenth century and early visitors tended to be scathing about such fruit as was grown, failing to realize that most Scots apples and pears were meant to be boiled and mashed rather than eaten raw. Had cider been a more popular drink, apples might have had greater prominence in the early Scots garden; nonetheless Priorwood's orchard features *Malus domestica* 'Court Pendu Plat', beloved of the Romans, along with such local cultivars as the early seventeenth-century *Malus domestica* 'White Melrose', which is believed to have been raised by the local monks. Among the other rarities, Royal Russet dates back to the sixteenth century, while Oslin is thought to be the original Pippin. An annual Apple Day allows visitors to sample old varieties, while the shop sells the rest of the harvest.

A ticket to Priorwood also entitles visitors entry to **Harmony Garden**, the walled Georgian property just down the hill.

Royal Botanic Garden, Edinburgh

Royal Botanic Garden, Inverleith Row, Edinburgh EH3 5LR

Open Nov to Feb, 10–4, but closed 25 Dec and 1 Jan; Mar, 10–6; Apr to Sep, 10–7; Oct, 10–6; no dogs other than guide dogs

Fee free; glasshouses: £3.50, conc. £3

Off the A902, 1m N of city centre; entrances at Inverleith Row and Arboretum Place

Edinburgh

T: (0131) 552 7171   E: info@rbge.org.uk   W: www.rbge.org.uk

The first botanic gardens were established in southern Europe in the sixteenth century, but it took Britain nearly a century to catch up. Established in 1670 on a small plot by Holyrood Palace, this is Scotland's oldest and Britain's second-oldest botanic garden, the first being the Oxford Physic Garden, which was founded in 1621.

The Royal Botanic Garden, Edinburgh, was founded by physicians Sir Andrew Balfour and Sir Robert Sibbald – the latter was physician to Charles II. Keen to combat the charlatanism which plagued Scots medicine at the time, their initial intention was simply to produce medicinal plants. The garden soon expanded to accommodate the teaching of students and the study of plants, resulting in Sibbald's *Scotia Illustrata* (1682), a survey of the geography, archaeology and flora of Scotland, commissioned by the King. The following year James Sutherland, director of the garden, published his *Hortus Medicus Edinburgensis*, or a *Catalogue of all the Plants in the Physic Garden at Edinburgh*. His purpose was philanthropic: 'that I might thereby let the World know what Plants I could furnish to others...so all who apply themselves to promote Natural History with me, might be encouraged to assist me in so good a designe by making interchange of Plants...'

Apparently Sutherland's interest in plants exceeded his interest in presentation; despite the garden's 2,700 species, the traveller Thomas Morer, in *A Short Account of Scotland* (1689), described it as 'the rudest piece of ground I ever saw with that name', decrying the paucity of walks, walls and hedging. As his comments attest, botanic gardens were seen as places of beauty as well as utility, though clearly utility was stressed by the pragmatic Scots, particularly in the early years.

Since its founding, the botanic garden outgrew three sites before settling in its current home, a 75-acre hillside to the north of the city centre. When this new garden was established by Sir John Hope in 1760 it contained only 5 acres, though that in itself was a major advance on the 40-foot-square plot of the original site.

Through the eighteenth century, as imports arrived from all over the world, plants were increasingly grown for their own sake rather than simply for medical purposes. During this period private collectors and commercial nurseries became increasingly important in the classification, propagation and dissemination of botanical specimens. Before making their way to the botanic garden, new species often went to private collectors such as the Naesmyths at **Dawyck,** or to commercial nurseries such as Austin & McAslan, which sponsored many plant-hunting expeditions.

By the nineteenth century, as plant-hunters moved from the tropics to the more temperate areas of the Himalayas, the Far East and the Americas, Edinburgh's botanic garden began to accumulate rhododendrons and primulas. Towards the end of the century the glasshouses and laboratories were expanded, and the arboretum, woodland and copse were created, as were the peat, heath and rock gardens. In the twentieth century a strikingly modern palm house, a library and a herbarium were added, and the specialist gardens at **Logan**, **Dawyck** and **Benmore** were brought under Edinburgh's umbrella.

Though today's botanic garden is magnificently sited with spectacular views across the city, the local soil is thin and sandy, while its rainfall, at 24 inches per year, is well below average. Nonetheless the garden offers demonstration gardens for the general public, while sculpture exhibitions, decorative landscaping and a large pond, complete with nesting swans, ensure year-round interest. The glass winter garden provides refuge in the coldest months and the spectacular long border is a source of summer inspiration. Innovations continue, with the recent installation of spectacular steel gates at the east entrance, designed by local architect Ben Tindall. Depicting the *Rhododendron calophytum*, a native of Sichuan in western China, these gates celebrate Edinburgh's famous rhododendron collection, the largest in the world with over 400 species.

Edinburgh City Council recently adopted the blue poppy *Meconopsis sheldonii* as the city's floral emblem. While the colour of its petals resembles the blue of the Scottish flag, the flower was chosen primarily because of its links with the Royal Botanic Garden, which first cultivated the meconopsis in the nineteenth century and in the 1930s identified the cross between *M. grandis* and *M. betonicifolia*, naming it *M. sheldonii*.

St Mary's Pleasaunce

St Mary's Pleasaunce,
Sidegate, Haddington,
East Lothian EH41 4BU

Open all year,
dawn–sunset; no dogs

Fee free

Central Haddington, off
A1, on the Edinburgh to
Dunbar road, behind
Haddington House

East Lothian

The late Duke of Hamilton donated the orchard of his seventeenth-century Haddington House to the Haddington Garden Trust on the understanding that they would develop it as 'an old Scottish garden' and preserve it as a public precinct. Renamed St Mary's after the fourteenth-century abbey next door, this modern-day 'pleasaunce' is clearly much loved by the local community.

E. H. M. Cox, in his *History of Gardening in Scotland* (1935), asserts that by 1245 the *pomaria* of Haddington Monastery were internationally famed and already old – a reminder that for centuries the monks were the repositories of horticultural wisdom in this northern kingdom. While the monks would bring apples and pears from their English and French houses, they also bred their own varieties, among which the Arbroath Oslin, developed by the monks of Arbroath Abbey, remained a local favourite for centuries.

This rich arboreal heritage has been honoured in the current orchard. In the seventeenth century apples, cherries and pears – hard cooking pears, not the soft eating fruit of today – were widely grown; plums were less common, and peaches and apricots were restricted to gardens with heated sheds or sheltered walls. The sturdy apple house at the rear of the pleasaunce still belongs to the Dukes of Hamilton; its thick walls would have kept the apples safely sheltered from the fiercest winter frosts. The orchard also features medlars, whose hard, bitter fruit was left on the tree until it was almost rotten. Though the public is encouraged to take the fruit as it ripens, Haddington's medlars are largely ignored today.

Herbs are the second major focus, and the pleasaunce features a sunken garden with geometric beds planted up with contemporary culinary and medicinal herbs. These beds are charmingly annotated with quotes from the herbalists John Gerard (1597–1612) and John Parkinson (1567–1650), informing visitors, for example, that lavender is good against 'all the griefes and paines of the head and braine that proceed from a cold cause' and santolina 'being drunk in wine, is a good medicine against the poison of all serpents and venemos beastes'.

Among the many roses in the pleasaunce is the lovely pink and white striped *Rosa mundi*, named, it is said, for Henry II's mistress Fair Rosamund, whom he kept hidden in a labyrinth in Woodstock Palace. Some say that the jealous Queen Eleanor fatally poisoned the young girl; others say that she retired to a nunnery, where, on her death, her grave was inscribed 'Rosa Mundi': Rose of the World. Experts tend to subscribe to the less romantic theory, espoused by Sir Thomas Hanmer in a book of 1659, that the rose was first found 'in Norfolk a few years since upon a branch of the common Red Rose'.

The lawn is planted with interesting specimens such as the tulip tree *Liriodendron tulipifera*, first imported to Britain from the New World by John Tradescant the Younger in the mid-seventeenth century. There is also a black mulberry, *Morus nigra*, promoted by James I in his efforts to develop a silk industry in Britain. By the time it was understood that silk worms preferred a different variety, black mulberries had been planted in many prison yards – the inmates' morning exercise giving rise to the well-known nursery rhyme 'Here We Go Round the Mulberry Bush'.

On the south side of the pleasaunce a flagged path leads through a hornbeam alley, down a laburnum walk to the churchyard beyond. The massive brick wall linking the pleasaunce to the churchyard is reputed to have been built by French prisoners captured during the Napoleonic Wars. There is also a wild meadow with a modern mount which visitors can climb to get a view over the enclosure to the surrounding countryside.

Scone Palace, Perth
PH2 6BD

Open 1 Apr to 31 Oct,
9.30–5.30

Fee grounds: £4, children
£2.75; palace: £7.50,
children 4.50

2 miles N of Perth on A93

Scone Palace

Perth and Kinross

T: (01738) 552300   E: visits@scone-palace.co.uk
W: www.scone-palace.co.uk

Still the private domain of the Earls of Mansfield, Scone Palace is best known to horticulturists as the childhood home of David Douglas, who began his career as a gardener's boy on the grounds. One of the world's greatest plant-hunters, Douglas introduced some of the most important trees in modern forestry, including the Douglas fir, *Pseudotsuga menziesii*, and the Sitka spruce, *Picea sitchensis*. He transformed the British garden with such popular delights as the flowering currant, *Ribes sanguineum*, the Californian poppy, *Eschscholtzia californica*, and *Lupinus polyphyllus* – from which most modern lupins descend.

The palace grounds are beautifully maintained despite, or perhaps because of, the busloads of tourists who descend daily to view the Moot or Boot Hill. Though thoughts on the name differ, this artificial mound, the site of the earliest Scottish parliaments or *moots*, was allegedly created by earth which clansmen brought in their *boots* to swear their allegiance to the king. On the same theme is a replica of the Stone of Scone, a rock brought in 846 by Kenneth MacAlpin, Scotland's first king. Until the thirteenth century, when Edward I removed it to Westminster Abbey, all Scottish monarchs were crowned on the stone.

Ancient arches, Celtic crosses and various graveyards add to the historic air, while recent rose and butterfly gardens – the latter a woodland glade planted with butterfly favourites – are clearly designed to entertain visitors with less interest in the past. In the same vein, a stunning laburnum tunnel with a tall central chamber leads towards the highlight of recent planting – the maze. Laid out by today's master maze-maker, Adrian Fisher, the unusual star shape is inspired by the Mansfield family emblem, while the 6,500 feet of green and copper beech hedging are laid out to resemble the Earl of Mansfield's tartan. The sound of running water draws visitors towards the heart of the maze, where they are rewarded with the sight of the naked water nymph Aretusa frolicking in a fountain.

In the late nineteenth century an acre of the kitchen garden was given over to the cultivation of lily-of-the-valley, with plants

David Douglas

In a nation of great plant-hunters, David Douglas (1799–1834) was one of the greatest. Born on the estate of **Scone Palace**, he trained at the **Glasgow Botanic Garden** under Dr William Jackson Hooker. In 1823 the Horticultural Society (it became 'Royal' in 1861) sent him to New York to collect fruit trees. Two years later he journeyed to the west coast of North America, where he was joined by his countryman and fellow explorer Thomas Drummond. Here Douglas collected so many species of conifer that he joked in a letter to Hooker, 'You will begin to think that I manufacture Pines at my pleasure.' He also introduced the flowering currant, *Ribes sanguineum*, and the bramble, *Ribes spectabilis*, which later created such havoc at **Dawyck**. Among garden flowers he introduced the Californian poppy, *Eschscholtzia californica*, various lupins, penstemons and clarkias, *Cornus alba*, *Mahonia aquifolium* and the monkey flower, *Mimulus moschatus*, which has naturalized so freely that many think it a native plant.

In 1829 Douglas returned to North America, where he survived obstreperous Mexican authorities, warring Indian tribes and a river whirlpool which cost him his canoe, notes and seeds. On his way back to England, he stopped off in Hawaii, where he was gored to death by a wild bull when he fell into a pit-trap while exploring the forest. Though it cost him his life, his final journey yielded the red larkspur, *Delphinium cardinale*, the poached-egg plant, *Limnanthes douglasii*, and the elegant shrub *Garrya ellip-*

being lifted and forced over succeeding weeks to ensure a constant supply of buttonholes and posies for the house. Sadly there is no evidence of such luxury today.

The parkland, spreading over 100 acres, is a tree-lover's paradise. The main pinetum, planted in 1848, contains a giant sequoia about 160 feet tall and the original Douglas fir, *Pseudotsuga menziesii*, a specimen grown from seed sent by David Douglas from the Columbia River in 1826. In 2002 this tree was designated one of fifty Great British Trees by the Tree Council as part of a scheme to generate interest in our dendrological heritage.

In 1977 a second pinetum was planted with over sixty specimens. There is also a fine acer collection, and the usual woodland walks through rhododendrons and azaleas under-planted with primroses and daffodils. Morning and evening the park is animated by the screeching of peacocks, including one magnificent, haughty, rare white cock that resembles a dowager in drag.

Shepherd House, Inveresk, East Lothian EH21 7TH

Shepherd House

East Lothian

T: (0131) 665 2570   E: ann@fraser2570.freeserve.co.uk
W: www.shepherdhousegarden.co.uk

Open 17 Apr to 28 Jun, Tues and Thurs 2–4; also by appointment and on certain days for Scotland's Gardens Scheme

Fee £3, children free

7m E of Edinburgh on A1, then A6064 towards Dalkeith; in Inveresk village, opposite Inveresk Gardens, at junction of main road and Crookston Road

This seventeenth-century town house has a small though appropriately formal front garden of neat, gravel-filled, box-edged parterres surrounding standard roses. The 1-acre walled garden tucked away at the back, however, is entirely different: a delicious mélange of horticultural influences. Colour-themed beds next to the house draw their inspiration from Gertrude Jekyll, who would have applauded the heady combination of the purple bearded iris 'Queschee' with the oriental poppy 'Patty's Plum'. Beside this a herb parterre is clipped, as tradition decrees, on Derby Day. An alpine wall, inspired by the **Royal Botanic Garden, Edinburgh**, is backed by a row of espaliered crab apple trees, an idea drawn from the potager at Alnwick Castle.

The main axis is a 120-foot-long Alhambra-like stone water rill, beginning in a frog fountain and ending in a rectangular pool near the house. Around this, arbours and trellises support old roses, while island beds are planted variously in hot and cool colours. An oval hole, cut into the clipped hedge to frame a wall-mounted ammonite, was inspired by the *claire-voie* at **Crathes**. At the back of the garden woodland paths weave through an orchard where ancient trees play host to climbing roses as spring bulbs and fine orchids poke through the long grass beneath. Recent clearing has left a tall stump from which an owl has been carved; elsewhere copper flowers and bronze hens peek from the undergrowth, challenging the Blue Silkie chickens that scratch about in the orchard. First recorded by Marco Polo, who mistook their downy feathers for fur, these delightful fowl produce creamy-pink eggs.

The garden route ends in two impressive potagers, reminiscent of Rosemary Verey's work in the 1980s. Though the inspirations are legion, Shepherd House garden is unique; brilliantly drawn together with an artist's appreciation of colour, texture and form, this delightful town garden feels much larger than it is.

Stobo Water Garden

Scottish Borders

Tel: (01721) 760245

Formerly the pleasure grounds for Stobo Castle, Stobo Water Garden is a delightful example of the oriental trend in Edwardian horticulture. The opening of Japan to the West in the 1860s sparked a fascination with all things Japanese which expressed itself horticulturally in everything from tortured bonsai and lily-strangled suburban pools to rural parklands filled with acers, prunus and camellias.

The fashion for Japanese gardens was particularly strong in Scotland, where the mercantile past ensured familiarity with the oriental aesthetic. The damp west coast provided ideal growing conditions, while inspiration was stoked by romantic plant-hunters like Reginald Farrer and such books as his *The Gardens of Asia* (1904). Charles Rennie Mackintosh's elegant Art Nouveau **Hill House** owes much to the oriental aesthetic, while **Broughton House** offers an extraordinary combination of cottage garden and Japanese woodland. At the beginning of the twentieth century a firm of Japanese landscapers was hired to create the garden at **Kildrummy**, and at the same period **Benmore**'s duck pond was transformed into a Japanese water garden. The oriental aesthetic continued to influence Scottish horticulture, as seen in such recent creations as the Japanese garden at **Biggar Park**, but Stobo represents one of the most authentic and restrained examples of the style.

The name Stobo could not be less oriental, *stub* being the Old English for 'stump'; *stobo* means 'hollow of stumps', indicating that even in the Middle Ages this region was full of trees. Set in a sheltered glen, the Japanese garden at Stobo was begun in the late nineteenth century by Hylton Philipson, the owner of Stobo Castle and a keen amateur landscape gardener. For his water effects, Philipson dammed the Weston Burn on its journey to the Tweed, creating a series of still pools and dramatic cascades. The oriental effect is enhanced with a rustic pavilion, stone lanterns,

Stobo Water Garden,
Stobo, Scottish Borders
EH45 8NY

Open by appointment and on certain days for Scotland's Gardens Scheme

Fee £3, children free

7m W of Peebles on B712

wooden bridges, meandering paths and stepping stones precariously placed – an effect which Sir Geoffrey Jellicoe would use in his mid-century designs, claiming that gardens should provoke fear and engender risk.

Plantings of acers, prunus, umbrella pines, azaleas and rhododendrons complete the effect, and not a bonsai in sight. The genius of this garden is its layout. Approaching from below, one is never aware of the boundaries; each twist in the path offers new surprises as pools, cascades, bridges and paths are suddenly revealed. An elegant fretwork balustrade at the top of the garden recalls the restrained, geometric style of Charles Rennie Mackintosh. And behind this, the biggest surprise of all – a large, tranquil, quintessentially Scottish loch, surrounded with grazing sheep.

The water garden is set in a larger estate filled with mature oaks, sycamores and some unusual hardwoods, such as curly-leafed beech. Among its other treasures are several castor oil trees and a *Cercidiphyllum japonica*. Known in its native Japan as the katsura, this species was introduced to the West in 1861. Prized for its vibrant autumn tints and the subtle caramel scent exuded by its decaying leaves, katsuras must enjoy the Border climate as **Kailzie** and **Dawyck** also feature these rarities.

With no professional help, Stobo's 4-acre garden is maintained by the owners; indeed, one of the great virtues of a natural landscape is its low maintenance and sustainability, features that might explain the survival of this particular garden through a century of swings in horticultural fashion.

Traquair House,
Innerleithen, Scottish
Borders EH44 6PW

Open Apr to Nov (times
vary, so phone or email
first)

Fee free entry to house and
grounds

29m S of Edinburgh, on
B709 just S of Walkerburn

Traquair

Scottish Borders

T: (01896) 830323   E: enquiries@traquair.co.uk   W: www.traquair.co.uk

The oldest inhabited house in Scotland, Traquair is known primarily for its romantic castle, which is steeped in Jacobite history. For those interested in horticulture, however, Traquair offers the fascinating prospect of an unrestored garden. The name means 'homestead on the river', *tre* meaning 'a dwelling', while *quair* derives from *vedra*, 'clear one'. Though Traquair was built on the banks of the river, in 1628 the owner petitioned his friend the king for permission to divert the river away from the house; today the Well Pool marks the original river bed.

Fishing, hawking and hunting have been enjoyed on the estate since it was first mentioned as a royal hunting lodge in the twelfth century. The bears that support the family coat of arms recall the joys of hunting, though bears have been extinct in Britain for over a millennium. Bears also flank the main gate, which was closed in 1744, behind Bonnie Prince Charlie, with the vow that it would stay not open until a Stuart king reigned.

The still closed gate gives on to a large rectangular paddock, bisected by an avenue, beyond which a simple lawn fronts the gated courtyard. Roses and fuchsias embellish the austere walls, but the real horticultural treasure is hidden away at the back of the house. Here a narrow terrace is bounded on each end by a pair of matching garden pavilions. A few roses struggling against the buttressing wall suggest that the terrace was once a long, ornamental walk. This overlooks a flat area, probably once a formal parterre. In 1980 the area was designed as a maze, inspired, one assumes, by the need to attract paying visitors. Some 1,500 Leylandii cypresses were planted, but when two-thirds of these died in severe frost the following winter they were replaced with beech trees, creating an odd combination of deciduous and evergreen.

A woodland walk meanders through an ancient arboretum where the old beech trees have been supplemented with Douglas firs, *Pseudotsuga menziesii*, whose seeds were first collected from the American West in the late 1820s by Scots plant-hunter David Douglas. The woods have been under-planted with rhododendrons – probably during the Victorian craze for bulking out forest walks with dense floral shrubs. The woodland also contains some ancient, atmospheric yews. To the east of the house is a croquet lawn and beside it a children's play area containing a rustic heather-thatched hut from the mid-nineteenth century. The gardener's cottage of 1745 has been turned into a tea room, while the old walled garden behind it is largely laid to lawn and orchard, probably a result of wartime labour shortages that required the ploughing up of unproductive flowers. Under a gnarled apple tree stands a striking statue of a horse, *Epona* (Rachel Long, 1999). Constructed of old, rusting machine parts, it evokes both dignity and decay...which sum up the estate itself.

NORTH-WEST SCOTLAND

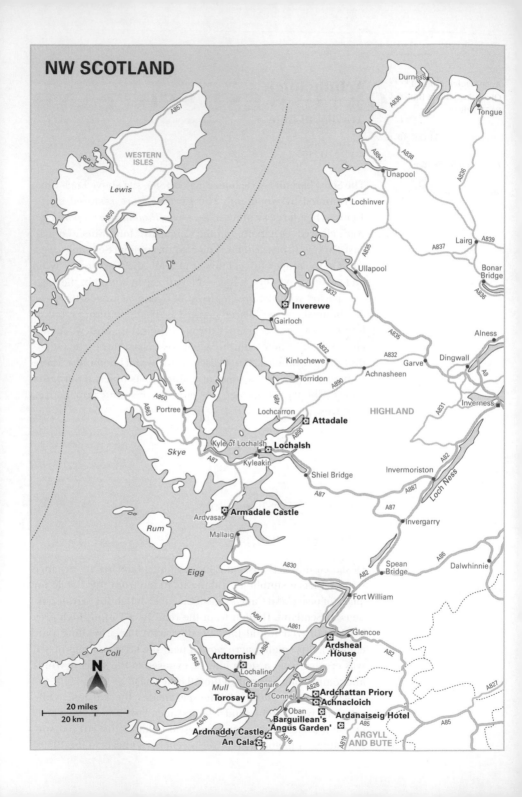

Achnacloich, Connel,
Oban, Argyll and Bute
PA37 1PR

Open 8 Apr to 31 Oct, 10–6

Fee £2, children free

9m E of Oban

Achnacloich

Argyll and Bute

T: (01631) 710221

The Scots baronial-style house, dated 1885, sits above Loch Etive surrounded by woodland. The gardens were restored in the 1950s, when large swathes of invasive *Rhododendron ponticum* were cleared. Originating in the Caucasus Mountains of northeast Turkey, *R. ponticum* was planted throughout Scotland's west coast in the nineteenth century to provide shelter from the wind and cover for wildlife. It has only really been tamed in the postwar period with the development of chemical weedkillers and mechanical scythes. Three marked walks demanding more or less stamina guide visitors through the estate and woodland clearings are filled with the usual west coast flora: rhododendrons and magnolias, bluebells, primroses and anemones. There is also an oak wood, a stand of mature Scots pines, a burn and ponds. The walled garden has gone to seed and now houses beehives.

An Cala, Easdale,
Isle of Seil, Argyll and Bute
PA34 4RF

Open 1 Apr to 31 Oct, 10–6

Fee £2

On B844, off A816, 16m
SW of Oban

An Cala

Isle of Seil, Argyll and Bute

T: (01852) 300237   W: www.gardens-of-argyll.co.uk

Designed in the 1930s, An Cala combines Edwardian elegance with Art Deco simplicity. Taking its name from the Gaelic for 'place of peace', An Cala is one of the most delightful private gardens in Scotland. Hidden from the road by a 15-foot-high grey brick wall (red would have clashed with the prevailing slate colours), this small 5-acre garden near the slate quarries of Seil was created from a steep hillside exposed to the searing winds and tempestuous storms of the Atlantic coast.

The languid odour of lilies permeates the garden, while retaining walls, arches and arbours, open lawns and island beds create a series of intimate spaces to balance the rugged surroundings. A plethora of flowering cherries attests to the 1930s' love of chinoiserie; the oriental feeling is enhanced by a large fishbowl and a formal lily pond which fronts a whimsical pavilion filled with decorative pine-cone and twig work. From the lower garden slate steps ascend to a balustraded woodland walk filled with conifers and under-planted with azaleas and rhododendrons. A paved upper terrace offers magnificent sea views, while a wooden gazebo presides from the topmost lawn, where a flock of ingenious chicken-wire sheep safely graze on a secluded patch of grass.

On the lowest level three brewery cottages were combined to make a single dwelling; covered in traditional white roughcast, it provides a perfect background to the pink and white roses which smother it in spring. The bleaching green in front was filled with topsoil and flattened to create lawns and herbaceous beds. Though many of the older west coast gardens are said to have been created with soil brought as ship's ballast from Ireland, An Cala's soil came from no further than Ayrshire in the south. This lower garden is stuffed with roses, geraniums and sweet peas and crowned with a charming *doocot*, but water is the presiding force throughout; it tumbles, shoots, glides and falls down the cliff into ponds, pools and canals, ending in an elegant stone-lined stream which descends in stepped channels towards the sea.

Ardanaiseig Hotel Gardens

Argyll and Bute

T: (01866) 833333   E: info@ardanaiseig.com   W: www.ardanaiseig.com

This early nineteenth-century baronial-style mansion was originally known as New Inverewe, since it was built for a nephew of the Campbells of Inverewe. When the estate was sold to industrialist John Ainsworth in 1879, it was renamed Ardanaiseig – meaning 'the point of the ferry'. Following the fate of many grand estates, the place has recently been turned into a luxury hotel. A flat raised lawn – all that remains of previous formal parterres – offers fabulous views across Loch Awe. An open theatre and boat house suggest extravagant Edwardian

Ardanaiseig Hotel,
Kilchrenan by Taynuilt,
Argyll and Bute PA35 1HE

Open Apr to Oct, 9–8

Fee £2, honesty box

Take A85 E from Oban to B845 (1m E of Taynuilt), then B845 to Kilchrenan and left on single-track road for 3m entertainments, though today the place oozes an air of bourgeois sobriety. The loch itself, which is remarkably clear, is linked to magical powers in legends smacking of Celtic blarney and canny salesmanship. The kitchen garden, a discreet distance from the house, has unusual curved walls, despite the widespread conviction that curved walls trap frost. As well as the usual fruit, flowers and vegetables, it harbours a glorious Judas tree, *Cercis siliquastrum* – rare this far north – and a sumac, *Rhus verniciflua* – an odd choice for a small, enclosed space since its sap is a severe skin irritant.

The main horticultural attraction is a 20-acre woodland garden. Part of a much larger plantation, the woodland had succumbed to neglect but is slowly being restored. The mild climate and acid soil support a typical Victorian mixture of azaleas and rhododendrons – magnificent in spring, when the under-planting of snow-drops, daffodils and bluebells coincide with the flowering of the shrubs. The estate also boasts a wide range of specimen trees (the hotel provides maps and free plans). A huge Sitka spruce, 140 feet high and nearly 25 feet wide, recalls the Victorian passion for this vigorous conifer. Native to the American North-West, the Sitka spruce was discovered by Perth-born Archibald Menzies, when he was acting as surgeon and naturalist on Captain George Vancouver's 1790 voyage round the world. The Sitka soon became the most commonly planted conifer in Britain, particularly suited to Scotland's moorlands. Versatile, hardy and adaptable, its sharp needles deter browsing animals and it grows much faster than the three native conifers – yew, juniper and Scots pine. Reaching heights of 160 feet, it can gain over 4 feet per year and a single acre of Sitka spruce can produce 50 tons of timber. Used in both the construction and paper industries, it is also rather beautiful.

The woodland contains various fir trees popular with the Victorians – *Abies nordmanniana*, *A. grandis* and *A. procera*, a swamp cypress, *Taxodium distichum*, a Japanese red cedar, *Cryptomeria japonica*, and an incense cedar, *Calocedrus decurrens*. A picturesque cemetery, buried deep in the woods, presents family and domestic staff lying together in perpetuity, suggesting a degree of social harmony perhaps rare in today's egalitarian society.

Ardchattan Priory Garden

Argyll and Bute

T: (01796) 481355   W: www.gardens-of-argyll.co.uk

Ardchattan Priory, Oban,
Argyll and Bute PA37 1RQ

Open 24 Apr to 31 Oct, 9–5

Fee £2.50, children free
(garden and priory ruins)

13m NE of Oban; from N
side of Connel Bridge take
A828 N, then first right
and follow Bonawe road
6m

The garden at Ardchattan provides a picture of the life of a medieval monk. Delightfully placed overlooking Loch Etive, it has existed since 1230, when the attached Valliscaulian priory was founded. The *Ordinale Conventus Vallis Caulium* – a schedule followed by the houses of the order – indicates that gardens were an integral part of daily life: 'When tierce has been sung let them repair to the refectory...After their meal let them rest upon their beds until the office of Nones. After Nones let them go to their Collation, after Collation every one may work in the garden or cell assigned to him until the first bell for vespers...' Ardchattan was one of only three Valliscaulian houses in Britain, all of which are sited in the remote north of Scotland. The Valliscaulians cut themselves off from the outside world, existing on the rent from their lands and parishes; not surprisingly, this notoriously strict order never attracted more than a handful of monks. Kale leaves carved into various parts of Ardchattan's buildings pay tribute to the order's early dependence on its mother house in Val des Choux – valley of kale – in France.

Though the priory became a private house after the Reformation, the garden is infused with its monastic history. A pair of fine old yews, wreathed in roses, marks the entrance to the priory. Trees over 400 years old line the Monk's Walk, an avenue that runs parallel to the loch and must have provided cold exercise on a winter's day. More recent additions of rhododendrons, acers, embothrium and philadelphus along the south side suggest Victorian planting to liven up the area with spring scent and autumn colour. The Prior's Walk, beside the present car park, was lined with plane trees till they were uprooted by a particularly severe winter storm fifty years ago; it has since been replanted with a mixture of ornamental shrubs and trees. The Monks' Pond off the entrance drive – now a sunken lawn – dates from the thirteenth century, when it was used for holding the Friday fish.

The large open lawn to the front of the house was first laid out in 1830, though island beds and backing shrubs suggest post-war redesign. Only a narrow road and a stretch of shingle beach separate the lawn from the Loch. The land is flat, the earth free-draining and the climate mild and propitious for plants. The lawn itself boasts an ancient oak and a Spanish chestnut, *Castanea sativa*. Roses, honeysuckle and a large magnolia scent the garden, which is flanked by herbaceous borders, a rose bed and a rockery.

The walled garden beyond the priory now houses a tennis court and various cows; an espaliered apple tree at one end is the only remnant of its earlier incarnation as a kitchen garden. Fifteen years ago the old tennis court, beyond the dairy, was turned into a wild garden and planted with thirty different varieties of sorbus. A lone monkey puzzle, *Araucaria araucana*, attests to earlier Victorian planting. Introduced by Archibald Menzies in the late eighteenth century, the monkey puzzle, which originates on the dry volcanic slopes of the Andes, obtained its common name in the mid-nineteenth century when a visitor to the Cornish garden where one of the first saplings was growing remarked, 'It would take a monkey to climb that tree.' One of Scotland's earliest monkey puzzle trees was cosseted in a conservatory at **Blair Castle** for two decades till more intrepid gardeners demonstrated that the species could cope with the northern climate.

While Ardchattan boasts magnificent views and a wide variety of plants, the ruined chapel – included in the garden admission price – is also worth a visit. Wandering through the grounds, with their ancient trees and picturesque ruins, it is easy to believe the legend that Robert the Bruce held a parliament at Ardchattan in 1308 – the last at which Gaelic was spoken.

Ardmaddy Castle,
Easedale, nr Oban,
Argyll and Bute PA34 4QY

Open all year, 9–sunset

Fee £2.50, children 50p

8m S of Oban on A816,
take signpost for Easedale,
1½m off the B844, signed

Ardmaddy Castle

Argyll and Bute

T: (01852) 300353   E: c.m.struthers@lineone.net
W: www.gardens-of-argyll.co.uk

Reached by a narrow winding road on the shore of Seil Sound, the fifteenth-century castle of Ardmaddy sits on a promontory overlooking the sea on one side and the walled garden on the other. In the eighteenth century the estate marked the western

Celtic Bardery: Manufacturing the Highland Myth

With the Act of Union in 1707, Scots intellectuals began to fear that Scotland would lose her national identity. Looking to the past for inspiration, they began celebrating the simplicity and integrity of the Scottish peasant. Some even attempted to promote the idea of the Scots as the true fathers of democracy for having resisted the Romans in the early years of British history. As the most primitive part of the country, and the furthest from the corrupting influence of the decadent south, the Highlands became the focus of their attentions. Consciously and unconsciously, writers, artists and intellectuals began the packaging and promoting of the region that continues to this day.

The romanticizing movement reached its apex with the publication, in 1762, of James Macpherson's *Poems of Ossian*. Purporting to be translations of ancient Gaelic oral poetry, Macpherson presented an epic of noble lives and lofty landscapes. While his stories ranged from loose translation to complete invention, they caught the mood of the moment. His hero, Ossian, depicted as a Celtic Homer, was embraced throughout Europe and nowhere more avidly than among Scotland's artists. Alexander Runciman took the Ossian stories as his primary subject, David Allan painted simple peasant folk in exalted Highland settings, and Charles Steuart and Jacob More focused on the landscape itself, depicting the Highlands as both classical and sublime, a rival to any Italian *campagna* or Swiss summit.

By the early nineteenth century, essayist Thomas Babington Macaulay was warning, 'No traveller ventures into that country without making his will.' Within decades, however, 'that country' had metamorphosed from a rugged landscape of fiercely independent Highland chiefs into a playground for the English aristocracy. Though helped by advances in rail transport and then motor cars, this transformation was largely due to Queen Victoria and her favourite artist, Edwin Landseer. A series of paintings through the late nineteenth century show the landscape being subjugated by the canny monarch. *Queen Victoria Sketching at Loch Lagan* (1847) depicts an obsequious huntsman presenting the young woman with a slaughtered stag: the monarch of this glen is unequivocally Victoria. Three years later *Royal Sports on Hill and Loch* has the dead stag prostrate at the Queen's feet, while game bags and fishing rods suggest the species of air and sea about to be sacrificed to her.

By the mid-nineteenth century, though more than half the population of Scotland lived in industrial, urban or suburban environments, the popular images of the day continued to depict happy peasants living at one with the land. Like Sir Walter Scott's **Abbotsford** in the south, **Balmoral** played a large part in promoting this Arcadian myth. By embracing the Highlands, Queen Victoria denied the historic antagonism between England and Scotland. When she sported the tartan and the bagpipes, she obscured the fact that such emblems of national identity had been prohibited by the Act of Proscription of 1747 and were not made legal again until 1782. In celebrating the landscape, she reinforced her dominion over it, diminishing the Highlands from Macaulay's fearsome wilderness to a decorative backdrop for her annual autumn retreat.

boundary of the Earl of Breadalbane's domain, allowing him to ride the breadth of Scotland entirely on his own land. When the present owners inherited the property twenty-five years ago, they demolished various Victorian extensions and restored the medieval keep. The 1½-acre walled garden probably dates from the late eighteenth century. Sited at the base of a steep hill planted with camellias, rhododendrons and other flowering shrubs, it tapers to accommodate the burn running beside it. When the owners arrived, the garden was overrun with weeds, but despite the prevailing advice to turn it over to sheep, they set out to create a traditional west coast garden.

The original box hedges were restored and a lawn created, lined at one end with a deep border of white and yellow potentilla. Visitors enter through a magnificent vegetable garden with fruit cages arranged in a cruciform round a circular stone urn, recalling the dipping well which would have featured in the original garden. Herbaceous borders are being established, bulked out with rhododendrons. Acid soil and a rainy climate dictate the plants, but an effort has been made to ensure flowering interest from spring through to autumn.

The boggy ground beyond the wall has been transformed with ponds surrounded by candelabra primulas, astilbes, hostas and grasses, while the burn-side walk offers ferny banks filled in late summer with bright-orange crocosmia.

Further on a stately, tree-lined avenue leads to a tiny graveyard in a clearing. Here headstones list and tumble down a rough slope, while magnificent sea views open out beyond. A nearby bench invites contemplation of the fact that the great British gardens have always contained an element of *memento mori*. Unlike the French and Italians, who pursue permanence with architectural formality and clipped evergreens, British gardeners – filling their spaces with deciduous trees and herbaceous borders – celebrate the changing seasons of growth and decay. This quality is particularly evident in Scotland: from **Little Sparta**'s inscriptions through the memorials littering **Balmoral** to the impetus behind **Barguillean's Angus Garden,** Scotland's melancholic temperament finds poignant expression in her gardens.

Ardsheal House

Argyll and Bute

T: (01631) 740227   E: info@ardsheal.co.uk

Ardsheal House,
Kentallen, Argyll and Bute
PA38 4BX

Open phone or email first,
as it has recently been
closed for renovation

Fee £2.50

Signed from A828 in
village of Kentallen

Currently under restoration, Ardsheal's walled garden promises to be a spectacular amalgam of Victorian plants and contemporary design. Approached by a long drive through native woodland, the elegant Stuart mansion – now a bed and breakfast – sits on a rocky height overlooking green fields with Loch Linnhe shimmering beyond. The old tennis court has been turned into a car park; a pond and a bog garden are recent creations, dragged from the low marshy ground; and there are beehives situated just outside the garden wall, from where they can pollinate the trees beyond without disturbing visitors.

Carved from a rock face on one side and enclosed by hedges on the other three, the walled garden offers the traditional mixture of pleasure and utility, with a gazebo, rose beds and decorative flowers sharing the space with fruit, vegetables and herbs. A stately row of palm trees attests to the warm microclimate, while a low hedge of step-over apples provides a more traditional note. A rockery has been created in the rock face, a 100-foot herbaceous border lines the opposite side and a fruit tunnel defines the central allée. The dipping pond has been planted up to create a water garden, while fruit trees grow from slate-lined squares in-filled with overlapping shells – the contrast of grey slate and white shell, of curves and lines, turns the mundane orchard into an abstract work of art.

Beyond the house a set of steps – ingeniously formed by sections of tree trunk with a wire tracing across the surface to prevent them becoming slippery – leads through the woods to shoreline meadows and a tree house, which is really just a shed on a low-lying branch.

Ardtornish

Ardtornish, Lochaline,
Morvern, Argyll and Bute
PA34 5UZ

Argyll and Bute

Open daily 1 Mar to
30 Nov, 8–8

T: (01967) 421288   E: tourism@ardtornish.co.uk   W: www.ardtornish.co.uk

Fee £3

9m SW of Fort William on
A82, take Corran ferry,
13m on A861, right on
A884 for 19m, 2m before
Lochaline

Surrounded by magnificent Highland scenery, this Victorian mansion commands spectacular views along Loch Aline to the hills of Mull, and though much reduced by post-war exigencies, the grounds still give a hint of early twentieth-century splendours. The wide, shallow River Rannoch at the bottom of the garden has been channelled into a fishery and the walled garden, on a flat plateau beyond the estate road, has been turned into a commercial nursery. The 28-acre gardens once employed twelve gardeners and several horses; today they are laid to informal woodland with the usual shrubs and rhododendrons – species and hybrid – nestled amid sheltering conifers. Some of the twentieth-century additions were gifts from Sir John Stirling Maxwell of **Pollok House**, and the vibrant cerise-flowered hybrid rhododendron 'Jock' is named after Sir Maxwell's son-in-law.

In the 1930s several formal beds of pampas grass and *Hydrangea hortensis* were removed and the oak wood to the west of the house, already planted with such popular spring-flowering rhododendrons as 'Pink Pearl' and 'Cynthia', was given an extended season with late-flowering azaleas. Eucryphia, escallonia, enkianthus and cmbothrium all flourish even though the Gulf Stream's mediating warmth is weak in this area. A constant battle with the ubiquitous *Rhododendron ponticum* has yielded some clearings and in spring the woodland is carpeted with snowdrops, daffodils and bluebells.

The house is sited on a rocky ledge, with a lawn in front giving over to a precipitous slope, while narrow paths wind up the rhododendron-planted cliff behind to provide panoramic views of the loch. The old iron stag in the distance was a target, not a sculpture, though art is represented in an intriguing contemporary ironwork balustrade which leads from the lawn to a narrow terrace filled with an outsized terracotta pot. From here the path descends to the primula garden below. This area has recently been filled with hostas and meconopsis, while *Gunnera manicata* thrives in the damp ground at the base of the cliff. With leaves of up to 12 feet wide, the largest of any plant in cultivation, this species was introduced from Brazil in 1867 and soon became a Victorian favourite.

Woodland walks encompass an alpine meadow, a rhododendron glen, a birch avenue and a eucryphia plantation, while an elegant Edwardian boathouse on the loch beyond suggests more pleasure than utility.

Armadale Castle Gardens

Isle of Skye, Highland

T: (01471) 844305 or 844227   E: office@clandonald.com
W: www.clandonald.com

Armadale is not so much a garden as the corporate headquarters for the Clan Donald. The late eighteenth-century castle is now a picturesque ruin, sitting amid manicured lawns and discreetly labelled trees. A Chilean lantern tree, *Crinodendron hookerianum*, planted in 1983, suggests a prescient attempt to expand the horticultural interest. An enormous Sitka spruce, *Picea sitchensis*, towers 120 feet high, while a Japanese cedar, *Cryptomeria japonica*, and a cypress, *Chamaecyparis nootkatensis*, add to the arboreal interest. The long border and terraced walk flank the lawn and an ornamental pond has recently been created from the old laundry stream.

The clan archives are housed in the award-winning Museum of the Isles, which – with its poignant tale of mismanagement, eviction, exile and emigration – is the main reason for visiting Armadale. This simple, modern building is unobtrusively sited in a woodland clearing which was probably the bleaching ground, as the ruins of old laundry lie nearby.

Several marked nature trails lead through bluebell-threaded woods and cultivated farmland. From the high viewpoints, especially in the setting sun, the fields reveal traces of the earlier *runrig* system of land cultivation, whereby strips of land were divided into parallel *runs*, or channels, and *rigs*, or ridges, creating a corrugated effect. Parcelled out by annual ballot to vary the distribution of the poorest land, the system was both inefficient and unecological. As the strips apportioned to each man were not necessarily contiguous, much time was wasted moving between them, while the annual redistribution of land removed

Armadale Castle,
Armadale, Sleat,
Isle of Skye, Highland
IV45 8RS

Open 2 Apr to 26 Oct,
9.30–5.30 (last admission 5)

Fee £5.00, conc. £3.80 (incl. museum)

By ferry from Mallaig (1½ hours) or 24m S of Kyle of Lochalsh on A851 any incentive to improve one's allotted piece beyond short-term fertilization.

In coastal areas seaweed was used as fertilizer; in inland areas the ground was often burned periodically – a counterproductive act which ultimately deprived the land of all its fertility. During his celebrated Scottish tour of 1773, Dr Johnson observed that the Highlands consisted of two things: '…stone and water. There is indeed a little earth above the stone in some places, but very little, and the stone is always appearing. It is like a man in rags, the naked skin is always peeping through.'

Attadale, Strathcarron,
Highland IV54 8YX

Open Apr to Oct except
Sun, 10–5.30

Fee £4.50, children £1

18m NE of Kyle of
Lochalsh on A890
between South Strome
and Strathcarron

Attadale

Highland

T: (01520) 722217   E: info@attadale.com   W: www.attadale.com

Three centuries' worth of horticulture is present within this delightful 20-acre garden backed by steep cliffs, overlooking the sea and the Isle of Skye. The formal, sunken rose garden in front of the house is a vestige of Georgian formality, while the ha-ha which separates it from the adjacent field speaks of late eighteenth-century naturalism. The stone field drains, now surrounded by woods, are early nineteenth-century agricultural improvement, while the rhododendron plantations are late nineteenth-century whim, as are the specimen conifers – particularly the Wellingtonias, tsugas and redwoods, which were then pouring in from America. The elegant eighteenth-century house has suffered various Victorian additions, including a baronial tower added by Hamburg banker Baron Schröder, who purchased the place in the 1890s, when the fashion for acquiring Scottish sporting estates swept across Europe. In the 1950s the estate passed into the family of the current owners, who have been developing it ever since.

A series of devastating storms in the 1980s felled many of the older trees and in the clearings new gardens have sprung up. The mill stream running beside the entrance drive was transformed into an elegant water garden, planted with various gunneras – the gigantic *manicata*, the smaller *chilensis* and the dwarf *magellanica* from the southern coast of Argentina. Primulas and iris proliferate in spring, while rheums and rodgersias provide autumn colour. The rhododendron walk above is backed with sheltering conifers, while cherry, maple, rowan and birch provide spring flowers, autumn foliage and interesting bark. Above this a stone lookout, constructed in 2002, harmonizes with the rugged Highland scenery.

Behind the house a kitchen garden is laid in gravel with raised beds and neat box edging. Presiding over one end of the garden is a sensual, stacked-slate sculpture of an urn. Created by the Dumfries sculptor Joe Smith, it recalls the craft of dry-stone walling and pairs with an obelisk, by the same sculptor, in the sunken garden at the front. Beyond the kitchen garden, a shade garden features a geodesic dome housing a collection of exotic ferns, while hardier ferns survive in the damp shadow of the cliff behind.

From here a woodland walk wanders through the old rhododendron dell. Among many notable trees, this area boasts a 100-year-old Wellingtonia, *Sequoiadendron giganteum*; there is also a magnificent Californian redwood, *Sequoia sempervirens*, which, though less than fifty years old, already towers over the landscape. In their native California, sequoias reach over 325 feet in height, though in Scotland they are unlikely to grow much beyond 160 feet. One of the largest living organisms on the land, the sequoia can live for 3,000 years if its spongy, soft, protective bark is not damaged. The oldest accurately dated specimen, felled in California in 1892, had 3,212 annual rings. Given their potential lifespan, Attadale's sequoias are mere saplings, but with the clean air, mild climate, abundant rainfall and long hours of summer sunlight they might well succeed their American ancestors in age, if not in height.

A Japanese garden in a low-lying area at the heart of the woods was created when the A890 was built nearby, blocking the drains. When new drains were installed and gravelled over, the oriental flavour was exploited with the addition of venerable rocks, raked sand and a limited plant palette, including cloud-pruned azaleas and miniature conifers. The distant hills are framed to bring in 'borrowed landscape', and the all-important running stream was given basin and cup for visitors to purify themselves before proceeding to the tea ceremony.

Produce is sold in the restored steadings, while a self-service café offers garden books for browsers. Contemporary sculptures dot the landscape, adding a twenty-first-century touch to this charming mélange of horticultural passions and styles.

Barguillean's Angus
Garden, Taynuilt,
Argyll and Bute, PA35 1JS

Barguillean's Angus Garden

Argyll and Bute

Open all year, 9–sunset

Fee £2, children free

T: (01866) 822048   E: info@barguillean.wanadoo.co.uk
W: www.barguillean.co.uk

3m S off A85 at Taynuilt
Hotel, signed 'Glen Lonan'

More a woodland than a garden, this landscape is a memorial to a twenty-eight-year-old journalist, Angus Macdonald, killed by terrorists in Cyprus in 1956. Created by his mother, Betty Macdonald of Barguillean, the garden demonstrates the redemptive power of horticulture. The 9-acre woodland surrounds an 11-acre loch nestled in the Glen Lonan hills. The landscape has been gently shaped with cedar steps, mown grass paths, open glades and unobtrusive lookouts. Three colour-coded paths guide visitors around the site, where rhododendrons, azaleas and other flowering shrubs, unusual trees and some conifers have been added to the native woodland of oak and birch. Fallen trees are left to decay, nourishing the flora and fauna. An under-planting of spring bulbs offers seasonal interest, while the abundance of moss, ferns and lichen gives a primordial feel which is somehow consoling. The memorial element figures in a large, exuberant bell honouring Betty Macdonald and a bench dedicated to her husband; his sister and her son are also commemorated. Subtly inserted into the landscape, these features display the discreet hand of man in a sylvan scene.

Inverewe, Poolewe,
Highland IV22 2LR

Inverewe (NTS)

Highland

Open Good Fri to 31 Oct,
9.30–9 or sunset if earlier;
otherwise 9.30–4

Fee £8, conc. £5

On A832, by Poolewe, 6m
NE of Gairloch

T: (01445) 781200   E: inverewe@nts.org.uk   W: www.nts.org.uk

One of Scotland's most famous gardens, Inverewe is a triumph of patience, faith and imagination. Despite being further north than Moscow, this barren patch of red sandstone on the edge of Loch Ewe is warmed by the North Atlantic Drift, enabling it to host such varied exotica as Chile's *Cryptocarya alba* with its subtle resin scent, the privet-like Chinese shrub *Symplocos pyrifolia*

Robert Fortune and the Lure of China

Since the early sixteenth century, when Portuguese explorers returned from China with oranges, the oriental kingdom fascinated Europe's horticulturists. Sailors brought back intriguing plants from coastal towns, but Europeans were forbidden to travel inland until the eighteenth century, when the Jesuits established themselves in Peking and secured permission to journey into the interior. The tantalizing accounts, paintings, seeds and plants these missionaries sent back to Paris inspired Britain's Horticultural Society to establish a Chinese Committee. Despite being barred from the country, the members produced a list of desirable plants and a catalogue of Chinese nurseries for the day when they could enter mainland China. In 1842, with the end of the first Opium War, the Treaty of Nanking gave Britain the island of Hong Kong, favourable trading conditions and freedom to travel 20 miles inland from the treaty ports. The following year the Horticultural Society sent Berwickshire-born Robert Fortune (1813–80) to collect new varieties of garden plants.

Fortune had been trained in Edinburgh at the **Botanic Garden** before moving south to serve as Deputy Superintendent at the Horticultural Society's gardens in Chiswick. Despite having neither travel experience nor any knowledge of foreign languages, Fortune embraced the challenge. Adopting Chinese dress, he penetrated the interior, surviving storms, fever, pirates and xenophobic crowds to return with such delights as white wisteria, winter jasmine, 'Japanese' anemone, forsythia, weigela, winter-flowering honeysuckles, various viburnums and chrysanthemums. Over several trips to Japan and China he added many other cultivated plants to the list and mastered such horticultural arts as the cultivation of chrysanthemums and the dwarfing of conifers.

In 1846 Fortune was appointed Curator of the Chelsea Physic Garden. Two years later the East India Company commissioned him to return to China, to infiltrate the elusive tea industry. Disguising himself as a Chinese person from a distant province, he learned the secrets of tea growing, then acquired 2,000 plants and 1,700 seedlings, and convinced several experts to work for him. Smuggling the plants out of Shanghai, he sent them to the Himalayas in Nathaniel Ward's newly invented glass cases.

Robert Fortune was the first plant-hunter to use Wardian cases for the maritime transportation of plants. Previously specimens had been stored on ships' decks in slatted wooden boxes, suffering the effects of limited light, salt spray, temperature fluctuations and hungry rats. Ward's 'closely glazed cases' were filled with damp soil and moisture-retaining mosses, then sealed against the elements. By enabling the transportation of exotic plants across long distances, they revolutionized European horticulture and enabled the establishment of lucrative plant-based businesses, such as the tea and rubber industries, far from the plants' native habitats.

Fortune went on to write several books about his travels, the most famous of which is *A Residence among the Chinese* (1852). In total he introduced over 120 species to Western gardens, though the only plant he collected from the wild was the rhododendron which bears his name, *R. fortunei*.

and the Tasmanian groundsel tree, *Brachyglottis brunonis*. When Osgood Mackenzie acquired the estate in 1862, it was windswept moorland with a single willow tree rising from the stunted heather. With patience and foresight, he installed deer and rabbit fences, then planted 60 acres of sheltering trees, mostly Scots and Corsican pine – reluctantly accepting that certain foreign conifers were hardier than the native Scots pine, yew and juniper. Like many at the time, Mackenzie also freely employed the robust – and invasive – *Rhododendron ponticum* to provide fast, effective shelter. Today it is deployed with care, as where it creates a closely clipped hedge along the top of the walled garden to screen the wind and salt spray from the Mediterranean border below.

While the aptly named Am Ploc Ard peninsula – 'the high lump' – was metamorphosing into sheltering woodland, Mackenzie built himself a turreted Scots baronial mansion. Fifteen years later, he began clearing the new woods to create his garden. Rhododendrons dominate, the wonderful ochre bark and arching limbs of *R. sinogrande* vying with the noble *R. nobleanum* for supremacy in the woodland walk, while the striking blue of hydrangeas and Himalayan poppies link the skies above to the loch below. Exotics such as the red Chilean firebush, *Embothrium coccineum*, and the lantern tree, *Crinodendron hookerianum*, brighten dull patches.

On a hill above the house Mackenzie indulged Victorian taste in a 'bambooselum'; though the area is now dominated by tree ferns and eucalyptus, an impenetrable thicket of ancient bamboos still sits at its heart. The highlight of the garden is probably the magnificent tiered, walled kitchen garden which was built into a steep slope over the beach round Loch Ewe. Open on three sides to the sea, the garden was laboriously created with creel-loads of soil brought in by boat, a process described by Mackenzie in his classic gardening book, *A Hundred Years in the Highlands*, published in 1922 just before his death. Here vegetables jostle with herbaceous plants and espaliered fruit trees are interspersed with lavender along the upper wall, while internal divisions are created by swagged roses and clipped box hedges. From the lower wall, doors open to the loch beyond, providing easy access for the gardeners, who would have had to haul in the heavy seaweed that was used as fertilizer. Today benches are provided, giving views over the shore with its fishing nets stretching across brown, wrack-covered rocks.

Mackenzie's original baronial mansion was destroyed by fire in1914 and the stones were used to construct the rock garden below. When Mackenzie died, his daughter Mairi Sawyer took over the estate. In 1937 she had the present house built in the distinctive Dutch South African homestead style. The marriage breakup of both Mackenzie and his daughter and the deaths of her two children gave rise to the legend that the family had been cursed for dislodging crofters to create the garden. Like many before her, however, Sawyer found solace in gardening and became one of Scotland's greatest horticulturists; she continued developing Inverewe until 1952, the year before her death, when she turned it over to the National Trust for Scotland.

A Peace Plot from 1919 commemorating the First World War introduces the memorial element common in Scots gardens. The wet valley hosts one of the largest *Gunnera manicata* in Britain; an American collection, pond gardens, peat banks, pine and azalea walks are just a few of the other horticultural features on offer, while a midge-eater discreetly placed in the woodland makes summer visits much more pleasant than they would have been in Mackenzie's time. An exit sign in half a dozen languages exhorting drivers to drive on the left indicates the range of Inverewe's appeal. Despite the full force of the National Trust's commercial activities, with a visitor centre, gift shop, restaurant, café and bus and camper parking, Inverewe retains the elegance and enchantment of an Edwardian country estate.

Lochalsh Woodland Garden (NTS)

Lochalsh, Balmacara, Highland IV40 8DN

Highland

Open estate: all year; woodland garden: all year, 9–sunset

T: (01599) 566325 E: balmacara@nts.org.uk W: www.nts.org.uk

Fee £3, conc. £2

Lochalsh Woodland Garden provides interesting woodland walks and glorious sea views to Skye. The 13-acre estate is situated on a steep site overlooking Loch Alsh. In the late nineteenth century, when the house was built, the slope behind was planted with a shelter belt of oak, Scots pine and beech. While these now provide a mature canopy protecting more tender species, the mass of roots, combined with the thin soil and rocky site, can make the garden very dry in summer.

3m E of Kyle of Lochalsh, off A87

In 1953 the estate was given to the National Trust for Scotland and ten years later plant collector Euan Cox of **Glendoick** began developing the plantings, experimenting with a range of rhododendrons, including the tender, fragrant, late-flowering 'Maddenia', for which he had collected wild seed in China and the Himalayas.

Given the prevalence of woodland and rhododendron gardens along the west coast, the National Trust wisely decided to concentrate on other features, expanding plantings of bamboo, fuchsia, hydrangea and hardy ferns – all favourite Victorian plants that flourish in the sheltered microclimate created by the forest. The old steadings have been restored to provide an information centre, while woodland walks lead past the bamboo, rhododendron and fern plantations to a forest of century-old pines.

The car park in the upper woodland often echoes with the drumming of woodpeckers desperately seeking mates. Below this a fuchsia-lined road leads from the village into the estate. The sunken lawn beside the house (not open to the public) offers sheltered views, while a small pool and stream ensure the cooling sound of running water. The lawn is surrounded by shrub and flower borders, featuring magnificent hydrangeas in every shade of blue – the acid soil guards against any hint of pink, though the actual shade of the flowers is determined by aluminium in the soil as well as by the acidity. Treated essentially as pot plants in the nineteenth century, hydrangeas are now grown as hardy shrubs throughout the Highlands.

The recently planted Coach House Garden is a small ornamental space with flowering shrubs and herbaceous plants; a barrier of bamboo offers some protection from wind and salt spray blowing off the loch, though the rotting-corpse odour of *Olearia waikariensis* permeates this space on hot, late summer mornings.

ع‏ی ع‏ی ع‏ی

Torosay

Isle of Mull, Argyll and Bute

T: (01680) 812421   E: torosay@aol.com
W: www.holidaymull.dor/members/torosay

With the plethora of woodland walks among Scotland's west coast gardens, it is rather refreshing to come upon Torosay's formal Italianate gardens. The name Torosay derives from the Gaelic *torr rasach*, 'hill of shrubs', and certainly the formal gardens provide a striking contrast to the rugged Highland scenery. The baronial-style castle, designed by David Bryce, was constructed in 1858, replacing a more modest Georgian house. Initially only a grassy slope linked the castle to the eighteenth-century walled garden below, but at the turn of the twentieth century the then owner, Walter Murray Guthrie, commissioned Robert Lorimer to design three Italianate terraces and a statue walk to connect them.

The top terrace descends to the fountain terrace, with its sturdy, flanking banqueting houses, one of which harbours a *doocot* in the roof and a grotto in the basement. This, in turn, descends to the Lion Terrace, guarded by two large crouching stone lions known as Smiler and Growler. Herbaceous borders flank the terraces, roses cloak the supporting walls and a series of austerely planted urns embellish the garden wall. The walled garden itself contains a delightful domed gazebo with a classical pergola supporting a heavy wisteria. Subject to flooding during tidal surges caused by the spring tides, this low-lying garden is often waterlogged and drainage has to be carefully managed.

To the east of the house, the magnificent sculpture walk displays one of Britain's finest collections of Italian rococo statuary. The nineteen statues by Antonio Bonazza (1698–1765) were discovered by Guthrie in a derelict garden near Padua. These were shipped as ballast from Genoa to Glasgow, then on to Mull. One wonders what the estate workers made of the elegant eight-eenth-century figures: fishmonger, bakers and hunters are interspersed with more mysterious creatures – a masked, cloaked male and a delightful, pregnant, Picassoesque female. The sculpture walk is backed by an elegant hedge of *Fuchsia magellanica*. The hardiest of the fuchsias, *magellanica* can survive temperatures as low as 14°F. In its native Chile, it

Torosay, Craignure,
Isle of Mull,
Argyll and Bute PA65 6AY

Open gardens: all year, 9–7 or sunset if earlier; castle: 1 Apr to 31 Oct, 10.30–5

Fee gardens: £4.75, children £2.50 (reduced rate for admission by honesty box when castle closed); castle and gardens: £5.50, children £3

On A849 7m S of Fishnish ferry, 1½m S of Craignure

reaches heights of 15 feet or more, while in cultivation it forms a lower, denser shrub – ideal hedging for Scotland's windy, west coast.

Woodland walks surround the formal garden, where the acid soil encourages rhododendrons and azaleas. Among the many delights is the hydrangea dell – a sea of striking blue colours. The Gulf Stream ensures a mild, wet climate that supports a wide range of plants, including an Australian and a New Zealand collection. To the east a Japanese garden, created in the 1960s, exploits the oriental idea of 'borrowed landscape', incorporating picturesque views of Duart Castle across the bay. Beyond the main garden a 5-acre Chilean wood is being created with the **Royal Botanic Garden, Edinburgh**.

NORTH-EAST SCOTLAND

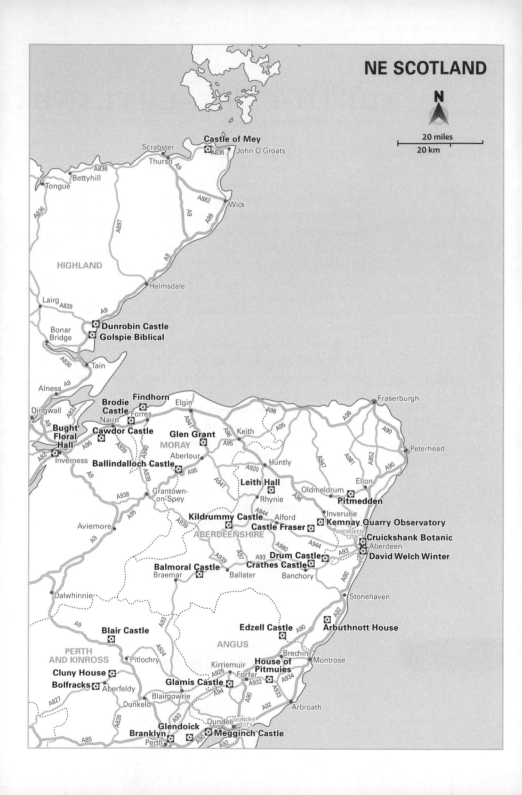

NE SCOTLAND

N

20 miles
20 km

Castle of Mey
Scrabster
Thurso
A836
John O'Groats
A9

Bettyhill
A836
Tongue

A882
A897
A9
A99
Wick

HIGHLAND

A9
Helmsdale

Lairg A839
A9
Bonar Bridge
Dunrobin Castle
Golspie Biblical

A836
Tain

Alness A9
A832
Dingwall
A9
Findhorn
Fraserburgh

Brodie Castle
Elgin
A98
A98
A9
Bught Floral Hall
Nairn
Forres
A941
A96
Keith
A95
A96
A981
A90
Peterhead
Cawdor Castle
A938
Glen Grant
MORAY
A95
A952
A90
Inverness
A96
A939
A940
Aberlour
Huntly
A947
A920
Ballindalloch Castle
A95
Ellon

A9
A938
A941
Leith Hall
Oldmeldrum
Grantown-on-Spey
Rhynie
A96
Pitmedden

Aviemore
A95
A939
Kildrummy Castle
A944
Alford
Inverurie
Kemnay Quarry Observatory
ABERDEENSHIRE
Castle Fraser
ABERDEEN CITY
Cruickshank Botanic
A980
A944
A93
Aberdeen
Dalwhinnie
A9
A939
Balmoral Castle
A97
A93
Drum Castle
David Welch Winter
Braemar
Ballater
Crathes Castle
Banchory
A90

Stonehaven

A9
A92
Blair Castle
Edzell Castle
A90
Arbuthnott House
PERTH AND KINROSS
ANGUS

A924
Brechin
Cluny House
Pitlochry
Kirriemuir
House of Pitmuies
Montrose
Bolfracks
A826
Forfar
A932
A934
Aberfeldy
Glamis Castle
A933
A827
Blairgowrie
A94
A90
A92
Dunkeld
Arbroath
A826
Glendoick
Dundee
DUNDEE CITY
Branklyn
Megginch Castle
A85
Perth
A92

Arbuthnott House,
Laurencekirk, Kincardine
and Deeside AB30 1PA

Open garden: all year, 9–5;
house: check for opening
days; no dogs

Fee garden: £2,
children £1;
house and garden: £4.50

3m W of Inverbervie
on B967

Arbuthnott House

Kincardine and Deeside

T: (01561) 361226   W: www.arbuthnott.co.uk

Beyond magnificent entrance gates, a long rhododendron-lined drive leads to Arbuthnott House, home of the Arbuthnott family since 1190. The fifteenth-century castle and courtyard replaced an earlier fortified house, while a classical sandstone façade was added in the eighteenth century. The front is laid to parkland and a 5-acre walled garden extends from the side of the house down a vertiginous slope to the millstream below. Directly abutting the dwelling in the old Scots manner, the garden allowed the inhabitants to observe the horticultural seasons from the comfort of their salon.

The kitchen garden at the top of the slope combines fruit, vegetables, cutting flowers, herbaceous borders and rose beds, while the back wall shelters fan-trained fruit trees, wisteria and several elegant *Actinidia kolomikta*. In one recently restored Victorian greenhouse jasmine and citrus trees over-winter; in another, large camellias have potting-up tables constructed around their trunks. Thick hedges provide shelter and a venerable Lebanese cedar presides.

Below the kitchen garden, wide grass avenues traverse the slope, giving views to the hills beyond. From the far bank of the millstream these avenues suggest the Union Jack – a popular motif in early eighteenth-century gardens, celebrating the 1707 Act of Union between Scotland and England. The statuesque metal stag by the bottom gate is for target practice, while the millstream beyond offers mown walks along ferny banks past several striking laburnums.

⁓ ⁓ ⁓

Ballindalloch Castle

Aberdeenshire

T: (01807) 500205   E: enquiries@ballindallochcastle.co.uk
W: www.ballindallochcastle.co.uk

Ballindalloch demonstrates the transformation in Scotland from medieval fortified dwelling to Victorian sporting estate. Legend has it that when the laird first attempted to erect his castle it was mysteriously blown down several times till the faeries advised him to 'build it in the coo-haugh'; the site was duly moved to the cow field below and the resulting castle stands to this day.

The castle is approached by an impressive tree-lined drive, giving on to a meadow recently planted with prunus and sorbus for spring flowers and autumn berries. Beside the car park an unusual square *doocot*, dated 1696, holds over 800 nesting boxes – a sign of the estate's early importance. An enormous emerald lawn exploits Scotland's cool, wet summers, providing a perfect foil to the castle's austere towers. The castle wall is flanked by a simple herbaceous border, while swagged roses lead to the rockery, created in the 1930s, when scree, rock and alpine gardens were in vogue.

A rhododendron-lined path meanders to the old walled garden, a long way from the castle for the kitchen staff of old. Recently replanted as a rose garden, its lawns, statuary and a central rosery round a tiered fountain lend an air of Edwardian elegance. Beds are under-planted with dianthus, nepeta and the lavender shrubs which John Reid recommended in *The Scots Gard'ner* (1683). A sweet-pea arch adds variety, while an orchard and espaliered fruit trees recall the earlier function as a kitchen garden. Greenhouses beyond harbour tender roses, camellias and grapes, while beehives guarantee pollination.

One of the most picturesque elements of Ballindalloch is the stocky black Aberdeen Angus cattle which graze in the 'coo haugh'. First bred in 1860 to create hardy, hornless, meaty cows, Aberdeen Angus are descended from native Scots cattle traditionally found in the north-east, the 'Doddies' of Angus and the 'Hummlies' of Buchan. Ballindalloch boasts the oldest continuous herd in existence, sharing a bull with the late Queen Mother's herd at the **Castle of Mey**. Despite the prevalence of these beasts in the landscape of the north-east, the Scots,

Ballindalloch Castle,
Grantown-on-Spey
Aberdeenshire AB37 9AX

Open Good Fri to 30 Sep
except Sat, 10.30–5

Fee grounds: £3.50,
children £2;
castle and grounds: £7,
children £3.50

Bridge of Avon, off A95
between Keith and
Grantown-on-Spey

unlike their neighbours to the south, are not great beef-eaters. Among the poorer classes beef was eaten only at Martinmas, the 11 November celebration of St Martin. Indeed, it is possible that the name itself derives from the Gaelic *mart* or 'cow', acknowledging the annual autumn slaughter of livestock for which there was no winter fodder.

As well as the usual woodlands, Ballindalloch offers riverside walks along the Avon and fishing in the salmon-rich Spey. It also boasts a champion nine-hole golf course recalling how Victorian country houses were virtual sports clubs, providing such entertainments as stalking, fishing, riding, climbing and trekking before the requisite Highland ball.

Balmoral Castle, Ballater, Aberdeenshire AB35 5TB

Open 1 Apr to 31 Jul, 10–5

Fee £7 incl. exhibitions, children £3

7m W of Ballater on A93

Balmoral Castle

Aberdeenshire

T: (01339) 742534 E: info@balmoralcastle.com W: www.balmoralcastle.com

Balmoral and its rugged landscape played a major role in creating the modern image of Scotland. In 1848 Queen Victoria took the lease on Balmoral Castle on the advice of her physician, who thought the climate might improve her rheumatism – he also happened to be related to the leaseholder. Within four years Victoria and Albert had purchased Balmoral, along with several neighbouring estates. Immediately they set about designing a new castle large enough to accommodate their growing family.

Balmoral, Gaelic for 'majestic dwelling', sits on a strip of meadow, bordered in front by the River Dee and guarded behind by the heights of Craig-Gowan. Picturesque if a little gloomy, the estate was known to Victoria as 'this dear paradise'. As she confided to her diary, 'the wilderness, the solitariness of everything is so delightful, so refreshing...' While she found comfort in its peace and isolation, Albert was drawn to the outdoor life, where the hiking and hunting reminded him of his beloved Saxe-Coburg. Charles Grenville wrote about their life in the Highlands, 'They live there without any state whatever...not merely like private gentlefolks, but like very small gentlefolks...with the greatest simplicity and ease...She is running in and out of the house all day long, and often goes about alone, walks into the cottages, sits down and chats with the old women.'

In 1855, when the new castle was complete, Victoria and Albert designed the 3-acre grounds around it. The Queen occupied herself with a rustic cottage and garden, while the Prince Consort oversaw the building of new stables and a dairy, as well as a new bridge over the Dee, designed by Isambard Kingdom Brunel. Albert also superintended the plantations. With a penchant for the sorts of trees which populate Grimms' fairy tales, he planted the half-mile entrance drive with such melancholy firs as *Abies alba*, *Abies grandis* and *Abies concolor* var. *Iowiana*.

When Albert died, the Queen sought refuge in Balmoral, to the irritation of her English subjects, who were less tolerant than the Scots of their sovereign's protracted mourning. Thereafter few changes were made beyond the addition of a small number of staff cottages: Baile na Coille was built for Victoria's beloved Scots servant John Brown and Karim Cottage for her beloved Indian secretary, the Munshi Abdul Karim. Victoria's major effect on the landscape was a series of monuments: a cairn in 1862 honouring her consort; five more commemorating the marriages of each of her children; a further obelisk and a statue to Albert; a statue to John Brown, who died in 1883; several memorials to family dogs; a statue of the Queen in 1887 for her Golden Jubilee; a cross in memory of her son Alfred, who died in 1900; and an obelisk in memory of the Queen after her death in 1901.

Since then the garden has been a litmus of horticultural fashion. A pinetum was planted in the 1920s; in the 1930s Queen Mary created the sunken rose garden; in the 1970s Queen Elizabeth added a water garden. In 1998 the Ballroom Terrace was planted with yellow herbs for Elizabeth's Golden Wedding anniversary; four years later the Victorian conservatory was restored to celebrate her Golden Jubilee; and recently Prince Philip added the large kitchen garden.

Though the planting is generally natural in style, herbaceous borders around the castle are designed to flourish in August, when the royal family is in residence. Bowing to the needs of the paying public, the rose garden is now planted for year-round interest, with a spring flourish of dwarf daffodils in serried ranks down the central path, where the memorial theme is continued with a pair of silver weeping pears.

The kitchen garden reveals a diplomatic compromise between the English tendency to separate pleasure from utility and the Scots habit of integrating the two. Huge cut-flower beds are interspersed with enviable vegetable plots. Thin lines of oats and wheat were sown several years ago, after the Queen remarked to her gardener that nobody brings sheaves to the harvest festival held in the local church at the end of her annual summer stay.

While woodland paths and riverside walks attest to the solemn beauty of the estate, one striking feature of the landscape is the Balmoral War Memorial near the entrance gate; designed in 1922, its double line of swastikas is a reminder that before the symbol was tainted by Nazi ideology, it was an ancient Aryan emblem of luck.

Blair Castle, Blair Atholl, Pitlochry, Perth and Kinross PH18 5TL

Open 1 Apr to 26 Oct, 9.30–4.30; 27 Oct to 31 Mar, Tues and Sat only (check opening hours); closed Christmas and New Year weeks

Fee grounds: £2.50, children £1.30; house and grounds: £7.50, children £ 4.70

35m N of Perth on A9

Blair Castle

Perth and Kinross

T: (01796) 481207 E: bookings@blair-castle.co.uk W: www.blair-castle.co.uk

Blair in Gaelic means 'a field' or 'a battlefield', either of which would be appropriate for Blair Castle, the ancestral home of the Dukes of Atholl. The central tower dates from the thirteenth century and was built by a squatter while the Earl was off on crusade. The castellation and grand entrance are typical nineteenth-century embellishments. As with most grand estates of such age, Blair has seen its share of history. In 1336 Edward III stayed en route to subdue the Highlands. In 1546 Mary Queen of Scots' visit was celebrated with a hunt in Glen Tilt at which 360 deer and five wolves were slain. During the Civil War, when the family supported the monarch, Cromwell's troops captured the castle and held it for eight years until the Restoration in 1660, at which point the Earl was made a Marquis for his loyalty. His son was made a Duke for loyalty to Queen Anne, only to be imprisoned several years later for opposing the 1707 Act of Union with England. In 1745 Bonnie Prince Charlie rested at Blair during his southward march; the castle was then besieged during the Jacobite uprising, and when stability was finally established the Dukes of Atholl turned their attentions from politics to policies.

The gardens at Blair Castle are an unusual hybrid of formal, romantic and picturesque. The 2,500-acre estate was originally designed in 1730 by the 2nd Duke of Atholl. Following the French style, he laid out several formal avenues radiating from the castle. The first of these, established in 1737, leads to Diana's Grove. This magnificent wilderness surrounds a statue of the Roman huntress Diana – a copy of the original by John Cheere, replaced after it was damaged in the great storm of 1893. Evolving from the Renaissance *bosquet*, a wilderness was a formal wood, often geometric in shape, traversed by avenues and embellished with statuary. Like a labyrinth or maze, it provided a place of seclusion in the ordered symmetry of the formal garden. Though **Drumlanrig** still has its wilderness, these are rare survivals in British horticulture, as most were turned into informal woodlands in the landscape style of the mid-eighteenth century. While it still preserves the essential air of mystery and surprise, Blair's wilderness was originally filled with tall, broad-leaved trees which would have cast a dappled light, rather than the dense, dark gloom created by the conifers of the current nineteenth-century planting.

Blair's second formal avenue, established in 1742, leads up a hill across the park to a statue of Hercules, also by John Cheere, placed at the highest point as an eye-catcher. Originally known as the Hercules Walk, this avenue was planted in the manner advocated by Philip Southcote: 'with trees not very thick but the ground underneath them to be full of flowering shrubs and all other sorts of flowers'. Southcote promoted the *ferme ornée* style, which combined the pleasurable and the profitable to create an ornamental landscape; farm buildings were given picturesque façades and utilitarian hedges were enlivened with climbers, decorative shrubs and flanking flower beds.

During the turmoil of the late 1740s a formal garden to the side of the castle was grassed over, but in 1758, after the Jacobite uprisings had been put down, the Duke proceeded with his improvements, adding a 9-acre walled garden to the side of the Hercules Walk. Within its formal enclosure, this Hercules Garden demonstrates the shift from the classical to the romantic taste. A rectangular pool was canalized to create a water garden. This was embellished with two islands, one planted in dark conifers and the other in light deciduous trees. There were also several peninsulas supporting rustic fowl huts, a Chinese bridge and an elegant ogee-roofed pavilion. A *claire-voie* in the high surrounding wall was originally infilled with multicoloured chinoiserie railings. The garden may well have been inspired by the willow pattern china imported to England in the latter half of the eighteenth century prompting a brief vogue for oriental bridges, willow trees, boats, islands and tea houses. In any case, by 1795 the railings had been replaced by iron bars and the feeling today is more rococo than oriental, with a pair of eighteenth-century pastoral figures, a quartet of stone putti, gravel paths and herbaceous borders.

A third vista from the castle leads north, towards 'The Whim', a two-dimensional folly pierced with gothic arches and supported by pavilions. Erected in 1761, this intriguing eye-catcher is reminiscent of **Mellerstain**'s 'Hundy Mundy', created thirty years before. As the 2nd Duke died in 1764, the Whim was probably his final gesture in the transformation of the estate from medieval castle to picturesque Georgian landscape. The 2nd Duke is also credited with planting Scotland's first European larch, *Larix decidua.* Imported from the Tyrol, it was sited by the Diana Grove in 1737 and today measures 98 feet tall. (Those who care about such records should note that **Dawyck** lays claim to a *Larix decidua* planted in 1725 in the presence of the great Swedish botanist Carl Linnaeus.) Subsequent dukes continued improving the property, none more than the 4th Duke of Atholl, who, between 1774 and 1830, clothed the land within and beyond his estates with conifer plantations. Nicknamed the 'Planting Duke', he allegedly planted over fourteen million larches with a view to selling them to the British Navy. Unfortunately, while they were still saplings the first iron steamship was built, scuppering his hopes of riches. The Duke also planted thirteen million trees of other species, restoring thousands of acres of woodland which had been destroyed by centuries of misuse. Credited with pioneering the commercial reforestation of Scotland, he is also accused of pioneering the excessive conifer planting which disfigures the nation to this day. This lack of arboreal diversity was lamented by Scotland's *enfant terrible*, the late Ian Hamilton Finlay, in a teasing inscription, BRING BACK THE BIRCH, which hangs in a grove in **Little Sparta**.

Remarkably, the gardens at Blair Castle were largely spared changes in fashion, remaining much as they were designed in the eighteenth century. Today the splendid Hercules Garden is being restored with buttressing yew hedges, herbaceous borders, gravel paths and an orderly orchard. The apple store has been turned into a museum featuring images of family life at Blair and the summer pavilion has an archival display with nineteenth-century photos of curling on the canal. In 1998 the overgrown avenues were cut back to restore the views from the castle, revealing Hercules and Diana presiding over their respective garden and grove. Blair also has a deer park, children's playground, nature trails and picnic sites.

Bolfracks

Perth and Kinross

T: (01887) 820344

Bolfracks, Aberfeldy, Perth and Kinross PH15 2EX

Open 1 Apr to 31 Oct, 10–6

Fee £2.50, children free

3m W of Aberfeldy on A827

Boll comes from the Norse for 'a farmstead' and Bolfracks is indeed a Georgian farmhouse, to which a castellated gothic front was added in the 1830s. A formal lawn to the west suggests early eighteenth-century formality, as do the walled garden and the burial ground, dated 1708. The gardens, spreading north and east, are 1930s in design, with elegant fan-shaped steps, gravel paths, rockeries, several decorative bridges and a rustic pavilion. The wilder area to the north-west contains a woodland garden, meadows filled with spring bulbs, shrubberies and a planted burn-side running into a boggy pond. The burial ground houses a mausoleum with a plaque to 'Douglas Hutchinson 1918–2001 who lived at Bolfracks, planted trees and made a garden'. Guarded by a pair of weathered gnomes, a *Ceanothus* 'Gloire de Versailles' enlivens its austere façade, while some decorative sorbus and acers add seasonal colour. The vibrant heather-covered slope to the south attests to the acidity of the local soil, as does the abundance of rhododendrons and azaleas dotted about the property.

A magnificent double herbaceous border separates the informal woodland from the walled garden to the east. Here the top walk offers fine views of the silvery Tay. Separate rose and sundial gardens and a central lawn are defined by a hedge of *Prunus pissardii*. An ornamental plum originating in the Balkans, this deciduous tree makes a dramatic purple-red hedge if firmly clipped **House of Pitmuies** has a similar hedge, again used to good effect backing a herbaceous border. The lower half of the slope is given over to a less formal area of lawn, shrub borders

Deer Parks

While deer were originally considered royal beasts and could only be hunted in the king's forests, as early as the Middle Ages the crown began granting licences to landowners to create deer parks. Varying from several acres with a few groves of sheltering trees to vast enclosures encompassing whole forests, deer parks were surrounded by protective ditches, with the infill soil used to build flanking earth banks topped with pales. Periodic gaps in the paling – deer leaps – enabled deer to enter but not leave the enclosure. Deer parks soon became essential to the economy of large estates, providing fresh meat as well as timber; indeed, the status of the great medieval barons was measured, to a large extent, by the size and number of their deer parks.

By the mid-sixteenth century it had become more profitable to breed cows than to pasture deer, and even when the newly rich created deer parks for entertainment, they limited the size to leave land for the more profitable activities of agriculture and grazing. During the Commonwealth deer parks were reviled as elitist and many were destroyed, their palings pulled down, their trees felled and their deer stolen. However, with the picturesque movement of the eighteenth century deer parks returned to favour, and in the nineteenth century, when many Scottish estates were turned into sporting enterprises, the depleted stocks of native red deer were supplemented with smaller Asian Sika deer imported from Eastern Europe.

Scotland's red deer, the largest and most common species of wild deer in Britain, descend from the huge European stags that crossed the dry valley of the North Sea millennia ago. At that time Scotland was covered in forest that was home to moose, beaver, lynx, bear, wolves and boar. By the tenth century bears had been rendered extinct, by the seventeenth century the wild boars were wiped out and the last wolf was shot in 1743. Today deer are the only large mammals to survive from those ancient forests. Over the years, as their habitat was destroyed, they grew smaller to adapt to diminished food supplies and shelter. Nonetheless, their numbers have multiplied since the Second World War and many fear the effect of their overgrazing on forestry, agriculture and wildlife, as well as the safety hazard they present on rural roads. In 1959 the Red Deer Commission was established to monitor and control the deer population, and since then deer stalking has become a lucrative element in Scotland's tourist industry, helping to conserve the natural habitat and ensure the vitality of the deer population as well as bringing income to many estates.

and specimen trees, including the luminous birch *Betula utilis* var. *jacquemontii*. A bed of *Erica arborea*, the rare tree heather, grows near the top of the west lawn and hedges of heavily scented *Rosa rugosa* add an air of informality. Though the average rainfall is an unexceptional 42 inches, the garden's exposed north-facing site is subject to biting winds and late frosts; nonetheless within its sheltering trees Bolfracks offers a delightful combination of elegance and romance.

Branklyn Garden (NTS)

Perth and Kinross

T: (01738) 625535   E: smcnamara@nts.org.uk
W: www.branklyngarden.org.uk

Branklyn Garden, 116
Dundee Road (A85),
Perth and Kinross
PH2 7BB

Open 1 Apr to 31 Oct, 10–5

Fee £5, conc. £4

Outskirts of Perth on A85
towards Dundee

This densely planted 2-acre garden is an unexpected treasure in the city of Perth. In 1922 Dorothy and John Renton bought the steep west-facing plot, part of an old orchard just above the main road. Though the first priority was to screen the property, the Rentons were soon seduced by gardening, with Dorothy taking the role of designer while John became the labourer. They developed a particular passion for Sino-Himalayan plants after receiving seeds from the Ludlow and Sherriff expeditions to south-east Tibet and Bhutan. With its sheltered site, light loam soil and average annual rainfall of 30 inches, Branklyn's conditions are favourable to ericaceous plants, and over the years the Rentons amassed impressive collections of primulas, meconopsis and dwarf rhododendrons.

In the southern end of the garden they copied the idea, pioneered at **Logan**, of making beds with peat-block walls for acid-loving plants. Since the use of peat has subsequently been deemed ecologically irresponsible, such beds are now a rarity. In 1925 the Rentons created a rock garden; soon after, they replaced their tennis court with scree beds. The fashion for rock gardens was inspired by Reginald Farrer (1880–1920), whose florid accounts of his plant-hunting expeditions enchanted Edwardian gardeners. When the Rentons were creating their gardens, Farrer's *The English Rock Garden* (1918) was still a classic, though the author had died in Burma several years before.

At Branklyn design was always secondary to plants; as Dorothy explained, 'the principal aim has been to give plants the proper conditions – it is primarily a home-from-home for plants'. A lower path leads past a cascade to the pond and bog garden. This area boasts an amazing palette of spring-flowering primulas beneath a rare, pink-barked birch, *Betula albosinensis* var. *septentrionalis*, grown from seed collected in China. An upper path, round the top of the garden, passes troughs full of alpines and several ancient fruit trees from the original orchard.

In 1954 the Royal Horticultural Society recognized Dorothy Renton's success in cultivating difficult plants by awarding her the prestigious Veitch Memorial Medal. Instituted in 1870 and named for the great dynasty of nurserymen, the Veitch is one of the RHS's highest awards. In 1960 Dorothy Renton also received the Scottish Horticultural Medal from the Royal Caledonian Horticultural Society. On the death of the owners in 1968, Branklyn was bequeathed to the National Trust for Scotland. While carefully preserving the Rentons' personal touch, the Trust has added thousands of plants to the collection.

Brodie Castle, Brodie,
Forres, Moray IV36 2TE

Brodie Castle Gardens (NTS)

Open castle: Easter
weekend and
1 Jul to 31 Aug, 10.30–5;
1 to 30 Sep, Sun–Thur
10.30–5;
grounds: all year,
9.30–sunset

Fee castle: £8, conc. £5;
grounds: free

Off A96, 4½m W of Forres
and 24m E of Inverness

Moray

T: (01309) 641371   E: brodiecastle@nts.org.uk   W: www.nts.org.uk

Though it has no seductive herbaceous borders, Brodie Castle Gardens will be of interest to landscape historians. This 176-acre estate has vestiges of formal and informal gardens with a shrubbery, a lake and a walled garden. The sixteenth-century Z-plan castle is abutted on the east by a walled garden which probably served for fortification as well as pleasure in the tempestuous early days. The large walled kitchen garden was planted far from the house in Victorian times to protect the inhabitants from the sight and smell of that utilitarian space. Though the garden itself disintegrated during the Second World War, broken lines of espaliered fruit trees and disintegrating greenhouses attest to earlier productivity, while a 'Cathedral walk' along the north wall ends in an unusual multifaceted sundial.

An elegant wing was added to the castle in the seventeenth century, indicating a time of peace, wealth and refinement – features reflected in the designed landscape to the west, with its formal lawn and elegant beech and lime avenue. In 1730 the view was completed with a lake, though a 1769 estate map indicates a wilderness and a serpentine approach were also part of the ambitious design. A ha-ha at the southern edge of the lawn reflects the eighteenth-century landscape style, its ditch and sunken fence obviating the need for obtrusive walls while preventing livestock from straying on to the lawn.

By the mid-nineteenth century the lake had silted up and lost its crisp edges, creating a more natural outline in keeping with

Victorian romanticism; in the 1870s the pond was enlarged and made more regular. At about the same time the shrubbery was created to screen the kitchen garden from the house. A shrubbery plan, available at the entrance, indicates the specimen trees; a blue Atlas cedar, Sitka spruce, some redwoods and a Nootka cypress reveal the Victorian passion for evergreens, while a sweep of hardy but invasive *Rhododendron ponticum* was probably planted to protect more tender species. There is also an unusual bamboo house created by hollowing out the centre of a grove of *Arundinaria anceps*; when such hardy bamboos were introduced to Europe in 1823 they quickly spread throughout the continent, flourishing even in northern Scotland's frost-free pockets.

The National Trust for Scotland acquired the Brodie estate in the 1980s and has recently begun an extensive restoration programme. The lake was restored to the outline indicated on an 1870s estate map, with an island created in the centre as a wildlife refuge. Bird hides allow visitors to observe more discreet fowl, though swans swim freely about the lake. While the forest had become overrun with conifers, a few exotic trees indicated an earlier ornamental garden. The National Trust restored the lakeside with a mixed forest, including exotics which would have been found in the policies of a Victorian estate, such as ginkgo and the inevitable monkey puzzle, *Araucaria araucana*, discovered by Scottish plant-hunter Archibald Menzies while he was acting surgeon and botanist on Captain George Vancouver's 1792 expedition along the west coast of America.

In its effort to vary the identity of its properties, the Trust has concentrated on woodland planting at Brodie, providing colour from spring to autumn with a variety of different leaf and tree shapes. The castle grounds themselves focus on daffodils, recalling the horticultural passion of the 24th Brodie of Brodie, who raised thousands of varieties in the early twentieth century. Though these were originally planted out in neat trial beds in the kitchen garden, today they line the great west avenue in a dazzling display of annual exuberance.

Oddly enough, the daffodil is a key tool for garden historians. By identifying different species and knowing the date each was bred or introduced to this country, experts can gauge the age of a garden. Daffodils were first introduced to Britain by the Romans, who used their sap as an ointment, though it contains crystals which are more likely to irritate than soothe today's

Heather

Deriving its name from its heath-land habitat, heather flourishes in Scotland's acid soil. Fortunately the plant is very versatile and figures prominently in Scots rural life. If picked when still pliable, young heather shoots can be woven or twisted into such domestic items as brooms, baskets, saddles and rope. In the ice house heather was laid between layers of ice to provide insulation; in the home it was used for insulation, thatching and bedding. Heather can also be made into dye, creating a range of colours from pale cream through gold to brown. In some Hebridean islands heather bark was used for tanning leather and to this day crofters burn heather as kindling.

Because of its durability, heather was used to build roads in boggy areas, forming an intermediate layer between brushwood at the bottom and gravel on top. It was also used to line field drains and to stabilize sand dunes. Extract of heather is said to be anti-inflammatory, diuretic and sedative. In folk medicine it was macerated in alcohol to make a liniment for arthritis and rheumatism; it was also used to treat baldness, dandruff, diarrhoea and hay fever.

In his *Poems of Ossian*, James Macpherson recounts the legend of the white heather. Ossian's daughter Malvina had fallen in love with a warrior who was then killed in battle, but before his death he sent her a spray of heather as a token of his love. On receiving the spray, Malvina ran across the hillsides weeping, and where her tears fell they turned the purple heather white. When she saw this, Malvina vowed that the white heather would bring good fortune to all who found it, and to this day white heather is supposed to be lucky.

Heather is the general name for plants of the *Ericaceae* family – *erica* from the Greek *eriko*, 'I break', because of its brittle stems. At the beginning of the twentieth century only 250 cultivars were known, but in the past hundred years that number has multiplied tenfold, with cultivars occurring naturally as well as being selectively bred. Of the three genera of *Ericaceae*, Scotland's most common heather, *Calluna*, takes its name from the Greek *kalluno*, 'to cleanse', suggesting an antiseptic property to add to its many virtues. *Calluna* has only one species, *Calluna vulgaris*, commonly called 'ling'. The second genus, *Erica*, has more than 700 species, including the tree heaths *Erica arborea* and *Erica australis*, which can grow up to 6½ feet tall. The third group, *Daboecia*, was named after Dabeoc, son of a Welsh chief who founded a monastery in Ireland, where *Daboecia cantabrica* originates.

more tender skin. The pale, frilly, double-flowered 'Van Sion' was popular in the early seventeenth century, predating by half a century the Dutch influence of William of Orange; in contrast, today's large, upright, orange hybrids demonstrate a modern taste for bold, brash flowers. Smaller, older varieties do best in Scotland, where the wind can blow through their wide, raggedy heads without destroying them. One of the Brodie's own developments, the pink-trumpeted white daffodil 'Helena Brodie', was extremely popular in its time.

Bught Floral Hall

Highland

Tel: (01463) 222755   E: info@invernessfloralhall.com
W: www.invernessfloralhall.com

Though floral halls, like winter gardens, suggest Victorian show-pieces built largely of glass and designed for inclement weather, Bught Floral Hall is primarily a place of flowers. Built in 1992, this climatically controlled greenhouse features a subtropical landscape with grotto, waterfall and tropical fish pond filled with lugubrious koi. Ferns flourish, as do palms and other exotics, while a display bench presents a changing selection of plants. Demonstration gardens include scree, alpine and heather beds, a water garden, herbaceous border and rhododendron area. An innovative pest-control programme uses live predators – that is, other insects – to prevent pests and diseases. With its exuberant white statuary, classical columns and luscious palms, Bught Floral Hall resembles a Hollywood version of a decadent Roman palace. As with the **David Welch Winter Gardens** in Aberdeen, this jungle-like space is a perfect place to pass a cold winter's afternoon. There is also a separate, award-winning cactus house. Both are set within a walled garden with lawns, arbours, raised beds and colourful floral displays.

Bught Floral Hall,
Bught Park, Bught Lane,
Inverness IV3 5SS

Open Apr to Oct, 10–5;
Nov to Mar, 10–4,
except for Christmas
and New Year weeks

Fee £1.75, conc. £1.25

About 1m N of city centre,
take signs to Inverness
Aquadome

Castle Fraser (NTS)

Aberdeenshire

T: (01330) 833463   E: information@nts.org.uk   W: www.nts.org.uk

Castle Fraser is one of Scotland's most romantic estates. The name of the castle, like that of its ancestral owners, can be dated back to a tenth-century Norman who served the king strawberries and was knighted for his service with the name 'fraiser'. As the need for defence gave way to political intrigue and then to pleasure, the original fortified tower was gradually extended with picturesque turrets and elegant halls. Castle Fraser boasts a secret chamber, known as the 'Laird's Lug' – 'lug' is Scots for

Castle Fraser, Sauchen,
Inverurie, Aberdeenshire
AB51 7LD

Open garden: all year, 9–6;
castle: Sun, Tues, Wed,
Thurs, Sat and Bank
Holiday weekends Fri and
Mon, Good Fri to 30 Jun,
12–5; 1 Jul to
31 Aug, 11–5; 1 to 30 Sep,
12–5

Fee garden: free; castle: £8,
conc. £5

Off A944, 4m N of
Dunecht, 16m W of
Aberdeen

ear – from which one could eavesdrop through a ventilation shaft on the room below. Indeed, this feature so delighted Sir Walter Scott that he included it in several of his novels. The castle also contains a secret chapel, several stuffed dogs and a history of heroic if misguided lairds. During the Wars of Independence Sir Simon Fraser was hanged, drawn and quartered for supporting 'Braveheart', Sir William Wallace. Five hundred years later, in 1746, Simon, 11th Lord Lovat, after taking part in the Jacobite uprising, became the last man to be beheaded in England. There is also a castle ghost – a murdered princess whose blood still stains the tower steps.

The romance of the castle is enhanced by a spectacular parkland setting. Though built in what was then bog, over the centuries the land was drained and forested and a mid-eighteenth-century military survey shows several formal tree-lined avenues. In 1794 the estate was redesigned in the picturesque fashion by Thomas White the Younger (1764–1811), who, like his father, promoted the landscape style of Lancelot 'Capability' Brown, with undulating lawns, ornamental groves and large, reflective lakes. Though the Whites designed dozens of estates throughout northern Britain, most of their Scottish landscapes have been lost in twentieth-century redevelopment. Ironically, Castle Fraser's redesign was undertaken just when the landscape style was falling out of favour as nationalists decried the obliteration of traditional Scots scenery to conform to an English pastoral ideal.

Even today the gothic castle sits a little uneasily within the classical serenity of the surrounding park. The walled garden is located far from the house in the English fashion. Carefully sited to maximize exposure to the sun, its impressive 12-foot-high walls are lined with brick to retain the heat. The north wall, unusually, is built of granite to withstand the biting winds. A Victorian greenhouse survived the First World War, though sadly not the second. A recent infestation of pernicious weeds inspired the head gardener to overhaul the whole space, restoring the late eighteenth-century paths while destroying an important twentieth-century border designed in the 1970s by Eric Robson. The current fashion for historical accuracy demonstrates one of the dilemmas facing the guardians of historic gardens: when undertaking restoration, to what period should they restore? Unlike other art forms, gardens are never fixed or finished; they exist in time, constantly evolving in a natural cycle of growth and

Scotland's Walled Gardens

Though walled gardens exist throughout Europe, Scotland's bitter winds, rough terrain and barren soil have made the walled garden an essential element of Scottish horticulture. In the late seventeenth century John Reid counselled readers of his *The Scots Gard'ner* to 'situate your house in healthy Soyl, near to a fresh spring, defended from the Impetuous-west winds, northern colds and eastern blasts'. Clearly shelter was a major consideration, though until the late sixteenth century the site for a house would depend primarily on how well it could be defended, then on its water supply, with its horticultural potential being a lesser consideration. In hilly regions the walled garden had to be located on the nearest piece of level ground, which was often some distance from the house; in flatter regions the gardens tended to abut the main dwelling. It was this style of attached walled garden, often associated with the baronial castles of the late Middle Ages, which romantics like Walter Scott and Robert Lorimer promoted as the national style.

With typical Scots pragmatism, the walled garden combined practicality and pleasure, producing decorative flowers as well as utilitarian fruit, vegetables and herbs – both culinary and medicinal. Given the roughness of the Scots terrain and the inclemency of the weather, the walled garden also offered a sheltered space for exercise and entertainment.

The 1603 union of the crowns of England and Scotland initiated a period of peace during which defensibility was no longer a primary consideration, so houses could be built on picturesque land, while gardens could be sited to take advantage of the sun – essential, as John Reid explained, to warm 'the cold, chilled, baren, rugged-natur'd ground'. Half a century later, in the building boom which followed the Restoration, walled gardens were once again sited away from the house, to allow for the formal parterres demanded by the tastes of the time.

When the naturalism of the eighteenth century swept away formality, the walled garden was still banished to allow for curving lawns, still lakes and picturesque groves. The siting of the garden some distance from the house spared landowners the odour of fertilizer and the sight of garden labourers; it also allowed for the cultivation of exotic flowers which might have jarred in the natural landscape. Sir Herbert Maxwell, in his *Scottish Gardens* (1911), describes an eighteenth-century tapestry of the flowers in Monreith Castle garden; an extensive list, including Madonna lilies, carnations, hyacinths, mulleins, primroses, auriculas, polyanthuses – known as 'spinks' in the Lowlands – anemones, moss roses, lychnis, geraniums, convolvulus, sunflowers, sweet williams, scabious, Canterbury bells and daffodils, it demonstrates the range of flora, both native and foreign, available to the eighteenth-century gardener.

The sentimental nationalism of the late eighteenth century engendered a revival of the medieval baronial style. Though Sir Walter Scott was among its most ardent admirers, the fashion persisted into the twentieth century. While some neo-baronial mansions were built with walled gardens abutting the house in the traditional manner, most kept their kitchen gardens firmly out of sight.

ରେ ରେ ରେ

With the house parties of the nineteenth century, walled gardens became extremely elaborate, producing all manner of exotic fruit and flora. Though hot beds were mentioned by John Reid, they didn't come into general use for another hundred years. By the mid-eighteenth century Justice James had devised a pineapple pit, raising the first pineapple in Scotland and creating a vogue for this unlikely fruit. There were also melon frames, such as those still at **Newhall**, and glass bells for forcing spring vegetables. Mushrooms could be provided through-out the winter – **Mertoun** still has its mushroom house beside the walled garden gate – while asparagus beds ensured supplies as early as December. Before greenhouses, fruit trees were espaliered against heat-absorbing garden walls, protected from winter frosts by portable lean-tos glazed with canvas, glass or oiled paper. Often, as at **Culross Palace** and **Kellie Castle**, bee skeps would be kept in wall niches to ensure pollination.

The layout of the walled garden was generally simple and practical, with a central avenue bisected by flower-lined paths. Larger gardens, such as those at **Culzean**, were subdivided with interior walls of brick or stone to maximize the fruit-growing potential. By the eighteenth century heated walls were widely used to cultivate such delicacies as grapes, peaches, figs and nectarines. When Victorian ingenuity popularized the greenhouse, these were often placed against the north wall to make the most of the southern sun. Some walled gardens also had arches at the base to allow fruit trees to spread their roots to the cooler earth outside.

Robert Lorimer (1864–1929) delighted in the traditional Scots walled garden with its mingling of fruit, flowers, vegetables, lawns, floral borders and orchards, declaring, '...the ideal plan is to have the park, with the sheep or beasts grazing in it, coming right under the windows at one side of the house and the gardens attached to the house at the other side.' The grounds he designed at **Kellie Castle** exemplify this combination of naturalism and formality, Edwardian exuberance and Scots austerity, while the walled garden at **Crathes** exhibits more pleasure than utility with stupendous, world-renowned flower borders.

In the twentieth century technical advances seemed to spell the end of the walled garden. Exotic produce could be imported year round for less than it cost to rear it at home. Higher wages, smaller households requiring less produce and cheap imports made working the land unprofitable. Maintenance was costly, horticultural skills were lost in two world wars, modern machinery could rarely squeeze into the gardens and when it did it damaged paths, edges and drainage systems. Many walled gardens were subcontracted out to commercial nurserymen, some were sold off for development and others were simply abandoned.

With the dawn of the twenty-first century, however, the future looks better. The recent vogue for organic and locally grown produce, the general interest in gardening and the appreciation of heritage have renewed interest in Scotland's walled gardens. Knowledgeable gardeners appreciate the soil in these enclosures, enriched by centuries of fertilizer and generations of careful cultivation. New conservation rules now prevent the destruction of walled gardens, while twenty-first-century romanticism might well recognize Scotland's walled gardens as among her most prized horticultural treasures.

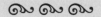

decay. Along the south side of the walled garden another important border, designed in the 1950s by James Russell, has been recently restored and modified to include such unusual tree peonies as *Paeonia suffruticosa* and *P. delavayi*, which flourish in local conditions.

Extensive woodland walks and the ubiquitous children's playground are being developed in the grounds. A devastating storm in 2002 destroyed some of the estate's oldest trees; while their replacements struggle to reach maturity, spring bulbs are flourishing in the clearings.

Castle of Mey

Highland

T: (01847) 851473   W: www.castleofmey.org.uk

Castle of Mey, Thurso, Highland KW14 8XH

Open 13 May to 27 Jul, 9 Aug to 28 Sep, Tues–Thurs, Sat 10.30–4

Fee £3, conc. 2.50; castle and grounds: £7.50, conc. £6.50, children £3

1½ m E of Mey, 6m west of John O'Groats on A836

The major horticultural distinction of the Castle of Mey is its location, on the most northerly part of mainland Britain in a region which, until the seventh century, was owned by Norse earls. Today the castle is renowned as the favourite dwelling of the late Queen Mother; indeed, it was the only property Her Royal Highness ever owned.

In 1556 the 4th Earl of Caithness acquired the Barony of Mey from the Bishop of Caithness and expanded the existing fortified store-house to create a traditional Z-plan castle. On this exposed northern site the threat of invasion was ever present; early on a secret passage was created for hasty escapes by sea, while the cannons later placed on the front lawn were designed to deter any chance of attack by Napoleon.

In 1952, while mourning the recent death of her husband George VI, the Queen Mother discovered the abandoned castle and vowed to restore it. One of her first changes was to reinstate the ancient name – for several centuries it had been known as Barrogill Castle. HRH also relieved the castle's austere façade, commissioning the cipher over the dining-room window which depicts her royal monogram flanked by the entwining emblems of Scotland's thistle and England's rose. This elegant carving is the work of Hew Lorimer (1907–93), son of the architect Sir Robert Lorimer. Schooled in the Arts and Craft tradition, with its emphasis on 'direct carving', Lorimer was apprenticed to the sculptor Eric Gill; his work, notable for its simplicity, eloquence and reverence for the natural world, embellishes many Scottish estates.

Despite its cold ground and harsh climate, the Castle of Mey has a garden with a long and illustrious history. In 1628 the traveller William Lithgow described the walled enclosure as 'a green-faced garden' and in 1762 the Bishop of Caithness extolled the fact there were 'plenty of apples, strawberries and cherries prospering within its bounds'. Today the 2-acre walled garden is a triumph of faith, hard work and 15-foot-high, sheltering walls. While a greenhouse ensures pot plants whatever the weather, the garden itself supplies kitchen and dining room, as well as providing an enclosed pleasaunce for walks in clement weather. Traditionally the flowers were timed to flourish in August, when the Queen Mother visited, though recently efforts have been made to extend the growing season for the paying public. Deep hedges divide the space, providing further protection. One of the resulting enclosures is the Shell Garden, so called because of the sea shells scattered here by the Queen Mother. These were subsequently replaced by a more stable surface of pebbles, but the garden remains a favourite resting place, with its herbaceous borders and colourful island beds filled with old-fashioned shrub roses. Elsewhere a traditional Caithness fence made of flagstones turned on end provides a warm backing to vibrant displays of antirrhinums.

Of the garden's more utilitarian produce, root vegetables prosper and cabbages are particularly prized among the surplus items sold by the gate. Fruit is chosen for its resistance to salt spray and biting wind; low-lying fruit such as currants, raspberries and strawberries survive remarkably well, as do gooseberries. At the turn of the twentieth century Gertrude Jekyll extolled 'this much neglected fruit', noting that the Scottish gooseberry 'comes to unusual excellence. It is a hardy thing, and appears to thrive better north of the Border than elsewhere.' She even advocated dedicated gooseberry gardens, filled with such romantic-sounding varieties as 'Red Champagne', 'Amber Yellow', 'Jolly Painter' and the trusty late 'Red Warrington', and suggested that gooseberry lovers grow the fruit in espalier form – an idea that does not appear to have been widely followed.

Just beyond the castle wall the late Queen Mother has been honoured in a memorial bench; carved of Caithness slate, it faces the Pentland Firth and the Orkneys beyond. The castle farm specializes in Aberdeen Angus cattle, a relatively recent breed descended from native cattle found in the north-east of Scotland. In 1937, with her husband, the Queen Mother became joint patron of the Aberdeen Angus Cattle Society. Over the years she built up her own pedigree herd and today these picturesque creatures graze the castle grounds.

Cawdor Castle Gardens

Highland

T: (01667) 404401   E: info@cawdorcastle.com   W: www.cawdorcastle.com

Cawdor Castle, Cawdor, Highland IV12 5RD

Open 1 May to 14 Oct, 10–5.30 (last admission 5)

Fee castle and gardens: £7.30, children £4.50

E of Inverness on A96 to Brockley, then 4m S on B9090

Cawdor Castle Gardens provide a potent mix of ancient history and contemporary symbolism. The name Cawdor evolved from the earlier *calder*, meaning 'a woodland stream'. Visitors will appreciate why Shakespeare's Macbeth was thrilled when the witches predicted he'd be the thane – or laird – of the estate. Land in the region was fiercely contested, as the earth is rich and the weather is said to be the best in the British Isles. Even the full thrust of contemporary commercial exploitation cannot diminish Cawdor's romance, and few will disagree with Sir Herbert Maxwell when he said that 'perfection is attained in a garden where the eye is gratified by beauty of form and colour, and the mind is stimulated by historic association; and such is the case at Cawdor Castle'.

Legend claims that when the thane was appointed Sheriff of Moray by James II, he decided to build himself a castle appropriate to his new status. Unsure where to site it, he was instructed in a dream to put his treasure on the back of an ass and build where the beast lay down. The ass settled beneath a grove of hawthorns and the castle was duly built. Cynics point out that the site was on high ground, providing a strong foundation, a defensible position and a good well – a lot for a mere ass to have discerned. Nonetheless the castle was indeed constructed around a small tree which carbon-dating links to the fourteenth century. The tree, however, was a holly, not the hawthorn of legend. Hardy and evergreen, the holly is a Christian symbol of life, though its iconography dates back to pagan times when it was used by the Romans in their December Saturnalia. It was also believed to provide protection against fairies, fiends and lightning, and it was this superstition that probably influenced the decision to retain the tree within the original castle walls, which are still discernible amid seventeenth- and eighteenth-century additions.

The first record of a garden at Cawdor is dated 1635, but as this enclosure is cut into a bank with medieval retaining walls, it was probably built with the original keep. The later walled garden, abutting the castle in the old Scots style, was an eighteenth-century addition. Today it is planted as a pleasure ground with lawns, grassy walks, arbours, pergolas, knots, an orchard and a thick peony border. Bright-red benches give an oriental flavour to this Edwardian assemblage, while the extraordinary height and vigour of the herbaceous plants attest to the benefits of Scotland's northern summer, with its cool, damp days and long hours of sunlight. The garden also boasts an abundance of *Rosa pimpinellifolia*, the Scots or Burnet rose, one of Britain's few native roses. The dry moat is silted up but ferns flourish in its damp embrace, while the fragile beauty of *Rosa banksiae* climbing the castle walls is enhanced by the grim grey towers rising above it.

In the 1980s, as supermarkets proliferated in the region, it was decided that the kitchen garden could be more effectively deployed entertaining the public than feeding the household. One-third of the space was turned into a holly maze, designed by Lord Cawdor, based on the pattern of an old Portuguese mosaic tile. Foot mazes often figured in the floor patterns of medieval churches, where they were intended to induce contemplation while suggesting the journey of life. Sadly, Cawdor's maze is now closed to the public as the designer underestimated the volume of visitors and the shallow roots of the holly plants cannot withstand the pressure of such crowds. The space beyond has been turned into a Garden of Earthly Delights. Taking its design from an old sampler, this uses only plants mentioned in Parkinson's 1629 *Paradisi in Sole, Paradisus Terrestris*. The Fall is suggested by a flanking orchard, an unusual thistle garden represents Purgatory and Paradise is found within a circular yew hedge. At the heart of this labyrinthine enclosure is a delightful white garden centred on a bronze cylinder fountain decorated with arcane images and set with scallop shells, again evoking pilgrimage and the journey of life.

Woodland walks surrounding the Cawdor Burn are filled with favourite Victorian trees, including western hemlock, *Tsuga heterophylla*, and Wellingtonia, *Sequoiadendron giganteum*.

Cluny House Garden

Perth and Kinross

Cluny House,
Aberfeldy,
Perth and Kinross
PH15 2JT

T: (01887) 820795   E: matcluny@aol.com

Open 1 Mar to 31 Oct, 10–6; no dogs

Fee £3.50, children free

From A9, turn off at Ballinluig on the A827; at Grandtully cross river, take two immediate lefts, then after 3m turn off right and go ½m up the hill

Cluny means 'a meadow' in Gaelic, though the jungle density of this particular garden belies its pastoral name; 6 acres of Himalayan plants now thrive in what was once a field. Cluny House Garden, created in the 1950s by the local vet and his wife, is being continued by their daughter today. A nineteenth-century shelter belt of conifers, beeches and oaks was planted when the house was built. Several Wellingtonias, a fern-leaf beech, *Fagus sylvaticum*, and a silver fir, *Abies alba*, attest to the Victorian love of large trees; indeed, one of the Wellingtonias, planted in 1850, already has a girth of 35 feet and is reputed to be the widest conifer in Britain. The effect of severe winters and late spring frosts is mitigated by a second, inner shelter belt of acers, birches and sorbuses under-planted with dense shrubs such as rhododendrons, viburnums, embothriums, eucryphias and enkianthus.

Chemicals are avoided and bark-lined paths wind through the woodland, enlivened by hydrangeas. Fritillaries, violets, primulas and North American trilliums thrive in the damp, dappled, woodland shade, as do the blue Himalayan poppies, whose startling colour develops to perfection in the acid soil. Many of the plants at Cluny House Garden were grown from seed; a fine Tibetan cherry, *Prunus Serrula* var. *tibetica*, was one of various seeds from the Ludlow–Sheriff expedition to Japan in the late 1940s. Cluny House also holds the national collection of Asiatic primulas.

ᔐᕽ ᔐᕽ

Crathes Castle (NTS)

Crathes Castle, Banchory,
Aberdeenshire AB31 5QJ

Open garden: all year,
9–sunset;
castle: Good Fri to 30 Sep,
10–5.30, 1 to 31 Oct, 10–4.30

Fee garden: £8, conc. £5;
castle and garden: £10,
conc. £7 (incl. castle)

15 W of Aberdeen, 3m E of
Banchory on A93

Aberdeenshire

T: (01330) 844525   E: crathes@nts.org.uk   W: www.nts.org.uk

This spectacular Edwardian garden, one of Scotland's finest, was given to the National Trust for Scotland in 1952 along with the 600-acre estate of Crathes. Dating from the late sixteenth century, the castle, a magnificent example of the Scottish baronial style, inspired Gertrude Jekyll to describe it as a fairy palace with rugged fortalice below and ethereal turrets aloft: '...the whole beautiful mass appears as if it had come into being in some far-away, wonderful, magical night'.

The estate was given by royal decree to the Burnards, or Burnetts, an Anglo-Saxon family who came to Scotland in the fourteenth century. Like his neighbour William de Irvine at **Drum Castle**, Alexander Burnard was rewarded for his loyalty by Robert the Bruce, who bestowed upon him the position of Royal Forester of Drum. In the mid-seventeenth century Robert Gordon of Straloch noted that Alexander's son, Thomas Burnett, the 1st Baronet, had 'covered the forbidding crags, laid it out with gardens and dotted it with pleasaunce'. In the eighteenth century chroniclers begin to remark on the 'delicate fruit' of the walled garden, its mild microclimate being unusual in the brutal north-east, especially in a site which is 350 feet above sea level. Although a yew hedge dated to 1702 indicates the presence of an earlier formal design, the first modern record of the garden itself appears in Gertrude Jekyll's *Colour Schemes for the Flower Garden* (1895). A decade later, in her inaccurately named *Some English Gardens* (1904), Jekyll returned to Crathes, describing the flower garden as bisected by a yew hedge, divided into upper and lower levels, with floral borders, grass lawns and a kitchen garden surrounding an ancient mulberry tree. Jekyll extolled the tunnel-like rose arches and masterful contrasts of bright flowers, dark velvet yews and weather-worn granite. She also praised the luxuriant phlox, pyrethrum, rudbeckia, tansy and Japanese anemones, which attest 'by their size and vigour' to a strong, loamy soil.

Over the succeeding decades the garden fell into disrepair, and in the 1920s the estate was passed on to Sir James Burnett, a keen collector with an interest in trees, whose wife, Lady Sybil, had a passion for herbaceous plants. Together the Burnetts redeveloped the 3½-acre walled garden.

Inspired by Hidcote in England, they created eight garden rooms, each with its own mood. The four oldest, found on the upper level, are divided by the eighteenth-century yew hedges. Major pruning was recently undertaken to prevent the overgrown hedges from collapsing in heavy snow.

The upper gardens are separated from the lower by a wall housing old greenhouses, restored in 1978 to their original designs. Today the greenhouses contain the national collection of Malmaison carnations. Rare in Scotland, these labour-intensive beauties are an emblem of Edwardian opulence. First raised in France during the Second Empire of the mid-nineteenth century, they are named for their resemblance to the popular Malmaison rose. Their poor cousin, the pink, has stronger national associations, having taken Paisley by storm in the early nineteenth century when the as-yet-unblackened skies shone on tiny plots of pinks, carefully nurtured by local weavers eschewing the lure of pub and cricket ground to incorporate the flowers' delicate features into their fine muslin shawls...if J. C. Loudon is to be believed.

Back to Crathes itself: though the walled garden abuts the castle in the Scots baronial style, the public entrance is to the side of the lawn, where a path leads directly into the lower level gardens though the white border – dramatically planted so its green foliage contrasts with a backing of purple prunus. A Portuguese laurel, *Prunus lusitanica*, halfway along this border acts as a focal point from which the double herbaceous border, planted in primary colours for summer interest, goes northwards. A double shrub border goes southwards and a June border of cottage flowers bisects the quartered lawn, leading to a seventeenth-century dovecot which Lady Sybil placed here as a picturesque endpoint.

A red garden to the west was created in 1978 and the golden garden across the shrub border was planned by Lady Sybil, but planted in 1973 by the National Trust for Scotland. *Viburnum opulus* 'Xanthocarpum', *Malus* 'Golden Hornet' and the yew, *Taxus baccata* 'Fastigiata Aurea', contribute golden hues to this area. Along the southern wall is a rare *Eleutherococcus trifoliatus*, planted by Sir James. The Camel Garden is so named for the humps in the ground, the Burnetts having chosen to work with the flow of the earth rather than levelling it to create a flat surface. Beyond this is the Trough Garden, which takes its name from the large stone pool at its centre.

On the top terrace the Upper Pool Garden, finished in 1932, was Lady Sybil's first creation – it displays an unusual palette of red, yellow and bronze-coloured plants. Beside it is the croquet lawn, which might once have been a bowling green. Across the yew hedge is the Rose Garden, with four triangular beds featuring floribunda and hybrid tea roses, and a large handkerchief tree, *Davidia involucrata*. The fourth quadrant of the upper terrace, the Fountain Garden, centres on an Italianate fountain; this area is discreetly planted with calm blue flowers, a welcome relief from the heady delights of the surrounding spaces.

The parkland, noted for its trees, bears little evidence of the havoc wrought by a severe gale in 1968. An illustration of 1798, now hanging in the castle kitchen, indicates a limekiln in the field beyond the old approach road. This would have been used for burning lime to create agricultural fertilizer, a common practice in this region, as evidenced by the limekiln still standing in the woods at **Pitmedden** nearby. Some 15 miles of woodland walks thread their way through the estate, one of which leads to the recently restored Caroline's Garden, a wild space dramatically sited beneath a granite cliff.

Cruickshank Botanic
Gardens, Aberdeen
University, St Machar
Drive, Aberdeen
AB24 3UU

Open all year, Mon–Fri
9–4.30; May to Sep,
Sat and Sun also, 2–5

Fee free

St Machar Drive, 1½ m N
of city centre in Old
Aberdeen, entrance in
Chanonry

Cruickshank Botanic Gardens

Aberdeen

T: (01224) 272704   E: n.gorman@abdn.ac.uk   W: www.abdn.ac.uk

In 1898 Miss Anne Cruickshank endowed this 6-acre garden to the University of Aberdeen for botanical research and the public good. In keeping with those early philanthropic ideals, the garden continues to open free to the public. Set behind magnificent iron gates in the charming cobbled streets of Old Aberdeen, the garden today is a favourite place for snogging students and blethering birds, whose chatter almost drowns the noise of city traffic beyond. The occasional cry of a seagull reminds visitors that the North Sea is barely a mile away.

The original garden, designed by George Nicholson of Kew, was eradicated during the First World War. In 1920 an

Edwardian layout was put in its place with a long wall, sunken garden and herbaceous border. Much of this was turned over to vegetable cultivation during the Second World War, but the garden has been restored yet again, with the winding paths, open lawns and discreet labelling of modern times.

In 1970 the garden was extended to include a rock garden, a terrace garden and a sunken rose garden. As befits a teaching institution, the rose garden displays different rose groups. In one bed old garden roses such as the Damask Rose 'Isphahan' and Moss rose 'Quatre Saisons' represent the Gallica, Damask, Alba, Centifolia and Moss roses which derive from a few European and west Asian species. In a second bed are the Chinese garden roses which were introduced into Europe at the end of the eighteenth century and hybridized with old roses to create Bourbons, Hybrid Perpetual Teas and Hybrids. In a third bed are species roses such as *Rosa moyesii* and Scots roses which have undergone little if any hybridization, while the fourth bed displays popular modern roses such as large-flowered Hybrid Tea and Floribunda cluster roses.

Unobtrusively placed by the main Cruickshank Building are three acid-loving beds backed by unusual peat walls, a legacy from the 1920s, when peat was not yet endangered.

Over the years the garden has expanded and today 4 of the 11 acres are planted as an arboretum. While the bracing location militates against large conifers, rhododendrons flourish, underplanted with hellebores, primulas and meconopsis. Today this delightful botanical garden is maintained by a meagre staff of three, a sad indication that the study of plants is being supplanted by contemporary subjects such as soil science – hardly surprising as industry endeavours to find ways to clean up toxic industrial sites.

A plaque on the Cruickshank Building commemorates Scotland's first professional plant collector, Francis Masson (1741–1805), who was born nearby.

Francis Masson

Born and raised in Old Aberdeen, Masson was working as a gardener at Kew in 1772 when Joseph Banks appointed him the Royal Botanic Garden's first official collector. Masson was sent on an expedition to the Cape of Good Hope in a ship captained by James Cook. Since South Africa was under control of the Dutch East India Company at the time, Britain knew little of its rich flora when Masson wrote home extolling the country 'enamalled with the greatest number of flowers I ever saw of exquisite beauty and fragrance'.

Since many of his early plants died on the voyage home, Masson began sending seeds; later he established a nursery in the Cape to house his plants between voyages. On plant-hunting expeditions into the interior, he collected over 100 varieties of Cape heath, gazanias, romuleas, pelargoniums, lobelias and proteas; he also introduced the white arum lily, *Zantedeschia aethiopica*, and *Senecio cruentus*, from which today's cinerarias descend. In the drier regions he discovered around forty species of *Stapelia*, becoming the world authority on these showy but foul-smelling succulents.

In 1775 Masson returned to Britain, having contributed nearly 500 new species to Kew's collection of living plants. The following year he set off for the Azores, the Canary Islands and the West Indies. Ten years later he returned to the Cape, though his explorations were curtailed by political uncertainties, in particular the widespread fear that the French might take over the Cape as they had Holland. In 1797, at an age when most men contemplate retirement, Masson embarked on an expedition to Canada. Attacked by French pirates, his ship was lost, though he and some of the crew were eventually rescued by a German ship. Among the many seeds he sent from Canada to Kew was the much-loved woodland *Trillium grandiflorum*. During the unusually severe winter of 1805 Masson wrote to Banks from Montreal, asking to be recalled, but he died before permission was granted.

David Welch Winter Gardens

Aberdeen

T: (01224) 585310   E: wintergardens@aberdeencity.gov.uk   W:
www.aberdeencity.gov.uk

Despite, or perhaps because of its storm-tossed northern location
and its grey granite architecture, Aberdeen has recently begun to
swathe itself in flowers, winning first place in the Britain in
Bloom competition a record number of times and earning the
epithet 'The Flower of Scotland'. The 44-acre Duthie Park in the
city centre demonstrates this municipal love of flora. A typical
Victorian creation, it was endowed in 1883 as a gift to the citizens
of Aberdeen from Lady Elizabeth Duthie to perpetuate the memory of her uncles and brothers. As Queen Victoria was recovering
from an accident on opening day, the park was inaugurated by
her daughter, Princess Beatrice. Among its many amenities were
a boating lake, a colourful bandstand and a drinking fountain,
now sadly dry, commemorating the good work of the Aberdeen
Temperance Society. In 1899 an elegant palm house was erected,
180 feet long and 90 feet wide, with a central dome rising nearly
50 feet high. In 1969, having been badly damaged in a gale, the
building was demolished for public safety. For many years after,
David Welch, director of Aberdeen's City Council, pushed to
replace the lamented palm house with a winter garden. Eventually his efforts paid off and the resulting David Welch Winter
Gardens are the largest indoor gardens in Europe, hosting flora
from around the world.

Though originally conceived as outdoor spaces planted with
evergreens for winter display, in Victorian times the winter garden was reinterpreted as a 'people's palace' – a glass exhibition
hall, embellished with potted plants, but designed primarily for
concerts and dances. The David Welch Winter Gardens go back
to the earlier idea, providing an enormous garden under glass.
The arid house contains the largest collection of giant cacti and
succulents in the UK, while the tropical house hosts an enormous collection of bromeliads, orchids and gingers. There is also
a fern house, a floral courtyard, a temperate house, a Japanese
Peace Garden and a Victorian Corridor bursting with fusty geraniums, spectacular hanging baskets and such favourite house
plants as fuchsias, streptocarpus, cyclamens and cinerarias.

David Welch Winter
Gardens, Duthie Park,
Aberdeen AB11 7TH

Open Apr to Aug,
9.30–7.30; Sep to Oct,
9.30–5.30; Nov to Mar,
9.30–4.30, but closed
Christmas Day and New
Year's Day

Fee free

Riverside Drive, Ferryhill
area of Aberdeen

Just beyond the Winter Gardens a rose mountain rises from a former flagpole mound. In spring it is draped in crocuses, followed by daffodils, but the mountain reaches full glory in summer, when its 120,000 roses, ranging across the colour spectrum, infuse the park with their intoxicating scent.

Drum Castle (NTS)

Drum Castle, Dromoak, Banchory, Aberdeenshire AB31 5EY

Aberdeenshire

Open garden: 31 Mar to 31 Oct, 10–6; castle: 31 Mar to 30 Jun, 1 Sep to 1 Oct, 12.30–5; 1 Jul to 31 Aug , 1–5 (last admission 4.15)

Fee garden: £2.50, conc. £1.90; castle and garden: £8, conc. £5

10m W of Aberdeen, 8m E of Banchory off A93

T: (01330) 811204   E: drum@nts.org.uk   W: www.drum-castle.org.uk

With a history stretching back 800 years, Drum Castle provides sporadic insights into the evolution of the Scottish landscape since the Middle Ages. Originally a royal hunting forest, the lands and Forest of Drum, along with the thirteenth-century keep, were granted by royal charter to William de Irvine, armour bearer to Robert the Bruce, in 1323. The castle derives its name from the Gaelic *druim*, meaning 'a ridge' or 'a knoll', describing the promontory, 400 feet above sea level, on which the castle sits. In the sixteenth century, wood from the estate was used in the constructing of James IV's fleet and in 1606 'wode of Drum' helped build the *Bon Accord* – the first large ship to be launched at Aberdeen.

In 1619 the Irvine family built the Jacobean manor house whose Victorian accretions were designed by David Bryce two centuries later. In 1975 the castle and its 400 acres were bequeathed to the National Trust for Scotland.

Though there is little documentation about the early gardens, the seventeenth-century historian John Spalding records that Covenanting soldiers in pursuit of the Royalists destroyed the 'pleasaunt garden planting' as they passed. In the late eighteenth century the grounds were landscaped with English-style parkland of open lawns and specimen trees – the laird being a subscriber to Edinburgh's Botanic Garden. Originally the 4½-acre walled kitchen garden was probably sited on the level ground in the south lawn, which in Victorian times was transformed into a croquet ground to accommodate the newly fashionable game. At this time the kitchen garden was probably moved to its present location, several hundred yards north-east and out of sight of the house. The same era saw the introduction of such novelty trees as the handkerchief tree, *Davidia involucrata*, which Ernest 'Chinese' Wilson introduced from western China in 1869. An impressive collection of conifers, also amassed in Victorian times, includes Brewer's weeping spruce, *Picea breweriana*, a Douglas fir, *Pseudotsuga menziesi*, and some spectacular sequoias. In the 1920s specimen rhododendrons were planted and in the 1930s the water garden was added to the walk from the castle to the walled garden.

By the 1980s the walled garden had succumbed to neglect. As two gardeners now had to do the work that eleven had previously done, maintaining 20 acres of gardens and policies, it was deemed impossible to restore a traditional kitchen garden. Given the proximity of **Crathes** with its splendid floral displays and **Pitmedden** with its historical restoration, the National Trust decided to create a 'garden of historic roses'.

Within its 13-foot-high walls the garden is divided into quadrants, each representing a different century. The seventeenth-century garden features gravel paths, topiary yews, Versailles planting tubs and a shallow, carved stone basin. These embellish tight parterres filled with wild rose types such as the Centifolia rose 'Pompon de Bourgogne', introduced before 1667. Though these old varieties tend to have the strongest scent, their decline in popularity is explained by the prominence of petal drop, black spot, mildew, rot and rust.

The eighteenth-century garden, based on a 1702 German illustration, has formal box-edged parterres round an elegant lion fountain. The nineteenth-century garden is enclosed with high yew hedges around loosely planted beds featuring such favourites as the Rugosa rose 'Blanc Double de Coubert' surrounded by nepeta, santolina and colourful pansies. The twentieth-century garden, Edwardian rather than modern, focuses on a sunken terrace round an ingenious sundial where visitors act as the gnomon, with their shadows pointing to the hour. Here alliums, forget-me-nots, anemones and – Gertrude Jekyll's favourite – bergenias complement such roses as the musk 'Pink Prosperity' from 1931. The gardens surround an elegant trellis-work gazebo based on that at Tyninghame, while the main axis terminates in a huge oriental bench designed by Hew Lorimer and similar to one he created for his own garden at **Kellie Castle**. An old tool shed in the corner has been cleverly redeployed as an interpretation centre.

The walled garden is approached by a recently planted avenue of variegated *Ilex alta clarensis* 'Golden King'. As the Irvine family crest contains three holly leaves, the holly motif is repeated throughout the garden. The 117-acre woodland to the north-west of the estate is one of the few vestiges of the ancient oak forest that once enveloped the Dee valley, providing refuge for wolves and wild boar. Along with the rare remaining oaks, the forest contains the traditional mixture of Scots pine, birch and picturesque, gnarled geans – wild cherries.

Dunrobin Castle

Dunrobin Castle, Golspie, Highland KW10 6SF

Open 1 Apr to 15 Oct, 10.30–4.30; Jun to Sep till 5.30; Apr, May, Jun, Sep, Oct, Sun from 12

Fee £7, children £5 (incl. castle)

50m N of Inverness, 1m N of Golspie on A9

Highland

T: (01408) 633177   E: info@dunrobincastle.net   W: www.dunrobincastle.net

The garden at Dunrobin Castle is a prime example of the Victorian interpretation of the grand French style. With thirteenth-century origins, Dunrobin claims to be the oldest inhabited house in Scotland – a distinction also claimed by **Traquair** in the south. Though sixteenth- and seventeenth-century accretions remain, the house was largely redesigned in 1845 by Sir Charles Barry, architect of London's Houses of Parliament. Notwithstanding Dunrobin's romantic gothic splendour, Barry was generally drawn to the formal style, particularly in horticulture, having designed such grand gardens as Shrubland Park, Harewood House and Cliveden. When invited to lay out the gardens at Dunrobin, he took Versailles as his inspiration, creating an architectural design of clipped evergreens, bisecting allées and geometric parterres that can best be appreciated from the castle terrace. Both formal and luxurious, the garden manages to hold its own against the spectacular panorama of the Moray Firth and the Cairngorm Mountains beyond.

While the steep site demanded protective balustrades and buttressing walls, a grand staircase, upright urns and fountains provide a vertical link to the castle above. The rose-covered retaining wall features the Duchess Border, a deep herbaceous bed designed in the 1920s and stuffed with such English favourites as potentillas, delphiniums, foxgloves, peonies and

Peat

Described by the Irish poet Seamus Heaney as 'brown butter', peat was for centuries Scotland's major source of domestic fuel for cooking and heating. Unlike coal, peat burns fast, releasing a lot of heat in a very short time. Generally it took three men three days to cut enough winter fuel for one household. Peat was also used for insulation and agriculture, being dug into the soil to provide nutrients and improve moisture retention.

Peat bogs developed over thousands of years from the slow accumulation of partially decayed vegetable matter. Growing at a rate of one millimetre per year, peat forms in marshy areas where the acidic conditions and waterlogging inhibit the decay of plant material. Despite thousands of years of peat extraction, it is only over the past half-century that Scotland's peat bogs have become endangered through afforestation, agriculture and mechanized peat-extracting machinery.

poppies. Further borders flank the main axis, which ends in the elegant wrought-iron Westminster Gates; presented in 1894 by the 1st Duke of Westminster, these open on to the Moray Firth.

The large circular north parterre was designed to evoke a Scottish shield, while the two rectangular parterres to the south have recently been redeveloped, replacing an old shrubbery with twenty massive wooden pyramids covered in roses, clematis and sweet peas. While nodding to the formal French aesthetic, these also suggest that feature beloved of today's avant-gardeners, the potager. Ornamental vegetables, herbs, clipped fruit trees and slatted park chairs reinforce the French atmosphere.

Several thriving *Gunnera manicata* attest to the efficacy of the Gulf Stream, which sweeps up Scotland's west coast and pushes round the north to expend its final surges of warmth in the Firth. In the seventeenth century Robert Gordon of Straloch, geographer to Charles I, described Dunrobin as follows: 'a house well seated upon a mote hard by the sea, with fair orchards, when ther be pleasant gardens planted with all kinds of froots, hearbs and floors…and abundance of good saphorn [saffron], tobacco and rosemarie, the froot being excellent, and cheeflie the pears and cherries'. Of the nineteenth-century makeover Sir Herbert Maxwell said, 'One is disposed to murmur at the taste of an age which swept away this old garden and its contents, to make way for terraces and parterres on a grand scale...nevertheless the ground lies so beautifully, the terrace stairs are so commanding, and the trees crowd so close to the tide, that the whole effect is very fine.'

An eighteenth-century summer house, just beyond the garden wall, is described by Maxwell as a 'Temple of Bacchus', a relic of the age of 'Gargantuan conviviality'. In the more sober Victorian era this was turned into a museum of zoological, botanical and geological treasures, recalling the earlier role of gardens as places of scientific study. Featuring Pictish stones, querns and inscriptions, odd seeds, cones and pods, but dominated by a ghoulish display of taxidermy, this is definitely not a place for the squeamish. Happily the falconry display, conducted several times a day at the bottom of the garden, eschews the use of live quarry. This ancient sport, developed to ensure elusive prey for the master's table, is demonstrated with a range of falcons, owls and eagles. The extensive landscaped parklands which surrounded the garden a century ago have reverted to woodland, now threaded with walks. The hapless stags whose heads ornament the castle interior came from Dunrobin Forest beyond.

Edzell Castle, Edzell, Brechin, Perth and Kinross DD9 7UE

Open 1 Apr to 30 Sep, 9.30–6.30; 1 Oct to 31 Mar, Mon–Sun 9.30–4.30

Fee £4, children £1.60

6m N of Brechin, A90 to B966

Edzell Castle

Perth and Kinross

T: (01356) 648631   W: www.historic-scotland.gov.uk

Traditional home of 'the lichtsome Lindsays', Edzell Castle is bound up in the tragic romance of Scotland's past. Mary Queen of Scots met her Privy Council here, James VI visited and Cromwell's soldiers requisitioned the castle during the Commonwealth. In 1715 the last Lindsay laird fell into debt and was forced to sell, ending his days as a stableman. The estate was then seized from its next owner, Lord Panmure, in punishment for his support of the Jacobite uprising. The York Building Society, which next took possession of the estate, went bankrupt and in 1764 the castle roof and floors were ripped up as the wood was sold to pay creditors. The castle quietly disintegrated until 1932, when HM Office of Works took over the ruin and set about restoring its historic garden.

An unusual place of emblems and inscriptions, Edzell is part of a horticultural tradition that winds through the eighteenth-century philosophers' gardens and resurfaces in the twentieth century with Ian Hamilton Finlay's **Little Sparta**. In the late seventeenth century John Ochterlony of Guynd described Edzell as a 'delicat gardine with walls sumptuously built of hewen stone polisht, with pictures and coates of armes in the walls, with a fine summer house with a house for a bath on the south corners thereof, far exceeding any new work of their times'.

The original sixteenth-century tower contained a barmkin – a courtyard built to defend cattle and labourers in turbulent times. In the early seventeenth century David Lindsay, Lord Edzell, added an extraordinarily cosmopolitan pleasaunce to his rustic dwelling. Educated at the Scots College of the Sorbonne and at Cambridge University, Lindsay was better travelled and better read than most of his compatriots. His pleasure garden displays emblematic bas-relief panels reflecting such influences as early sixteenth-century engravings from the Nuremberg studio of Albrecht Dürer. Indeed, so diligently did Edzell's carver imitate the engravings that he included the initials of the engraver, Georg Pencz, in the halberd of Mars's sword.

Though no record remains of the original planting, today the symbolic wall panels are the garden's major feature. Sir David Lindsay's coat of arms, his mottoes, his initials and those of his wife preside over the entrance, which also shows the date of the garden's construction: 1604. Niches for busts, now empty, are interspersed among the coping stones. The carvings reveal Sir David's interests in heraldry, astrology and numerology. The sacred number seven is particularly prominent. The eastern wall has seven panels representing the planetary gods: Mars, Jupiter, Saturn, Mercury, Venus, the Sun and Moon. The south wall represents the seven liberal arts, in which, no doubt, Sir David excelled: grammar, arithmetic, rhetoric, dialectic, music, geometry and astronomy. The west wall displays the seven cardinal virtues: faith, hope, charity, prudence, temperance, fortitude and justice. The decorative seven-pointed 'mullet' stars derive from the coat of arms of Sir David's ancestors, the Stirlings of Glenesk, on whose lands he discovered the valuable mineral deposits which financed the construction of his beloved garden. These stars contain central nesting holes to attract song birds, this being a garden of the senses as well as of the intellect.

The senses are also stimulated by an abundance of flowers placed on the vertical as well as the horizontal plane. Rows of recessed planting boxes inserted into the wall create the chequerboard motif of the Templar Knights of St John. Though some people think that these recesses may have been bee boles, most believe that bees would have been banished from the intimate confines of the pleasure garden. Certainly their skeps could easily have been placed in holes in the outer walls beside the fields for drying laundry. It is thought that in Sir David's time the inner recesses were planted with white flowers, probably alyssum, with the blocks between them painted blue to create a chequerboard effect. Today the recesses contain blue lobelia and white alyssum, evoking the Lindsay colours and, incidentally, those of Scotland's patron saint, Andrew.

The garden at Edzell was designed to be appreciated from the top floor of the banqueting house in the south-east corner. Despite their name, such pavilions were not intended for banquets in the current sense; they provided the excuse for a stroll round the garden after the main meal. The ground floor of the pavilion has an elegant vaulted ceiling as well as built-in benches for the taking of post-prandial sweetmeats. The upper room, well ventilated with a window in each wall and fireplace in one corner, was probably used as a summer sleeping chamber.

Opposite the banqueting pavilion lie the foundations of the bath house referred to by John Ochterlony of Guynd in his 1680 *Notes on Forfarshire*. An unusual feature for its time, the bath attests to Sir David's cosmopolitan tastes. Ochterlony also mentioned 'an excellent kitchine garden' and an 'orchard with diverse kinds of most excellent fruits', while the quality of the carvings on the outer walls of the privy garden suggest they faced on to equally grand spaces, such as archery courts or bowling greens. The original estate would have been much larger than the walled garden which remains today, as any country seat had to be virtually self-sufficient, requiring a dairy, brew house, laundry, stables, barns and labourers' dwellings as well as orchards, herb gardens and vegetable patches.

After centuries of disintegration and neglect, Edzell's privy garden was completely restored and replanted after the First World War. James Richardson, Scotland's Inspector of Ancient Monuments, oversaw the final design. Here, as at **Pitmedden**, he created a 1930s version of a seventeenth-century garden. A large clipped yew in the centre suggests a medieval mound, while raised terraces around the sides recall Elizabethan walks. Triangular beds in the corners feature a diplomatic mixture of English rose, Scots thistle, Irish shamrock and French fleur-de-lys. The central parterre is planted with anachronistic bright roses, while clipped box edges ingeniously spell out the Lindsay mottoes *Dum spiro spero* – While I breathe I hope – and *Endure forte* – Endure with strength. One can only hope these mottoes were some comfort to Sir David in his dotage. He died in 1610, impoverished by the construction of the garden, then bankrupted by the heavy fines he had to pay for his son's accidental murder of a man in a drunken brawl. The garden remains a poignant tribute to Sir David Lindsay's rare refinement.

Findhorn Community Gardens

Moray

T: (01304) 690311   E: enquiries@findhorn.org   W: www.findhorn.org

Findhorn Community, Findhorn, Forres, Moray IV36 3TZ

Open all year

Fee free

1½m E of Forres on A96, then 4m N on B9011; garden is just E of Findhorn town centre

Though it doesn't fit any traditional model of Scottish horticulture, the modern settlement at Findhorn can, in effect, be seen as one vast community garden. A remote Highland fishing village, Findhorn came to international attention in the 1960s when a trio of unemployed adults followed voices telling them to cultivate the land. Tales of giant cabbages filtered south and Findhorn became a gathering place for earth-worshippers, occultists, ecologists and other counter-culture groupies. Cynics note that throughout the north working men have created prized vegetables by filling ditches with compost and nurturing a single seed, but Findhorn's publicity sticks to the idea that their success was due to 'Eileen's inner guidance, Dorothy's contact with the intelligence of nature and Peter's determination'.

Though the days of super vegetables may be gone, Findhorn's commercial nursery, Cullerne Gardens, is a fine advertisement for organic principles, while various features throughout the village demonstrate a commitment to ecological living. Communal spaces are filled with wild flowers and deer wander freely. Housing ranges from the original caravans, now rusting picturesquely, through tin huts left from the site's earlier incarnation as an air force base, teepees, barrel houses created from obsolete whisky barrels and turf dwellings cut into the earth.

Findhorn also hosts Scotland's first straw bale house – an elegant building heated with solar panels. A spate of spacious new timber houses suggest a shift towards more bourgeois tastes. Indeed, from its hippie origins, Findhorn has evolved into an eco-village with an international profile, acknowledged by the United Nations and the Scottish Tourist Board. While some question its embrace of market principles and its isolation from the local community, Findhorn is, nonetheless, an extraordinary phenomenon; it demonstrates the riches that can be coaxed from a barren, sandy outcrop, particularly with the limitations of ecological, sustainable, organic methods.

Glamis Castle, Glamis,
Forfar, Angus DD8 1RJ

Glamis Castle

Open 18 Mar to 30 Dec 30,
11–5, but closed 24, 25 and
26 Dec

Angus

T: (01307) 840393   W: www.glamis-castle.co.uk

Fee castle and garden:
£5.30, conc. 4.30;
gardens free in Nov
and Dec

1m from Glamis on A94

Famed as the childhood home of the late Queen Mother, Glamis is also known as the setting for Shakespeare's *Macbeth*. A royal residence since the fourteenth century, the castle demonstrates the usual alterations as the medieval need for defence gave way to seventeenth-century formality, eighteenth-century elegance, nineteenth-century entertainments and, finally, twentieth-century economies.

Daniel Defoe, in his 1724 *A Tour thro' the whole Island of Great Britain*, remarked on the abundance of statuary: 'When you come to the outer gate you are surpris'd with the variety and beauty of the statues, busts, some of stone, some of brass, some gilded, some plain…' The imposing, mile-long approach avenue, planted in the formal style of the seventeenth century, was removed amid eighteenth-century 'improvements'. Sir Walter Scott, who invented many historical features for his estate at **Abbotsford**, deplored this attempt to reshape Glamis' ancient setting in the English style: 'A disciple of Kent [William Kent, the landscape designer] had the cruelty to render this splendid old mansion more parkish…to raze all those external defences, and to bring his mean and paltry gravel walk up to the very door, from which, deluded by the name, we may have imagined Lady Macbeth issuing forth to receive King Duncan.'

Highland Cattle

With their primitive, mammoth-like appearance, Highland cattle were thought to descend from the now extinct wild oxen or aurochs which once roamed northern Britain. However, recent DNA tests suggest that they are genetically closer to cows from Syria and Turkey, where the beast was first domesticated.

In the sixteenth and seventeenth centuries, the cattle trade was an important part of the Highland economy. Rent was often paid in butter and cheese, while surplus dairy produce could be bartered for other goods. In a process of transhumance similar to that found in the Swiss Alps, girls and women would lead the herds to high pastures in summer, living in shielings or rough bothies, making butter and cheese while the cattle fattened up for the autumn slaughter.

With their muscular bodies and short legs, Highland cattle were particularly suited to the long distances and rough terrain of the annual autumn journey from their highland grazing grounds to the markets in the south. Their thick outer coats gave protection from wind and water, while a second, inner, coat provided extra insulation and their fringe, or 'dossan', shielded their eyes from driving rain and snow. Though their toughness enabled them to withstand Scotland's winter weather, Highland cattle were threatened with extinction in the early nineteenth century when new, specialized breeds such as the Aberdeen Angus provided more meat. Saved by the Victorian fashion for the picturesque, these beasts were bred for long horns and golden colour – typically, Highland cows were black; indeed, in the Western Isles they were known as 'kyloes' or 'black cattle'.

Today Highland cattle are experiencing a renaissance. Unlike sheep or deer, cows control vegetation without destroying trees, so they are increasingly being used for low-maintenance land regeneration. Being both tough and self-sufficient, Highland cattle are particularly suitable for projects in severe climates such as the South American Andes and the Swiss Alps.

The defences to which he refers, a series of ornamental gates interspersed along the approach, had been repositioned around the edge of the policies in 1775. At about the same time the walled garden enclosing the forecourt was also banished to enhance the 'parkish' effect. The circular towers now marooned in the front lawn are relics of this earlier garden, as are the lead statues of James VI and Charles I which now flank the avenue. A ha-ha separates the castle from the policies, in which Highland cattle ruminate picturesquely. In the nineteenth century, perhaps inspired by Sir Walter's outcry, the formal avenue was reinstated.

The private, sunken garden on the east of the house, curiously known as the Dutch Garden, was laid out in the late nineteenth century in the Italianate style, with formal, box-edged flower parterres surrounding a statue of Mercury, messenger of the gods. The pinetum, planted about the same time, features the North American conifers which had recently been discovered by such intrepid plant hunters as Scotland's own David Douglas. Beside the pinetum runs the Water of Dean, a small burn which was canalized in the eighteenth century to drain surrounding farmland. The Victorian walled kitchen garden at the end of the pinetum supplied the castle with its fruit and vegetables until the 1970s, when it was laid to grass after labour costs, staff cuts and modern supermarkets rendered it obsolete.

The Italian Garden in the woods to the east of the castle was designed in 1907 by the wife of the 14th Earl. Despite its name, the garden draws its inspiration from France. Completely enclosed by yew hedges, it features a large, central fan-shaped parterre originally planted in rainbow colours though today it is filled with blue and silver herbs. Two pleached beech allées create diagonal axes between formal beds and box-edged parterres, filled, French fashion, with gravel. A spectacular herbaceous border, two sturdy pavilions, some simple stone urns and a central fountain complete the ensemble, which is accessed by ornamental gates commemorating the late Queen Mother's eightieth birthday.

A spectacular horse chestnut, *Aesculus hippocastanum*, in the east lawn was planted in 1746 at the time of the Battle of Culloden. In the car park is a rare cut-leaf beech, *Fagus sylvatica* 'Asplenifolia', rising 70 feet in height, while in front of the castle stand several massive yews, *Taxus baccata*, the largest of which is at least 300 years old. A dogs' graveyard, hidden beneath a noble fir, *Abies procera*, by the woodland walk, gives a domestic feeling to this monumental landscape.

Glen Grant Woodland Garden

Moray

T: (01340) 832118   E: glengrant.admin@chives.com

The Glen Grant Woodland Garden is a glorious piece of nine-teenth-century kitsch. A Victorian estate developed by a Victorian adventurer, it provides a fascinating insight into a vanished world. The 26-acre grounds were laid out in 1835 by John Grant, co-founder, with his brother, of the attached Glen Grant distill-ery. The bravado of this particular family is demonstrated by the fact that they gave their own name, rather than that of the local village, to their whisky. Whisky, which means 'water of life', is a product rooted in the landscape – a fact celebrated in the motto on each label of the malt: 'From the heath covered mountains of Scotia I come'.

In 1866 John's nephew James Grant, 'the Major', took over the estate and built himself a large baronial mansion in antici-pation of inheriting the family business. A notorious bon viveur, intrepid traveller and innovative entrepreneur, the Major ex-celled at fishing, shooting and hunting – he returned from one African safari with an abandoned native boy, whom he dressed in a suit and made his servant.

Over the years the Major developed his garden as a backdrop to his exhilarating life. Set in an open glen, bisected by a small ravine, the garden centres on the Back Burn, whose brown, peat-tinted waters resemble whisky itself. Fifteen gardeners meticu-lously tended the wilderness to ensure a natural look. A gravel path, meandering past the Victorian sluice gate, leads to a pictur-esque orchard whose ancient trees once provided so much fruit that the surplus had to be sold in Rothes. In the Major's day the lawns on this flat plateau would have been filled with colourful flower beds – carefully asymmetrical in deference to the infor-mal style. The burn itself was transformed into a water garden with bog planting, lily pools and rhododendron-covered slopes. The Major contributed specimens acquired on his travels: though a monkey puzzle and various blue spruces suggest rather conventional tastes.

The Major's major horticultural innovation was his 'faery hut', dramatically sited beside the waterfall halfway up the ravine and reached by a vertiginous track cut into the rock. Here guests would be invited for a post-prandial stroll; those who

Glen Grant Distillery
Co Ltd, Rothes, Aberlour,
Moray AB38 7BS

Open 12 Mar to 2 Nov,
9.30–5

Fee distillery and garden:
£3.50, (incl. £2 voucher
redeemable in the shop
against a 70cl bottle of
whisky) children free

10m S of Elgin on A941

made the treacherous ascent would be rewarded with a shot of the whisky, which was stored in a secret safe drilled into the rock itself. Less stimulating is the 'dram hut', a heather-thatched pavilion overlooking the linn at the base of the waterfall, with its own secret whisky supply.

A circular burn-side walk winds up through woodland to a high viewpoint, but flash flooding several years ago washed away the paths. Rabbit holes dug into the sandy hillside beyond the water garden have also undermined the bank, creating a risk of landslides. Though the garden is periodically closed for safety reasons, it is worth visiting if possible. The old distillery offices house an audio-visual programme, while black and white photos of mud villages, desert dunes and jungle clearings are oddly reminiscent of the Major's own heather-thatched huts and dramatic ravine.

Glendoick

Perth and Kinross

Glendoick, Glencarse,
Perth and Kinross
PH2 7NS

Open 9 Apr to 8 Jun,
Mon–Fri 10–4, and on
certain days for Scotland's
Gardens Scheme; no dogs

Fee £3, children free

On A90, 8m E of Perth,
1m E of Glencarse

T: nursery (01738) 860250; garden centre (01738) 860260
E: jane@glendoick.com W: www.glendoick.com

Glendoick is a commercial nursery hosting one of the largest collections of rhododendrons in Europe. The garden was founded in the 1920s, while the breeding programme, begun thirty years later, continues to this day, incorporating many specimens collected by the owners in China and the Himalayas. In spring, when the flowers are at their peak, the woodlands and garden are open to the public. Meconopsis, anemones and lilies – including the delicate pink and purple *Lilium mackliniae* and the spotted *Nomocharis pardanthina* 'Marei Sbec' – mingle with rhododendrons around the Georgian manor house. The walled garden, once an elegant Edwardian pleasaunce, now contains the trial beds for new hybrid rhododendrons.

At the heart of the woodland walk is the Den, an enclosed garden with a range of trilliums and other woodland plants supplementing masses of multicoloured rhododendrons against a backing of dark conifers. There is also a New Hybrid Rhododendron walk and an arboretum, planted in 1993.

The Doocot

The dovecot, or doocot as it is known in Scotland, provided year-round food and fertilizer, while requiring very little in the way of costs or maintenance. Doves were particularly valued for their flesh in winter, when the only other meat was dried, pickled, smoked or salted. Squabs – flightless young birds – were considered a delicacy and for centuries squab pie was virtually Scotland's national dish. Dove eggs were also useful, gathered from interior nesting boxes by means of a 'potence' or revolving ladder suspended from a central pole.

Doves – one's own or one's neighbours' – were traditionally lured into a new *doocot* by a bait of grain flavoured with cumin or old wine. In Islam doves are believed to be the souls of good men – which explains the tolerance shown to these messy creatures around the most exquisite mosques. More practically, dove droppings make powerful fertilizer. In Scotland dung gathered from the *doocot* floor was flailed to a powder and scattered on the fields. It was also employed in leather tanning, cloth dyeing and the making of gunpowder. To less effect perhaps, dove dung was applied to the head to cure baldness, while warm dove hearts, applied to the feet, were said to cure fever.

Though Bronze Age settlements appear to have had *doocots* and certainly the Romans used dovecots in Britain, Scotland's earliest extant examples are found in coastal caves. Since doves feed on grain, *doocots* are most common in arable areas such as Fife and the Borders, rather than in the rockier regions of the Highlands. The fact that so many have survived is more a testament to snobbery than to conservation. In the fifteenth century *doocots* could be built only by abbeys, monasteries, castles or baronies. Later, to raise money, the crown granted licences to owners of large estates; thus transformed to status symbols, *doocots* were often highly ornamented given their lowly function.

While the gentry vied to own them, *doocots* were generally resented by the peasants whose crops were ravaged by their inhabitants. Throughout the fifteenth century stringent punishments were meted out to frustrated farmers who attempted to protect their crops by killing thieving doves; by the end of the sixteenth century, the death penalty was prescribed for repeat offenders. In the late eighteenth century the sobering example of the French Revolution, followed, in the early nineteenth century, by food rationing during the Napoleonic Wars focused attention on the iniquity of dove-keeping. The importation of root vegetables such as turnips allowed livestock to be kept through the winter, reducing dependence on dove meat; at the same time improvements in livestock made domestic hens fatter and more productive than doves, so by the mid-nineteenth century the *doocot* was no longer necessary.

Rather than tearing them down, however, pragmatic Scotsmen redeployed them as pavilions, corn kilns, bothies and garden sheds. At Bonnington House the *doocot* was transformed into a 'fog house' – fog being a term for moss. With moss-lined walls and ceiling and moss-covered table and chairs, this rustic retreat was described by Dorothy Wordsworth in 1803 as 'snug as a bird's nest'. The thatched tea house at **Mellerstain** and the elegant garden shelter at **Kinross** are former *doocots*, while **Cawdor's** novel *doocot* was once a whisky barrel!

In earlier years *doocots* were placed in open ground, so they couldn't be ambushed by predators hiding in nearby shrubs or trees. In times of social unrest, they would be sited in the farm steadings or near the main house, where the doves could be protected by household staff, as at **The Hirsel** and **Ardchattan Priory**. By the late eighteenth century, when their decorative potential was exploited in designed landscapes, *doocots* were built in a dizzying array of shapes and styles. **House of Pitmuies** boasts a gothic style *doocot*, rather irreverently disguised as a chapel, while that at **Megginch** resembles a medieval market hall. **Inveraray's** elegant circular *doocot* harbours a ground-floor sitting room complete with fireplace.

In the nineteenth and twentieth centuries, once they had become decorative rather than practical, *doocots* were often sited in pleasure gardens, as at **Crathes**, where Lady Burnett moved an ancient example from the farmyard to her walled garden to create a decorative end to her new herbaceous borders. At **Torosay** Sir Robert Lorimer designed a pair of stately summer pavilions, one of which ingeniously houses a *doocot* in its roof and a grotto in its cellar. Put off perhaps by the prospect of dove dung, contemporary garden designers have shown little interest in this versatile garden feature.

Golspie Biblical Garden

Highland

T: (01408) 633001   E: acbarclay@beeb.net   W: www.golspie.org.uk

As a millennium project in this small Highland village, the local
Church of Scotland, with help from the Free Church, created a
communal Biblical Garden. Centrally located on the main street
and open to all, this charming project has a rather wide-ranging
interpretation of 'biblical'. Bronze fennel has a tag saying it is a
'biblical herb', sage is included because 'sage brush was the
model for the Jewish candlestick' and an old cypress tree is
justified because '*cupressus* was used by Solomon to burn in the
temple'. Several tamarisks bear a plaque reading, 'crystallized
sap from this tree was a possible source of manna'. Coriander
also slips in on the manna ticket – 'manna was like a seed of this
herb' – while poppies are, apparently, the 'flowers of the field'
mentioned in Isaiah. The pretty perennial polemonium, known
as Jacob's ladder, makes a predictable appearance, while roses
and lilies need no justification.

Wide gravel paths accommodate wheelchairs from the adjacent old people's home, a Celtic stone places the garden within
the Scots vernacular, while a handmade mosaic of fish, birds and
animals celebrates local artistry.

Golspie Biblical Garden,
Main Street, Golspie,
Highland KW10 6RH

Open all year

Fee free

10m N of Dornoch on A9;
garden is in Golspie town
centre

House of Pitmuies

Angus

T: (01241) 828245   E: ogilvie@pitmuies.com   W: www.pitmuies.com

House of Pitmuies is one of the most delightful private gardens
in Scotland. *Pit* is a Pictish word for farm, but while Pictish
stones indicate the area has been inhabited for at least a millennium, the house and garden date from the early eighteenth
century. Unusually, the walled garden encloses the house on two
sides; the other two façades overlook mature parkland. Entry
into the walled garden is past farm buildings which host an
intriguing rooftop carpet of ferns. An impressive kitchen garden,
done up in the 1970s in the fashionable potager style, has fruit

House of Pitmuies,
Guthrie, near Forfar,
Angus DD8 2SN

Open 1 Apr to 31 Oct, 10–5

Fee £2.50, children free

8m S of Brechin on A933,
1½m W of Friockheim on
A932

and vegetables in raised beds with decorative flower borders; an avenue of ancient apple trees under-planted with spring bulbs is the vestige of an earlier design.

The main garden, accessed through an iron gate, is framed by an arch of weeping silver pears, *Pyrus salicifolia*. The present layout is largely Victorian in origin, with the octagonal conservatory added in 1966 to link the house and gardens. A central axis is flanked by pastel-coloured herbaceous borders, backed by hedges of *Prunus cerasifera* 'Pissardii' – a deciduous tree which makes a striking dark-red hedge if kept firmly clipped. An old tennis court to the side has recently been planted with a large lawn, shrub borders and paved corners hosting a delightful range of dianthus and violas. A raised central bed, echoing the pool in the splendid rose garden in front of the house, links this new section of the garden to the rest of the design.

The rose garden encompasses three shallow terraces. Screened from the prevailing wind by a tall yew hedge, its east wall shelters shrubs under-planted with hellebores, hostas and fritillaries, while a variety of old and new roses surround the central fountain. The famous delphinium border, first planted in the 1920s, has produced prize-winning flowers in shows as far away as London. Like most other members of the buttercup family, the delphinium is poisonous, but the fact that its seeds were ground into a poultice against head lice helps explain its popularity in Scottish cottage gardens. The name, meaning 'little dolphin', was inspired by the curved spur of the wild species, which is lost in most modern hybrids.

A row of shiny-barked Tibetan cherry trees flanks the garden wall. Beyond, the old drying ground has been transformed into an alpine meadow. Carpeted with spring snowdrops and crocuses, this area fronts an intriguing chapel-like gothic wash house. A mown path leads to a strip of land between the Turbie Burn and Vinny Water. Dubbed Mesopotamia, 'the land between two rivers', this waterside walk meanders beneath stately trees past an unusual lectern-roofed dovecot. At the end of the walk is a small Victorian garden of hollies and monkey puzzles.

Across the burn a hornbeam walk leads past the house with its protective ha-ha to the Black Loch beyond. Planted with rhododendrons and azaleas, the loch harbours herons and swans as well as the more common ducks, rooks and squirrels. With its kitchen garden, formal gardens, Victorian garden, flower-filled policies, waterside and woodland walks, House of Pitmuies offers enormous charm and variety within a relatively small space.

Kemnay Quarry Observation Point

....

Aberdeenshire

T: (01464) 861372

Though not, strictly speaking, horticultural, the Kemnay Quarry Observation Point identifies a fascinating new direction in land-scape design. In 1996, to celebrate the 150th anniversary of the local quarry, a group of sculptors was invited to create works inspired by the site. Impressed by the barren landscape, three artists – John Maine, Brad Goldberg and Glen Unwin – went beyond the decorative use of stone to engage with the local history and topography. Naming their project 'Place of Origins', they moved over 100,000 tons of gravel and stone to create a hill on the rim of the quarry, spiralling into the air in a vertical reflection of the quarry's descent into the earth.

Being harder than marble, granite is rarely used for sculpture, so the artists lined the approach road with massive rocks to suggest the direction markers, paving slabs and gravestones for which granite is commonly used. The hill itself is built of mas-sive, rough-hewn boulders, some displaying the formal, vertical shafts created by drilling rods – an intriguing echo of classical columns. An ascending path offers a variety of aural and physi-cal textures, progressing from beaten earth, through gravel, to fine sand. A more direct route is provided by a rough set of steps – an echo of the grand staircase of the Renaissance garden. Grasses have begun to take root between the rocks and moss is growing on the exposed faces, giving the brash, raw site the imprimatur of age. At the summit, an observation point creates a visual link between the man-made quarry and the natural hills beyond. This intriguing transformation of landscape into land art is part of a contemporary trend towards reclaiming, restoring and reinterpreting obsolete industrial sites.

Kemnay, Aberdeenshire
AB51 5ST

Open all year

Fee free

¼m N on Paradise Road from High Street, down a dirt path

Kildrummy Castle , Alford,
Aberdeenshire AB33 8RA

Kildrummy Castle Gardens

Open Apr to Oct, 10–5

Aberdeenshire

Fee £2.50, children free

Off A97, 17m S of Huntley

T: (01975) 571203/571277   E: information@kildrummy-castle-gardens.co.uk

W: www.kildrummy-castle-gardens.co.uk

Brooding picturesquely from a rocky outcrop over the River Den, the thirteenth-century castle of Kildrummy was a royal seat, then an administrative outpost; it was damaged by Cromwell in the seventeenth century and in 1715 the Earl of Mar planned the disastrous Jacobite Rebellion from within its walls. When the uprising failed the Earl fled to France, abandoning his castle to neglect and decay. In 1731 the estate was bought by the Gordons of Wardhouse, who planted shelter belts of larch, silver fir and hemlock spruce against the north-east wind. In 1898 a new owner, the affluent soap manufacturer Colonel James Ogston, shored up the castle ruins, installed the replica of Aberdeen's Auld Brig o' Balgownie, which still bridges the Den, and created the baronial-style mansion below. Unsustainable as a private house in the post-war world, the mansion was turned into the hotel which presides today.

The garden itself is a palimpsest of early twentieth-century tastes. At the beginning of the century Ogston commissioned a Japanese garden. The opening of Japan to the West in 1868 generated widespread interest in oriental horticulture, a fashion which was particularly strong in Scotland, where the rough terrain plus a natural conservatism, respect for the past and tendency to imbue nature with spiritual qualities made the Scots particularly receptive to the oriental aesthetic. Like the owners of **Stobo**, Ogston imported a team of Japanese designers to transform the ravine around the Back Den into an elegant water garden. Lined with vibrant rhododendrons, the entrance drive introduces the oriental theme, which continues with cascades, streams and pools shaded by tall trees and lined with primulas, ligularia and other moisture-loving plants. In April the lower pool is ringed with *Lysichiton americanus*, whose yellow spathes slowly fade beneath the giant leaves.

In 1904 an alpine garden was created in the old stone quarry at the foot of the Den from which the castle had been built seven centuries before. In 1936 the rock garden was designed using glacial boulders from the Strathdon Hills nearby. The millstones, querns, Pictish stones and other lapidary treasures displayed in the museum were the contribution of General Ogston, who succeeded his brother. In 1953 a gale felled swathes of trees, creating clearings which were planted up with decorative shrubs to add variety to the woodland walks. Late frost and heavy snow continue to shape the landscape, though the steep ravine provides some shelter from the wind.

Leith Hall (NTS)

Aberdeenshire

T: (01464) 831216   E: leithhall@nts.org.uk   W: www.nts.org.uk

Leith Hall was built by the Leiths, a prosperous Edinburgh shipping family, in the middle of the seventeenth century. Its charming 6-acre walled garden, set some distance from the house, is shielded by a dense shelter belt, but when estate taxes and staff shortages in the inter-war years of the twentieth century made it impossible to maintain, half of the garden was leased out as a commercial nursery. Finally, in 1945 Leith Hall and its surrounding 280-acre estate were donated to the National Trust for Scotland.

Over the centuries the grounds at Leith Hall have altered, following shifts in family fortunes as well as changes in taste. A military map from the mid-eighteenth century shows the garden as a rectangular enclosure round the house, with a second enclosure up the hillside; plans from the end of that century reveal extensive formal gardens spreading north from the enlarged dwelling. Both house and gardens were further extended in the nineteenth century, as was the family name, when Hay was added to commemorate the great-uncle who bequeathed the money which allowed the embellishment of the estate. In the 1860s the east garden was extended and enclosed with the impressive walls which define it today, the glass houses were added within and the parkland without was planted up with deciduous and coniferous trees.

At the beginning of the twentieth century the improvements continued, chief among them the magnificent main gates, forged by a local blacksmith, with the monogrammed initials of Charles

Leith Hall, Huntly, Aberdeenshire AB54 4NQ

Open gardens: all year, 9.30–sunset; hall: Good Fri to Easter Mon, 12–5; 1 May to 30 Sep, Fri–Tues 12–5

Fee gardens £2.50, conc. £1.90; hall and gardens: £8, conc. £5

34m NW of Aberdeen, 1m W of Kennethmont on B9002

Edward Leith-Hay and his wife, Henrietta. Charles Leith-Hay constructed the rock garden crowning the hill to the west of the house in the 1920s, when the vogue for such features was at its height; under the National Trust this was replanted as a low-maintenance area with heathers and conifers replacing the earlier profusion of alpines and bold rocks.

Charles and Henrietta were responsible for the distinctive Moon Gate built into the north wall of the garden; though it frames nothing more than the old Aberdeen turnpike, this feature draws visitors up to the highest point of the garden, from where they can survey the garden itself, the hall and the magnificent country unfolding beyond. They also designed the whimsical zigzag border, with its deep, colourful herbaceous planting. The facing wall was originally planted with chrysanthemums, but as these Victorian favourites fell out of fashion they were replaced with plum trees, which have recently been replaced yet again with a magnificent blue stream of catmint composed of *Nepeta faassenii* and *N.* 'Six Hills Giant'.

The eastern boundary of the garden has an oriental flavour with a grass foot maze encircled by trees. An open shed nearby displays archaeological treasures, among which are Pictish stones worked by the ancient inhabitants of the region. More recent additions include the grass lawn into which is cut the design of the saltire or St Andrew's cross, to create a simple, formal parterre. Presiding over this area is a lead statue, cobbled together from various other statues in true eighteenth-century fashion, with tell-tale seams at neck and wrist.

With its internal hedges and dry stone walls the walled garden is a delightful place to wander, filled with serenading birds and horticultural surprises. The steep, south-facing site slopes towards woodland under-planted with bluebells and wild garlic, a pretty plant whose pungent odour belies its delicate flower. A poignant plaque in the car park explains that embedded in the presiding lime tree is a horseshoe hung there in 1854 by Colonel Alexander Leith-Hay the day he left for the Crimea in command of the Argyll and Sutherland Highlanders. The estate also offers woodland walks, stream, ponds and a bird observation hide.

Megginch Castle

Perth and Kinross

T: (01821) 642222

Megginch Castle, Errol,
Perth and Kinross
PH2 7SW

Open Apr to Oct, 2–5.30

Fee £3, children £1

8m E of Perth off the A90
on S side of road

Approached by a long avenue of oak, beech and wild cherry, Megginch offers a fascinating example of an old Scottish garden. The name means 'beautiful island' and centuries ago the region was indeed surrounded by marshland, though today it is part of the Carse of Gowrie, a fertile area known as 'the Garden of Scotland'. Accounts from 1460 record 'the tower and fortalice of Megginich', and today that same turreted castle provides a romantic backdrop to the garden. The indignant screech of imperious peacocks adds a note of gothic whimsy, while clumps of yew, said to be more than 1,000 years old, may indicate early Druidic occupation – the yew represents immortality in Druid culture. Others attribute the yew to the early Christian monks who first cultivated the estate. The top walled garden, created in 1575, is still in use, its brick walls harbouring figs and nectarines. The eighteenth-century garden beside it is largely laid to lawn, with herbaceous borders round the edges and an intriguing central bed within a low wall of upended wine bottles. An avenue of espaliered fruit trees is slowly breaking rank and a modern greenhouse houses a spectacular plumbago.

The lawn to the west of the castle has remnants of a formal garden with fountains, beds and fantastical topiary. To the side is an extraordinary crown-shaped form of clipped green and yellow yew; planted to commemorate Queen Victoria's 1887 Jubilee, it conceals a delightfully gloomy chamber within. Buried in the woodland, a small family chapel, built in 1672 and restored in the 1780s, replaces an earlier shrine to the Virgin, destroyed by reforming Protestants. The gothic stable yard contains an enchanting pagoda-like *doocot*. Crowned with a model of an East Indiaman ship, it recalls the oriental adventures of one of the nineteenth-century proprietors, Captain Robert Drummond, who is said to have brought back from China the first white Banksian roses and the first double pink camellias.

Pitmedden (NTS)

Pitmedden, Pitmedden
Village, Ellon,
Aberdeenshire AB41 7PD

Aberdeenshire

Open 1 May to 30 Sep,
10–5.30

T: (01651) 842352 E: information@nts.org.uk W: www.nts.org.uk

Fee £5, conc. £4
(incl. museum)

1m W of Pitmedden
Village on A920, 14m N
of Aberdeen

Pitmedden is an interesting exercise in historical reconstruction. When the National Trust for Scotland acquired the property in 1952, the donor, Major Keith James, had used it for many decades as a commercial market garden. The current Victorian house replaced a Georgian mansion, which in turn replaced the original fortified tower house. An inscription over the garden lintel indicates that a garden was begun on 2 May 1675, leading the Trust to create a seventeenth-century garden within the 3-acre walled enclosure. Sir Alexander Seton, creator of the original garden, was a contemporary of Sir William Bruce, who laid out the parterres of Holyrood Palace for Charles II. A Royalist, Bruce had spent much of the Commonwealth in Holland and France serving the exiled king. After the Restoration he returned to Scotland and promoted the French style in architecture and horticulture. Though no early plans exist, it is likely that Seton would have been inspired by Bruce's work at Holyrood, **Kinross** and Balcaskie.

Archaeological evidence revealed that both the upper and lower terraces had once been provided with stream-fed outlets, suggesting that each level possessed a water feature of some sort. Today the top garden consists of a lawn round a central fountain, flanked by two formal parterres. Developed in the early 1990s, the parterres reflect early seventeenth-century styles, as one is planted with period herbs such as lavender, camomile and thyme, while the other is filled with different-coloured gravels.

Down a double staircase, the Great Garden unfolds with four distinctly different parterres ranged around a central fountain. This area was designed to be appreciated from the main house and from the raised terrace along the north border – a parallel south terrace having long since disintegrated. The layout can also be viewed from the ogival pavilions at the east and west corners. These ingenious two-storey buildings straddle the garden's change in levels. From the top they appear to be decorative single-storey gazebos, but from below they are revealed to be double height, with the lower storey probably given over to such mundane tasks as the storage of garden tools and the over-wintering of apples. Accordingly, one of the gazebos is fitted out with table and chairs – as suggested by the seventeenth-century English horticulturist John Rea, not, as might be expected, for post-prandial sweetmeats, but for the gardener to use when cleaning and labelling bulbs.

High stone walls enclose the lower garden on all sides, providing protection from the north-east winds. The heat-retaining walls support a variety of espaliered and fan-trained fruit trees; some remain from the days of the mid-century market garden, but these are gradually being replaced with traditional Scottish varieties. The west wall is buttressed by magnificent clipped yew hedges, interspersed with early-flowering shrubs and climbers.

While three of the four parterres are copies of those at Holyrood, the fourth is based on Sir Alexander Seton's coat of arms. The design incorporates Seton's initials and those of his wife, Dame Margaret Lauder, surrounded by the mottoes *Sustento sanguine siga* – With blood I bear the standard – and *Merces haec certa laborum* – The sure reward of our labours. These mottoes are a horticultural tribute to Sir Alexander's father, John Seton, who died in 1639, 'shot thro the heart' while defending Charles I at the Battle of the Brig o' Dee. His sacrifice is also recalled in the weathervanes based on his crest which adorn the garden pavilions.

Some 3 miles of boxwood outline the elaborate parterres, planted up with 30,000 bright annuals. A far cry from the coloured gravel and simple herbs of Seton's time, this vibrancy was deemed necessary to entertain modern visitors. While the central fountains in the upper and lower gardens were provided by the National Trust, the rare, twenty-four-faceted sundial of 1675 was found on the property and is believed to have been part of the original design. Today it sits, appropriately enough, in the centre of the 'Tempus Fugit Parterre' – so named because of the motto carved in its east and west borders. Pitmedden's fountains and pavilions are surrounded, in the local style, with river stones split by hammer and laid flat side up.

Diligent visitors might notice similarities with **Edzell** nearby, another seventeenth–century garden redesigned in the mid-twentieth century by James Richardson, Scotland's Inspector of Ancient Monuments. Richardson favoured the use of emblems and mottoes, along with such historical anomalies as herbaceous borders and parterres filled with colourful annuals. A key figure in the preservation of Scotland's horticultural heritage,

Dr Richardson is commemorated in the decorative gate at the bottom of Pitmedden's Great Garden.

Pitmedden also contains a museum of farming life, a poignant reminder that most grand gardens were simply embellishments to agricultural estates. A small farm cottage done up with period furnishings, the museum offers a sobering picture of the farm labourer's life. As Thomas Hardy's *Tess of the D'Urbervilles* revealed, work was peripatetic, as short-term contracts meant unmarried labourers could find new employment every six months at the spring and autumn feeing markets, while married men could move on every year – a disruptive way of life, especially for wives and children.

Beyond the museum a modern herb garden and an apple walk provide further interest, while the wider grounds around the estate offer walks through mixed forests of native woodland, commercial spruce and ornamental trees. To the north, beyond the A920, a pond was fashioned from the disused limestone quarry which supplied the stone for the original house and garden walls. Beside this is a limekiln, which until the mid-nineteenth century provided fertilizer to counter the acidity of fields which had been heavily grazed – and urinated upon – by livestock. The kiln would be lined with dry wood and packed with layers of quarried limestone interspersed with layers of coal. A fire at the base would burn the lime to a rough powder. In the past most great estates along the eastern Scottish coast had their own limekilns, due, in part, to the proximity of the ports with their plentiful supplies of coal.

Glossary

allée/alley/avenue a formal path cut through trees or flanked by trees, hedges, walls or flower borders

arboretum a plantation or area of a garden dedicated to a collection of trees; arboreta were particularly popular in the nineteenth century, when imports were coming in from the Orient, North Africa and the Americas

balustrade a row of short columns, usually stone, forming an ornamental parapet to a terrace or balcony

banqueting house/hall/pavilion an ornamental building located within the garden, designed as a destination for post-prandial strolls; often sweetmeats were served here

baroque style a form of elegant ornamentation prevalent in the sixteenth and seventeenth centuries

belvedere/gazebo a decorative garden building sited to command extensive views of the surrounding countryside

bowling green a flat rectangular turf lawn used for bowling or other games

bosquet/bosco/grove/wilderness a designed woodland often studded with statuary and bisected by paths

broderie intricate parterre designs, evoking embroidery

canal a decorative rectangular water pool

casino/pavilion an ornamental garden house

claire-voie/clair-voyée a gap in a wall or hedge which frames the view beyond

English/landscape style parkland designed to look informal; usually contains a lake in the middle distance reflecting the main house on a slope above, with artfully placed clumps of trees and a distant shelter belt of woodland; pioneered in the eighteenth century, it swept across Europe, erasing many ancient formal gardens

eye-catcher a garden feature designed to stop the eye or direct it to a particular view

foot maze a two-dimensional maze pattern set into the ground or floor for visitors to contemplate as they trace its outline on foot

formal style a grand, symmetrical, geometric style, often very architectural, with terraces, balustrades, staircases, fountains, urns and statuary, inspired by Renaissance Italian gardens

folly a decorative garden building often of no particular use

gazebo *see* belvedere

grotto/nymphaeum an artificial cave, or rock niche, often embellished with intricate encrustations of fossils, volcanic rock and shells, dedicated to water nymphs

ha-ha a ditch which allows for uninterrupted 'borrowed' views of the countryside while preventing wildlife and livestock crossing into the garden

knot garden a formal space of low-growing hedges, such as lavender or box, clipped into symmetrical forms which are filled with flowers or coloured gravel

moon gate common in Chinese horticulture, a circular opening cut into a garden gate, door or wall, framing the landscape beyond while beckoning the viewer on

mount/mound an artificial hill providing viewers with a vantage point from which to appreciate the garden within and the landscape without

Palladian derived from Italian architect Andrea Palladio (1508–80), who reinterpreted the style of classical antiquity; his elegant, simple, balanced style was profoundly influential in eighteenth-century Britain

parterre a flat piece of ground filled with symmetrical ornamental beds, defined by low-cut hedges forming intricate patterns; similar to but larger than a knot garden

pergola a tunnel-like framework designed to support climbing plants, such as vines, roses, clematis, wisteria

pinetum an arboretum specializing in coniferous trees; popular in the nineteenth century, when imports such as the Douglas fir, *Pseudotsuga menziesii,* Monterey pine, *Pinus radiata,* and Wellingtonia, *Sequoiadendron giganteum,* were pouring in from the west coast of America

pleach to prune and train the branches of an avenue of trees so they intertwine to form a raised screen

pleasaunce/pleasure garden a pleasaunce is a Scottish word for an enclosed pleasure garden; often a private space close to the house, a pleasant ornamental area, distinct from parklands and utilitarian garden areas

picturesque style a rough, informal, wild style promoted by the Reverend William Gilpin, who defined picturesque as 'the sort of beauty that would look well in a picture'

policies the lands included in a Scottish estate

potager a decorative vegetable garden, associated with the formal French style

Renaissance style evolved in Italy between 1350 and1550; inspired by the humanist principles of reason, order and harmony, it used linear perspective and reinterpreted antique texts to create formal gardens subdivided geometrically and linked to the house through architectural devices such as pergolas, loggias and colonnades, while overlooking the surrounding countryside, often from a hilltop site

rococo style derived from the French word *rocaille*, meaning 'rock-work', rococo describes an ornate, frivolous, sinewy style full of charm and ornament, associated with the end of the baroque period in the late seventeenth century

rustic style a rough, natural style, often made of unworked materials such as stumps, logs, bark, heather or rough-hewn stones

steadings farm outbuildings

topiary the art of clipping trees and shrubs into ornamental shapes

trompe l'oeil painting or ornament which appears to be something it isn't; a trick of the eye

Victorian style reacting against the informal landscape style of the previous era, the nineteenth century rediscovered Italianate formality; the removal of the glass tax in 1845 allowed for the creation of vast glasshouses and conservatories in which to raise and propagate the tender exotics arriving from the New World; there was an emphasis on display, with vast bedding-out schemes, intricate parterres and a rich array of statuary; an interest in trees inspired the creation of dedicated pineta or more general arboreta

wilderness *see* bosquet

Biographical Notes

Robert Adam (1728–92) Scottish architect. The son of William and brother of John, Robert Adam became the most famous in this family of Edinburgh architects. The pre-eminent designer in Georgian England, his elegant neo-classical style embraced antique as well as Etruscan, Italian Renaissance and French motifs.

Sir Isaac Bayley Balfour (1853–1922) Scottish botanist; Professor of Botany at the universities of Glasgow and Edinburgh. In 1888 Balfour was appointed Regius Keeper of the Royal Botanic Garden, Edinburgh, which, under his direction, began to specialize in the Himalayan and Far Eastern flora for which it has become renowned.

Sir Charles Barry (1795–1860) English architect and garden designer. Barry promoted the Italian Renaissance style in mid-nineteenth-century country-house gardens, with architectural terraces, balustrades, loggias and grand staircases.

Sir Reginald Blomfield (1856–1942) English architect and garden designer. Blomfield promoted the grand, formal style and abhorred the naturalism popularized by William Robinson.

Lancelot 'Capability' Brown (1716–83) English landscape designer. The pioneer of the naturalistic style, Brown worked himself up from gardener at Stowe to become the most influential landscape designer of the eighteenth century. He destroyed many great, formal gardens to create the rolling parklands for which he was famed. Though his style was never particularly suited to the rugged terrain of Scotland, many Scottish landlords embraced his low-maintenance, easily sustainable style, choosing informal parkland over the labour-intensive formal gardens of the previous era.

Sir William Bruce (1630–1710) Scottish architect and garden designer. As a Royalist, Bruce followed Charles II into exile in the Low Countries, during which time he probably visited France. On the Restoration he was ennobled for his loyalty and appointed Surveyor-General of the King's Buildings in Scotland. In this position he promoted the formal French style in architecture and horticulture. His gardens at Balcaskie, Holyrood Palace and Kinross are characterized by a dominant axis, symmetrical layout, evergreen hedging and few flowers.

Sir John Clerk of Penicuik (1676–1755) Scottish politician, poet, composer and architect. Clerk was a leading supporter of the 1707 Act of Union between England and Scotland. The landscape-style 'improvements' he initiated at his own estate in the early eighteenth century were influential in promoting this essentially English approach among Scottish landowners.

Reverend William Gilpin (1724–1804) English garden designer. Gilpin promoted the picturesque approach to landscape design, advocating a rough, varied, wild style.

Sir William Jackson Hooker (1785–1865) English botanist and plant-hunter. From 1820 to 1841 Hooker held the Regius Chair of Botany at the University of Glasgow, where he helped design and develop the Botanic Gardens. In 1821 he brought out *Flora Scotica.* In 1841 he was appointed director of the Royal Botanic Gardens, Kew; his son, Joseph Dalton Hooker, succeeded him in the position.

Gertrude Jekyll (1843–1932) English garden designer, artist, plantswoman and garden writer. Jekyll pioneered deep herbaceous borders with subtle colour combinations and plants set out in drifts, virtually defining the Edwardian country-house garden style.

Sir Geoffrey Jellicoe (1900–1996) English landscape architect. Jellicoe combined Italian Renaissance design principles with modern sensibilities. Fascinated by Jungian theories, he injected allegory and symbolism into his later designs.

James Justice (18th century) Scots botanist and gardener. His books *The Scots Gardener's Directory* (1754) and *The British Gardeners Calendar* (1759) – qualified, respectively, as 'particularly adapted to the Climate of Scotland' and 'chiefly adapted to the Climate of North Britain' – reflect the *furor hortensis* or vogue for all things horticultural which overtook Scotland in the mid-eighteenth century. Appealing to the amateur, middle-class gardener, Justice explained all aspects of kitchen gardens, from orientation, exposure and layout to walls, frames and hotbeds. His *Calendar* advised on 'the Necessary Works in Every Month in the Kitchen, Fruit and Pleasure Gardens, and in the Nursery, Greenhouse and Stove, to which is added a Dissertation on Forest Trees and a catalogue of Seeds, Roots etc'. His own private garden, in Crichton near Edinburgh, was famous for its tender exotics and its tulips. Once, having planted auricula borders to provide nosegays, Justice declared that he had 'exceeded all the Blows [flowers] of any Auriculas ever seen in Scotland, in England or in Europe'. He also claimed to have been the first to grow pineapples as far north as Scotland and included a plan for a pineapple stove in his *Directory.*

Henry Home, Lord Kames (1696–1782) Scottish lawyer, philosopher and leading member of the Scottish Enlightenment. He took a particular interest in agriculture, transforming his own estate at Blair Drummond from mossy bog into productive farmland, adorned by one of the first deliberately informal gardens in Scotland. Eschewing the formality of his predecessors, he decried such artificial features as topiary and 'statues of wild beasts vomiting water', claiming, 'As gardening is not an inventive art, but an imitation of nature, or rather nature itself ornamented, it follows necessarily that everything unnatural ought to be rejected with disdain.'

William Kent (1685–1748) English architect, garden designer and pioneer of the informal approach to garden design. As Horace Walpole famously said of Kent, 'He lept the fence, and saw that all nature was a garden.' Kent was enormously influential in the development of the English landscape style, which reached its apogee in the work of Lancelot 'Capability' Brown. Kent retained classical follies and statuary in the landscape and was thus, perhaps, more influential in Scotland, where canny landowners were unlikely to jettison their expensive garden ornaments despite the prevailing vogue for Brownian naturalism.

Sir Robert Lorimer (1864–1929) Scottish architect and garden designer who combined Scottish vernacular styles with Italian Renaissance grandeur. Inspired by seventeenth-century Scottish horticulture, Lorimer delighted in walled gardens accessed directly from the dwelling. His style is characterized by symmetrical design, axial vistas, clipped hedges, geometric planting beds, floral borders, statuary and garden ornament. His son, Hew, became a distinguished sculptor, creating many works for Scottish gardens.

John Claudius Loudon (1783–1843) Scottish garden theorist and prodigious writer on garden matters. Loudon popularized gardening for the masses and coined the term 'gardenesque' to describe a style of planting in which individual trees, shrubs and flowers were isolated so their features could be best appreciated. His wife, Jane, a distinguished garden writer, founded *The Lady's Magazine of Gardening*.

Sir Herbert Maxwell (1845–1937) Born to a prominent Border family, Sir Herbert Maxwell was a politician, antiquarian, etymologist, angler, noted painter of both fish and flowers, and authority on plants and gardening. Though the twenty-first century has seen a surge of interest in Scottish horticulture, his 1911 *The Scottish Garden* was one of the first books to address the subject.

William Nesfield (1793–1881) English garden designer. Nesfield promoted the seventeenth-century French formal style with massive parterres embellished with clipped box patterns and filled with coloured gravel.

John Reid (17th century) Scottish gardener and garden writer. In 1683 Reid wrote *The Scots Gard'ner*. The first book ever devoted to gardening in Scotland, it is full of practical advice on preparing the site, levelling the ground, creating paths and walls, planting and cultivating fruit, vegetables and flowers.

William Robinson (1838–1935) Irish garden writer, publisher and designer who settled in England and became one of the most influential designers of the late nineteenth century. Reacting against Victorian formality, especially bedding schemes, which he descried as 'pastry-cook's gardening', Robinson promoted a more natural approach and advocated the mixing of exotics with native plants.

Sir Robert Sibbald (1641–1722) Scottish geographer, botanist and physician. In 1670 Sibbald helped to establish the Royal Botanic Garden in Edinburgh to propagate medicinal plants. In 1681 he founded the Royal College of Physicians there. He was also physician to King James VII and Cartographer-Royal of Scotland.

James Sutherland (1639–1719) Scottish botanist and first superintendent of the Royal Botanic Garden, Edinburgh. In 1683 Sutherland published *Hortus Medicus Edinburgensis or a Catalogue of all the Plants in the Physic Garden at Edinburgh*, describing approximately 3,000 plants; his aim was to promote the international exchange of plant material.

Thomas White the Elder (1736–1811) and **Thomas White the Younger** (1764–1831) English garden designers who worked mainly in Scotland and the north of England, interpreting Capability Brown's landscape style for the rugged northern terrain. Loudon accused them of destroying important formal features and ancient woodlands to impose a bland, English style on the picturesque countryside.

Acknowledgements

I would like to give particular thanks to Georgina Hobhouse who initiated this project and supported it through its early stages; I would also like to thank my husband, Michael, who navigated and interpreted the length and breadth of Scotland and my daughter, Jessica, who maintained her good humour throughout, despite the occasional anguished cry of 'Not another boring garden!' The gardeners and garden owners who showed me around and shared their passion are too numerous to mention, but I was particularly grateful to Trish Kennedy at Newhall, Sir Charles and Lady Fraser of Shepherd House, the Seymours at Stobo Castle Water Garden, Mrs David Barnes at Biggar Park and Major General and the Honourable Mrs Charles Ramsay at Bughtrig, who took me in and thawed me out with comforting cups of tea.

The publishers would like to thank the following colleagues, friends and family: Linda Dawes for her excellent maps, Michael Davenport, Leslie Levine and Annie Lee for their invaluable copy editing and proof reading, Diana LeCore for her index, Geoff Green for his endlessly patient technical help, Helen Blackmore for her blurb, John Blackmore for our website, Margaret Bluman, Jane Crawley, Margaret Popp Gordon Thomson, for their enthusiastic endorsement of the project and Mark Davis for his ever present support.

Index

Other titles by Barn Elms Publishing

Knot Gardens and Parterres

A history and how to make one today

Anne Jennings and Robin Whalley

This sumptuous book is a pioneering combination of intriguing history and practical gardening. Robin Whalley unravels the story of the knot garden as it transforms itself from the 'curious knot' of Tudor times into the magnificent embroidered layouts of the seventeenth century. The eighteenth-century landscape garden all but eliminated formal patterns, but they re-emerged with the flamboyant Victorian parterre.

Moving from history to practice, Anne Jennings then explores a structure that is always eye-catching. The options for a knot garden that can be brashly exuberant, romantically nostalgic or quietly simple and chic are clearly set out and every stage from initial planning, design and choice of plants to the nitty-gritty of care and maintenance is fully explained. It is no surprise that this book has so quickly become established as a classic.

'...beautifully produced and stuffed with precious information'
Patrick Taylor in the Sunday Telegraph

Pergolas, Arbours and Arches

Their history and how to make them

Paul Edwards and Katherine Swift

'Bringing together historians, designers and gardeners, this remarkable volume ... combines learning with practical concerns and historical images with superb new photography' – The Times

Structures built for climbing plants have existed since the earliest civilizations started using poles to support their vines. Five contributing experts tell us how pergolas and their like have been built, used and enjoyed at five key periods over the centuries – sometimes quite simple, sometimes amazingly elaborate, but always for pleasure.

Five of the finest pergolas in Britain today are then explored in detail by Katherine Swift, whose own garden features in the book. Finally Paul Edwards tells us about the appropriate plants and planting methods for these structures, before giving full drawings and notes on construction of six different structures he has himself designed – two of them for the National Trust.

'Like the Knot Garden book that preceded it, this is a lovely mixture of the inspirational and the practical' The English Garden

Alexander Pope: The Poet and the Landscape

Mavis Batey

Alexander Pope, the foremost poet of the new Augustan age, was responsible for a profound change in attitudes to nature and landscape. Mavis Batey – unrivalled in her understanding of relations between literature and landscape – explores Pope's gardening and grotto-making at home in Twickenham and unravels his connections with the leading garden makers of his time. 'Consult the genius of the place in all' was heard at Stowe, Chiswick, Marble Hill and Rousham and these and other English landscape gardens are beautifully illustrated throughout this original and enlightening book.

Jane Austen and the English landscape

Mavis Batey

Jane Austen started writing for the benefit of friends and family, bringing in references familiar to them all. One of the many delights of Mavis Batey's lovely book is that she is steeped in these subtleties. She shows how Jane Austen's characters reveal the prejudices of the day, with her heroines clearly reflecting the various aspects of 'Taste and Feeling' that were established attitudes. Garden and landscape design and the prevailing view of nature were influenced by these attitudes as much as any other aspect of life and Mavis Batey clearly elucidates Jane Austen's views from her texts and letters. The book is fully illustrated in colour throughout with rich and informative contemporary illustrations.

The Flowers of William Morris

Derek Baker

This book takes a close look at Morris's own gardens and the flowers he loved. After describing Morris's early life in Epping Forest and his student days at Oxford with Burne-Jones, Ruskin and the Pre-Raphaelites, the author concentrates on Morris's own homes: Red House, Kelmscott Manor in Oxfordshire, Kelmscott House in Hammersmith and the Abbey Works at Merton. We learn not only of Morris's great love for his gardens but also of his campaigning zeal as an early conservationist.

The last chapter looks at Morris's designs. Did he find inspiration for his designs from the flowers he could observe and draw, or did he work from medieval paintings, wood engravings and herbals? Beautifully illustrated in colour, this is a book for all who enjoy reading about gardens, design and the life of an extraordinary man.

How to contact us

Barn Elms Publishing can be contacted for orders in writing at
Flint House, 11 Chartfield Avenue, London SW15 6DT

For further information on our books see our website,
where orders can be placed and discounts are available.
www.barnelms.co.uk

Previous publications by the same author

Icons of Twentieth Century Landscape Design
(Frances Lincoln, 2006)

Marmalade Season
(Iron Press, 2003)

Moon Behind Shadows: Sir Claude Francis Barry
(Fine Art Promotions, 1999)

Live in the Flesh
(Lime Tree, 1992)

Let Us Leave Them Believing
(Methuen, 1991)

What He Really Wants Is a Dog
(Methuen, 1989)